COUNTRY CLUB MURDERS

VICTOR MOSS

Disclaimer

This book is strictly a fictional account of the police officers and detectives of the Denver Police Department including descriptions of physical settings and the Department's rules and procedures. This book is strictly for entertainment. All characters are imaginary, and any similarity to actual persons is simply a coincidence.

The author is not aware of any criminal or corrupt cops as described in the book. Instead, the author has deep admiration for the hard work and dedication of the men and women who chose to serve and protect society even though their lives may be taken away from them in an instant.

Dedication

To my wife, children and grandchildren who have given me support
and encouragement to keep writing.

Acknowledgments

I thank my daughter, Katherine Stafford and my friend, Melanie Tappen for their advice and suggested corrections. I also thank my sister and her husband, Mary and Duane Janssen for their encouragement and their useful comments and suggestions.

But above all, I have enormous praise for my wife, Rita Moss, for her support and the many hours she spent reading and discussing each segment. Her suggestions and editing were truly invaluable.

Contents

CHAPTER 1

Present day, Denver, Colorado.

THE BUTLER, Jarvis Benson, was busy setting up the massive dining table for an unusual event that his employer, William Hollister, had planned. Told not to make the affair formal, he used everyday china, tableware, and glasses. He was further instructed not to serve alcohol, only tap water. Consuela Rivera, the housekeeper and cook, brought in an elongated flower centerpiece made of white daisies and pink carnations. It was a casual arrangement and not the usual elaborate bouquet that she usually arranged for a dinner party. Hollister told her not to prepare appetizers or salads and only serve a pot roast with potatoes and carrots. For dessert, the guests would only receive green Jell-O.

Both Benson and Consuela knew that the dinner was of great importance to their boss. Being privy to the purpose of the dinner, because of their close relationship with Mr. Hollister, they gossiped between themselves how unpleasant the evening would be and braced themselves for terribly angry outbursts from the guests. After twenty years for Benson and thirteen for Consuela, they knew their employer well and sympathized with his plight. He treated them well with deserved respect, and they reciprocated. The employees knew their places and acted accordingly. They also knew who the expected guests were and how difficult and bitter the dinner would be for their employer.

The scheduled time for arrival was 7:00 p.m. and Mr. Hollister gave Benson specific instructions on what to do with the guests once they arrived. The first invitees came about ten minutes early. It was the eldest son, George, and his wife, Rhonda. "Hello, Benson, you're still looking good," George said. "How long has it been since last we saw you? Must have been at least a few months ago. Oh yeah, we saw you when you came by and delivered a gift from the old man."

"I believe that's right, sir. Would you please take a seat in the parlor?"

"What's this all about?" Rhonda asked, her face stern. "Coming here tonight is certainly very inconvenient. We had to drive all the way from Cherry Hills Village in this horrible traffic."

"Sorry madam. But it was important that you come."

The chimes of the doorbell rang out and the second eldest son, James, and his spouse, Kay, arrived. They gave warm and friendly smiles to Benson. Kay gave him a quick hug and James asked, "How's Dad feeling today? Is he okay?"

"Yes, sir, he's fine. Would you please join your brother and his wife?"

As the couple entered the sitting room, George and Rhonda stiffly nodded to them. Neither couple exchanged further words. Sitting opposite, both couples felt and acted uncomfortable. Finally, after a few minutes ticked by George gruffly blurted out, "So what's this dinner all about?"

"I don't have the foggiest," James uttered.

George stood up and approached Benson. "Now Benson, I demand to know why we're here?"

Benson shrugged, "Sorry sir, I'm not at liberty to say. You'll know in a few minutes."

At exactly 7:00 p.m., the eldest daughter, Cynthia Maxwell and her husband, Samuel arrived. "Why are we here exactly, Benson? You said it was very important. I had to cancel my book club meeting over this, and we had to drive down here all the way from Vail. Is something wrong with father?"

"Mr. Hollister desired to see you all."

"Well, he could have made it more convenient for us. He's all right, isn't he?" Benson didn't say a word, just nodded.

"Benson, I asked you a direct question. Is my father all right?"

"You will soon find out."

At 7:07 p.m., the youngest son, Darren, arrived, bringing a woman with him. He appeared a little tipsy as he said, "Hello there, old man. I'd like you to meet my new girlfriend, Tina Dionisio. Isn't she hot?" He pulled her closer to him and planted a kiss on her cheek. "I think we need a drink. Get us a couple martinis, would you, Benson? I think Tina would like at least a couple of olives in it."

"Sorry, sir, but no drinks will be served tonight."

"Aah, you gotta be kiddin' old man. I thought this would be a party. Why are we here anyway? Tina and I had great plans until you called and insisted that we come. Of course, when you said that if we came, we'd get a great gift, then I'm all for it. What is it? I hope it's a yacht." He exploded into a hearty laugh. Still laughing, he placed his arm around Benson's shoulder. "Go get us some drinks."

"I have instructions against that, sir. Please join the others in the parlor."

"Aw, come on, Tina, this place sucks, as always." He had almost walked out of the door when George came up and grabbed him by the arm and pulled him into the parlor.

"We need to talk," George said. "Something is going on here. I've got a bad feeling about it. When's the last time you saw Dad? Did he say anything to you?"

"Listen, bro. I try to talk to him as little as possible. He's always on my back about something or other. He doesn't like my lifestyle. He thinks I drink too much, and chase too many women, but I just like to have fun. After all, what's life all about? He probably won't like Tina, here." As he said that, he leaned over his girlfriend and nuzzled her neck. Embarrassed by his action, she pushed him away.

Rhonda said, her voice raspy, "You clown, Darren. Get serious for once in your life. Something is going on here and I don't think it's going to be pleasant."

Darren laughed, "You get serious if you want. I vote to enjoy life." He looked at Tina and smiled. "I want to enjoy life with you."

Tina blushed. She subconsciously glanced back at the front door. *This is awful. I want out of here. Why did I ever come along with him? He's obnoxious when he drinks.*

Benson waited until seven-fifteen for the youngest daughter, Ashley Hollister, to arrive. She still had not, but, nevertheless, he invited the guests to be seated at the dining table. After they took their seats, Benson notified William Hollister. The assembled sat in subdued conversation as they waited. After about five minutes, the old man shuffled in appearing grave, troubled, worn-out, grayer, and thinner than most of them remembered. He immediately noticed the empty chair. He also noticed a strange woman at the table. His children stood, tried to embrace him, but he briskly waved them away and told them to sit down. After they took their seats, at least a long minute passed before Cynthia spoke out sarcastically, "Well, hello to you as well. How long are we supposed to wait? We must get back home soon."

He glared at each of them. No one else said a word until finally, Darren broke the silence, "Dad, it's great to see you, but why are we here? What's this all about?" Then he laughed, "No wine, only water? Ha, you gotta be kidding."

William curtly answered, "Yes, only water. You had enough to drink." The severe answer left everyone silent, squirming and fidgeting on the Duncan Phyfe chairs. Suddenly the stillness was interrupted by the loud chimes of the doorbell. Ashley had finally arrived.

She came in laughing and as the baby of the family tried to act cutesy, "Hi Daddy, I'm so sorry for being late." Her hands flayed, theatrically. "I simply couldn't make up my mind what dress to wear. It was such a problem not knowing the occasion. Benson should've been more specific." Her smile faded abruptly after she noticed the somber crowd, her dark eyebrows raised as she asked, "What's wrong? Did someone die or something?"

"You're late. But then, I wouldn't have expected anything else from you." William's voice boomed. "Sit down!" He then gave Tina a pointed look and asked, "Darren, who is this woman?"

"Oh Dad, she's my good friend, Tina Dionisio. She's an investment banker and isn't she just gorgeous? I hope it's all right that I brought her. We both like to party, and I wanted her to see the house."

Sitting next to his father, George noticed William's lips quiver and his veined hands tremble. Placing a hand on his father's arm, he asked, "Why are you so riled up? You'll get a stroke. Just relax and tell us why we're here."

William pulled his arm away. He didn't answer George, instead, he turned to Benson and asked him to start serving supper. Now anxious, Ashley slipped into the chair at the end of the table looking to the others for an answer as to what was going on.

After Benson and Mrs. Rivera finished serving everyone, no one was in the mood to eat. The father barely touched his fork. He remained silent glaring at his children. The children were reluctant to talk and break the silence. All felt awkward.

After it appeared that they were through with their food, most of it uneaten, Benson brought out the green Jell-O topped with a dab of whipped cream. At that moment, William cleared his throat and began to speak, "After I say what I have to say, Benson will bring out envelopes for each of you, children, containing a gift of one-hundred-thousand dollars. Except for one of you, it is quite obvious that money is more important than love."

Objections from the group were immediate. Denials were swift. Breathing hard and heavy, Cynthia stood and screamed that they all loved their father. With tears in her eyes, Ashley cried out, "How can you say such an awful thing? We love you so much."

"Unfortunately," William continued, "Words are cheap. It's actions that count. And after all the years of watching you as adults, I know in my heart who genuinely loves me and who couldn't care less. I know most of you wouldn't have come unless you'd thought that you would get something out of it. That's why my invitation mentioned that there'd be a substantial gift. Even then, Benson had to text or call you to make sure you'd come. That's how uncertain we were."

"But Daddy," Ashley wailed. "I came over to see you a couple of days after Christmas. I brought you a tie, remember?"

"Yes, Ashley, I certainly remember. And it brought me great joy when you came. But you stayed only a few minutes, not asking how I was feeling or whether I was happy. Then, you begged me for money. I gave you a check and you grabbed it out of my hand, threw me one of your dramatic air kisses, said the perfunctory, 'Love you, Merry Christmas' and took off. Frankly, my little baby, you left me so saddened." Rivers of tears began flowing from Ashley. "Daddy, that's not fair."

"You all say you love me, but I've decided that for most of you, it's my money that you love. I admit that I would receive the obligatory call from you occasionally. But did we ever have a real conversation? No. Just, 'Hi Dad, how you doing? That's great. Have to run, call you later.' And those calls have become even more infrequent. Only one of you had invited me for Thanksgiving and Christmas. When is the last time that the rest of you invited me or came over and spent an evening with me? I can't remember when you'd just pop in to visit or invite me to a BBQ."

"William, it's not our fault," Rhonda protested. "We have busy lives wrapped up in our children. Don't be so doggone sensitive."

He stared hard at her, then at the rest. Taking a deep breath, he said, "I am extremely bitter. Very, very disappointed in you. I gave you everything you needed. I gave you security. And in that, I made a big mistake. And by your selfish actions, you plunged a dagger into my heart when I came to realize that I was just a money machine, an ATM, for you."

George began to object, but William demanded that everyone be quiet until he finished. "My hot-shot, social-society, children are too busy for their father. You can't understand how disappointed I am when I call and get a message that you're unavailable or too busy and will call me later. Later, most times, never came. I barely know my grandchildren. Now that they're grown, I never get a call from them because you never encouraged it."

Hollister paused as he took in some deep breaths, his voice shaky. "Only one couple here knows how precarious my health is right now. I asked them not to tell you as I wanted to tell you in person. Well, for your information, I have stage four prostate cancer. I'm fighting it, but the prognosis is very poor, and I don't know how much longer I'll live. The doctor says that maybe six months or maybe a little longer. But I don't want to give up."

"Oh Dad, you should've told me," Darren said. "I would've come right over."

Samuel Maxwell said, "That was awfully selfish of you to hold that information from us. You didn't give us a chance to support you."

Hollister looked hard at him. "Shouldn't you and my daughter have contacted me to inquire what I'm doing, how I'm feeling, and what my concerns are?" He looked around the table, "Except for one child, the rest of you didn't bother or think about me here all alone. No, too busy with your country clubs, parties, whatever, to bother to even think about me. If on rare occasions the bank failed to send the Trust check to you on time, then I certainly heard from you and sometimes the tone was such that I had better do something about it fast."

A loud murmur from the group elicited Hollister to shout, "Shut up! Let me continue. Cherish the money you'll receive today. Invest it wisely because except for one of you, it represents one-third of the money of the total that you'll receive after I die. Also, after sixty days, you will no longer receive your monthly trust payments."

"What! No, Dad, you can't do that! What's going to become of us!" Similar shouts were heard over and over. James had to restrain George whose fingers were balled into a fist from lunging at his father. Except for one child and his wife, all stood and yelled insults and swear words at their father, venom sprouting from angry eyes. Amid all the clamor he heard the voice of his eldest daughter, Cynthia, scream out that they will do whatever was necessary to stop him.

"Sit down and listen or no checks will be handed out tonight. Now sit! You need to know this so that you can make arrangements. You're all adults and it's about time that you stand on your own two feet and not have me carry you around like babies." They sat, all breathing heavily. "Darren just yelled out that I couldn't cut you off the trust. Well, I can. I set it up years ago as a revocable trust. That means it can be changed or terminated at my will. It was always my intent that you each had enough money for your education and some help to get on your feet. That's been accomplished. Now you're on your own." The group listened carefully, their heads bowed waiting for more drastic news, or, so to speak, the other shoe to drop.

"So, next week, I'm going to meet with my attorney. As I said, trust payments will terminate in two months. As far as heirs to my estate, only one of you had been loyal and concerned about me, not just my money. That one family came by almost daily to see how I'm doing and asked what they could do to help. They even offered to take me to their home to live so that I wouldn't be alone without a family." Everyone looked around the table to see who that would be. They suspected James was the one.

"In gratitude, I'm giving that child the bulk of my estate. As I said, your share will be an additional two hundred thousand. Some of the money will go to the Cancer Society, and an amount each to my faithful servants, Benson, and Consuela. Except for that one child, you're a bunch of miserable spoiled people and I guess I must take blame for that because your mother and I spoiled you. Maybe she might have even poisoned you against me after our bitter divorce. But you all should have at least the decency to know that I exist and need your companionship, comfort, and support." Every mouth hung wide open, too stunned to say anything.

"Now, I've also decided to sell this house while the market is red hot in Denver. Houses are selling like hotcakes, and I already had made other arrangements. I want you now to go up to the rooms you grew up in and take out whatever you might want. A lot of your high school and college stuff is still there. Benson left an empty box in each room for you to use. In the meantime, I'm going to go to my downstairs office. I want no one to come around to moan, complain, plead, cry, threaten me, or anything else. The door will be locked so don't bother me." He continued to glare at them for a long minute. Tears filled his eyes. Shoving his chair back, he stood with effort and shuffled out of the room. Benson informed everyone that they can go upstairs now. Tina was reluctant to go, but Darren insisted, and they followed the others upstairs.

CHAPTER 2

CLINT HAWK and Nora Ricci had just solved a complicated murder of a prominent socialite and her housekeeper and concentrated on preparing incident reports related thereto. Seated at their desks across the aisle from each other in the rectangular room of the Homicide Unit of District Six of the Denver Police Department, their train of thought was abruptly interrupted by their immediate supervisor, Lieutenant Ernest Perez, who was relatively new to the unit.

Hawk and Ricci were the ones that put an end to the corrupt cops in the unit, one of whom was the previous lieutenant, now jailed with no bail. Before Hawk became a detective, he served as a patrol officer while Nora Ricci transferred from Internal Affairs to be able to work with Hawk. Both in their early thirties and well-educated, they made up an excellent detective team, solving several crimes, and earning awards and accolades from the upper brass. Both were good-looking, always sharply dressed, and very professional; they made a striking couple.

Hawk and Nora looked up at the stout, square-shouldered, thick-necked Lieutenant Perez. A few strands of his dark hair fell over his smooth forehead. With a grim expression, he ordered, "Forget the reports for now. There's been a death in the country club area. I want you two to investigate."

Overhearing the conversation, Detective Mortimer Holliday strode up to Perez, coughing. It seemed that he coughed or sneezed whenever stressed. "What about me? I'd like to work with Clint and Nora again."

Perez thought for a moment, "All right, Holliday, for now anyway. Later, I'll team you up with Orlinski." Mortimer Holliday, a recent transfer from the Tampa Police Department, stood out from the rest of the detectives by his unusual personality, never smiling or laughing. His towering and gaunt stature, together with an eccentric appearance wearing decades-old apparel, all added to his strange and, at times, intimidating nature. He ended up at the Department because he met his fiancé, Josephine, on his one and only ocean cruise to the Bahamas where she asked him to marry her and move to her Denver home. No one in the unit knew exactly how he got the job, but there he was, and Perez had to make use of him somehow.

As the three detectives walked out of the station located at Washington and Colfax Streets, Mortimer declared, "It's great to be working with you two again." He caught up with Hawk, "Maybe you can tell people again that I'm a human lie detector as you did with a few of the suspects in the last case and they'd be afraid to lie."

"Yeah, that was sweet, all right," Hawk said.

Nora laughed, remembering how Tina Dionisio, one of the suspects in a murder of a woman in Cheesman Park area, fell for that fib.

Hawk sat behind the wheel of the unmarked Ford Interceptor, Nora in the front passenger seat and Mortimer with his long legs and feet scrunched in the back.

"Another death," Nora sighed. "It'd be nice to get a break at least until we have the time to finish our never-ending reports."

After turning left onto Speer Boulevard from Washington Street, Hawk asked, "Mortimer, do you remember this street? It's the one we took up to the Cherry Creek area."

"Oh, sure. Very pleasant there. I told Josephine about how impressive the buildings in that swanky area looked. I even asked if we could take a ride to the area since she hadn't been there for years."

"Did you go?' Nora asked, straining her neck around to face him.

"Oh, no. She said it was a total waste of gas money to drive there just to look at a bunch of buildings and rich elitists."

Nora said, "Gads, Mortimer, Josephine is a little hard on people."

"Oh." He remained silent for a minute, then said, "No, I think she really doesn't like to see people spend money."

"But that's what keeps the economy going," Hawk said, chuckling.

"Oh, you're right, but I can't change Josephine's mind."

The three remained quiet for a few minutes until Mortimer broke the silence, "I heard Lieutenant Perez mention the Country Club area. Nora, is that the place that you told me was the first black community in the Denver area? And where the city had a dump on which the expensive shopping center is now located?"

Nora answered, "No, Mortimer, that is further east, across University Boulevard. The Country Club was built where wheat fields existed. This was way out in the country during the turn of the twentieth century. The Country Club mansions, across from the Club, were built on land that was once used as a gentlemen's harness horseracing tract."

"When was that?"

"I believe the first ones went up in 1905 and continued for several years afterward. Your Josephine should buy a house there."

Mortimer sighed, "Josephine supposedly has millions, at least that's what she says, but she'd never spend money like that. She's very frugal…I'm trying to talk her into getting a new mattress for me. Said she'll try to find a second-hand one. No, there'll be no way she'd buy a big house. She's quite happy with her little bungalow in the Washington Park area."

Hawk turned left onto Franklin Street and drove through the interesting Mediterranean-style gateway. He loved to study architecture and this gate fascinated him. It sported straight lines and curved arches.

Nora admired the area with its wide streets and landscaped parkways. She again fantasized that she and Hawk would marry, come into money somehow and live in an upscale area such as the

Country Club. Her mother and grandmother in Pueblo, Colorado would be so proud. Deep in dreamland, she did not hear Hawk.

"Nora, Nora! I don't think the house is on Franklin. What's the address?"

"Sorry, Clint. I was deep in thought. It's on Gilpin."

"Oh, that's right. I'll just go over a block."

"Take your time, I just love to gawk at these houses. The architecture is so eclectic and if I had to choose a house, I couldn't do it. They're all so magnificent."

Hawk commented, "What you see is the Denver square style along with colonial, Mediterranean, Gothic, you name it."

Mortimer cleared his throat. "Yes, Nora, I see why you like the area. It's certainly impressive and peaceful. Tampa has some similar areas. That drive along Bayshore is phenomenal with the blueish waters of the bay to the south and the tall buildings of downtown in the distance."

"Love to see that," Nora said. "Maybe someday…what do you think, Clint? We should fly over some weekend."

"Sounds good. It would certainly be great to get away."

As they parked, a large, impressive house loomed in front of them. A police cruiser, a coroner's van, and the medical examiner's vehicle were parked in the wide driveway. They were greeted on the spacious, red-tiled covered porch by Hawk's competitor from his former days at the police academy and patrol, Corporal Hopkins. The husky, blond-hair corporal appeared disgusted when he spotted Hawk. "You again, de-tec-tive Hawk. I should've known they'd send you to irritate me."

"I guess you're just plain lucky, Dave."

"Yeah, just rub it in—you're the detective and I'm just a corporal. You think you're somethin' special just because you got the promotions, and I didn't."

"How many times are you going to repeat that to me? When in the hell will you get over it? Your time will come. Just hang in there." Hopkins gave him a gruff look. Hawk was used to Hopkins' attitude. At first, it bothered him that his old friend made him feel guilty, *but enough is enough,* he thought. "So, Corporal, what's going on here?".

"As far as I'm concerned, it's just an old man that croaked in his sleep, that's all. But the butler and the housekeeper insist that he was murdered by one of his kids. They made such a stink over it that I was dispatched here and evidently so was the ME. I didn't see any evidence of foul play here. We're all wasting our time; a funeral home should've taken him away by now."

"Nora said, "A butler and a housekeeper. Wow. I always thought that a butler existed only in the movies. Where are they now?"

"They're in the kitchen waiting for you…oh, here comes the butler now. And with that, since I don't think you'll need me, I'm taking off where I'm actually needed." Without saying goodbye, Hopkins turned and left.

A thin, grey-haired man in his early sixties, lithe build, dressed impeccably in a black suit with a white starched shirt and a solid dark blue tie, wearing thick, black-rimmed glasses, slowly approached the detectives. His rectangular face portrayed distress. In an English accent, but flat voice, he said, "I'm Benson, the butler. I assume you're the detectives." They nodded. "Thank you so much for coming. I'm sure that after I explain last evening's dinner with Mr. Hollister's children and spouses, you'll also agree that my employer was murdered. It's just too much of a coincidence."

Nora introduced herself, Hawk, and Holliday, saying, "We definitely want to hear you out, Mr. Benson, but first we'd need to see the decedent and join the Medical Examiner so that we can release the body."

"Just, Benson, madam."

"Yes, of course."

"Please follow me up to Mr. Hollister's bedroom." As they entered through the tall, heavy wooden arched door surrounded by granite, they stepped onto a white marble floor, inset with small black diamond marble tiles. The highly polished floor looked like ice, *I could skate on this,* Nora thought. At the end of the foyer was a wide spiral staircase with a wrought-iron banister and matching spindles, the steps in white marble. The unique staircase was encased by a round tower made of glass blocks. At the foot of the stairs stood a shiny black grand piano overshadowed by a magnificent white statue of Venus, the mythological goddess of love.

Benson turned right at the top of the stairs and led them into a large rectangular bedroom flanked by floor-to-ceiling windows. A long oblong rug covered the highly polished light oak floor. Closer to the door sat two soft upholstered chairs with matching footrests. At the end of the room stood a king-sized bed with a tall wooden headboard. The room was elegant, but the faint smell of death quickly overwhelmed the ambiance.

The medical examiner, a pleasant, older, full-bodied woman, Dr. Janeel Thompson, saw them and waddled over to them. "You again," she laughed. "We have to stop meeting like this over dead bodies. What's wrong with a restaurant or something?" She chuckled. "Nora, I see you scrunching your nose. The odor should bother me also, but over the thirty-three years on this job, I don't even notice it. But if we keep meeting like this, you won't notice it either. Although, I must say, what you're smelling mostly is vomit. Looks like the decedent threw up all over himself, the bed, and part of the floor."

"Yeah, it's pretty ripe in here, Janeel," Hawk said.

"Oh, poor boy, you'll survive." She snorted in laughter.

As Hawk and Nora approached the decedent. Mortimer stayed back. "Aren't you coming, Mortimer?"

"Oh, I don't think so, Nora. I'll stay close to the door if you don't mind. I sense evil in this room. I need to quietly concentrate on what might have transpired." With that said, Mortimer stood in one spot, raised his head toward the tall ceiling, and seemed to fall into a trance.

"What's wrong with him?" Benson whispered. "Is he alright?"

"I wonder about that myself," Janeel said.

"He's all right," Nora said. "That's how he concentrates." Janeel and Benson turned back and took another look at Mortimer. Benson's gray eyes stretched wide, while Janeel rolled her large black eyes.

"Okay, whatever," Janeel said. "Anyway, I just got here a few minutes before you, and from what I see so far is an old man who succumbed to the ravages of old age."

Benson screwed up his face and blurted out, "Oh no. He was only in his late seventies. Other than battling cancer, he was in fairly good shape. If you had seen his fuming children last night after he told them that he's cutting them off the trust and disinheriting them, you'd realize that he was murdered. Anger flowed hot and heavy. They were all here upstairs last night and one or all might have connived of a way to murder him. Consuela and I are convinced of it."

Mortimer suddenly became animated. "Yes, I agree. Evil existed here." With his unexpected outburst, everyone abruptly turned toward Mortimer. He looked back at them. "I'm serious. I feel it in my bones." Nora and Hawk exchanged glances, Nora raising her eyebrows.

"Well then, I better check the man out carefully," Janeel said, her expression semiserious. She studied Mortimer for a moment fascinated with his motionless stare at the ceiling. "Detective, are you some kind of psychic or something?"

Not taking his eyes off the ceiling he answered, "Oh, no. I'm not. But I'm very sensitive to vibrations that I feel when I'm still. It may be just intuition."

Janeel asked, "Are you always right?"

"No, unfortunately, I'm not. But most of the time, I can feel foul play."

CHAPTER 3

THE MEDICAL examiner shook her head and began a thorough inspection of the body. As Hawk, Ricci, and Benson watched, the ME seemed to focus on the decedent's left hand. Then she forced open his mouth and with the aid of a flashlight, looked inside. "Benson, do you know if Mr. Hollister was allergic to anything?"

"Yes. He was extremely allergic to aspirin. He almost died from taking it a few years ago. Why? Do you think someone slipped him an aspirin?"

"Possibly."

"But how? He waited for everyone to leave the house before he came out of his study."

Hawk asked, "Was he avoiding his children? What's that all about?"

Benson sighed. "It's a rather long story, sir, and I'd like to discuss it in a better setting than here. Consuela, the housekeeper, can join us in the library after you're finished. As a matter of fact, I'll go back down and wait for you there. Being in this room is hard on me. I can understand how tragic it was on Consuela when she discovered that our cherished employer had passed away."

Hawk waited for Benson to leave before he asked Janeel, "So what are you thinking?" Mortimer finally approached them but tried to avoid looking at the body.

"I'm thinking possibly that he had suffered from anaphylaxis, a severe allergic reaction, and succumbed from that. I see a few signs of that possibility. Whether it's enough to make a firm diagnosis, I'm not sure. But, for example, even though it's very faint, there is an indication of urticaria—"

"What is that?" Nora asked, puzzled. "It sounds awful."

Janeel chuckled. "Hives. I agree it's a nasty name for hives. Anyway, the vomit could be another sign and then after I checked his throat, I believed that there was an airway obstruction because of an excessive amount of mucus. I'll certainly do an autopsy, but whether I'll find any more than this, I'm not sure. Most times, it's hard to confirm anaphylaxis with an autopsy, but then maybe we'll find other indications such as visceral congestion or petechial hemorrhage."

Hawk said, "Okay, Janeel, you got me that time. You're really trying to impress us. What in the hell is petechial hemorrhage?"

Janeel chuckled again, "A pinpoint collection of blood in the skin. Pretty fancy term, isn't it?"

Nora laughed. "Yeah, and you love to throw those terms around to make us feel like idiots."

Hawk smiled at Nora's comment while he began to look around the bedroom. Afterward, he headed to the private bathroom. The large room had individual sections for the husband and the wife, full mirrors with ample counter space in each section. Hawk immediately spotted an open black container sitting at the end of the white marble countertop. It was a weekly pill organizer. He viewed that the days leading up to today were empty. There were three days left in the week and for those days, the compartments were filled with pills. Nora and Mortimer came in. "What'cha got?" Nora asked.

"Evidently, he took seven pills a day. One of these looks like the round white Bayer Aspirin, but slightly smaller if I remember correctly. If so, then it would certainly be easy to confuse the two."

"Do you think that someone substituted the pill he ordinarily took with aspirin?" Mortimer asked. "Makes it easy, doesn't it?"

"Could be, yes," Hawk said. "We must make sure that the crime lab thoroughly examines the bathroom and particularly the pill box. We might get lucky and there'd be a print or a hair strand."

"That'd be sweet," Nora remarked. "I'll call Chet Watkins from the crime lab and ask him to come by." While she waited for Chet to answer, Nora continued, "If it's that easy to confuse the two pills and based on Janeel's statement that he probably died from anaphylaxis being allergic to aspirin, then someone must've switched the meds."

Watkins did not answer after several rings, so Nora left a voice mail for him and his staff to thoroughly go over the bedroom and bathroom. Looking at Hawk, Nora asked, "But can we rule this a murder today? I'm not sure, are you, Clint?"

"Well, it might be farfetched, but yeah…would be an easy way to kill the old man with no one suspecting it. I'm not ready to call it a natural death…at least not yet."

"Many women carry aspirin in their handbags," Nora said. "And I suppose men carry them in a pocket if they're prone to pain. By habit, I'm sure the decedent grabbed the many pills as was his routine and swallowed them, never imagining that one of them was substituted with an aspirin."

"It's murder," Mortimer said. "I can feel it."

Hawk said, "I tend to agree. But until we know more, I guess we have to consider the death suspicious and leave it at that."

Janeel stuck her head through the door of the bathroom. "You having a high-level conference in here?" She laughed.

Nora said, "You know I love to laugh also, but I'm still squeamish about a dead body around. How can you laugh so easily with all the death that you see?"

"That's why I laugh. Otherwise, I'd cry. Listen, folks, can I have my men in the van take the body? I got a ton of work to do, and now another one. I imagine you'll want me to do an autopsy?"

"Yeah, please," Nora said. "We believe the death is suspicious."

Hawk agreed and mumbled as he walked away, "I think that's all we can do here for now. I'll get our tape and seal the bedroom off."

CHAPTER 4

BENSON MET Nora and Mortimer in the foyer as they descended the stairs. They waited for Hawk to finish taping the door to the bedroom before they followed Benson towards the library. As they walked, the butler said, "It's quiet there and we can talk. This morning I called all his children and informed them of the death. I expect at least someone to arrive."

They entered through another high-arched doorway, again outlined by stone, like that of the front door. The library was another long rectangular room with floor-to-ceiling bookshelves across from each other. At the end of the room hung two large paintings. Hawk studied art as a minor in college and thought he recognized them as paintings by an old Renaissance master, Masaccio, but was not sure. *If they're original, they're worth a fortune.* A long table made of mahogany with six matching armchairs upholstered in red leather stood in the center of the room, an aged red and blue Persian rug underneath.

Except for Mortimer who stood towering over them, the others sat down. Consuela entered the room. Her dark-brown eyes were puffy, her round face wretched, and her lips sagged. She tried to muster a smile but was not able. After introductions, Benson told them about the dinner that Mr. Hollister had arranged. "Mr. Hollister's purpose was to give them a piece of his mind, so to speak," Benson explained. "He was very bitter. Being sick for several months, not knowing how many months he had, he underwent radiation and chemotherapy. He was scheduled to begin another round of it, so he tried to reach out to his children and tell them what he faced. He wanted to tell them in person. But most of them were simply too busy to bother coming over. You can imagine how hurt he felt. He was a good man, a generous man that gave them everything and unfortunately, he spoiled them with a steady monthly stream of income from a trust that he set up specifically for them. It seemed to him that he was no longer necessary to them, only a nuisance they had to deal with.”

Looking sad, Nora said, “Oh my gosh! That’s simply awful. What kind of people are they?”

Consuela spoke up for the first time, “Terrible people, just terrible, except for one son and his wife. The rest thought only about themselves.”

“Mr. Hollister was never able to understand why they turned out that way,” Benson said. “I don’t know if anyone would. Mr. Hollister was bitter and disgusted with their selfish attitudes. He told them that he decided to revoke the trust and only give them a small portion of the estate. Tempers flared; anger became a scalding fury. I don’t remember exactly who it was, but someone threatened him with harm if he even tried it. Others threatened him with lawsuits.”

Benson continued, “This morning I called every one of them, left a message with most, that their father had died. The people I spoke with seemed truly upset, but then again, it might be all for show. Mr. Hollister told them that he’d cut them off next week and now with him dead, they must rejoice and believe that the trust payments would continue, and they’ll receive their share of the estate. I’m sure it entered someone’s head that if he were eliminated before he had a chance to change anything, the funds would continue, and that they’ll inherit. My understanding is that his estate is worth millions.”

The detectives listened, and Nora and Hawk took notes. Benson continued with a wry smile, “What they don’t know is that he had already revoked the trust and made out a new will. He wanted to see the reaction he would receive at the dinner and wanted to give them a chance for a week to see if they could convince him otherwise. That’s why he asked his lawyer, Alan Windsor, to keep the signed documents handy just in case he changed his mind.”

Mortimer asked, “How do you know all this? He was just your employer.”

"Yes, that's true, but over the years we became dear friends, same with Consuela. We were like family. Both Consuela and I live on the premises. We each have a room in the guest house in the back. He confided in us and shared his anxiety about his children."

Mortimer continued, "And since you were so close, you expect to receive an inheritance from him, is that correct?"

Benson took in a deep breath and furled his eyebrows. "He told us that in gratitude we'd be well provided for in his will, but both of us loved the man and certainly didn't want him to leave us. I assume you're accusing us of having a motive to kill him?"

"Yes, it appears that you do if you anticipate a sum of money from his estate."

Devastated by the accusation, Benson pushed his hand across his full gray hair in frustration. He looked at all the detectives, "Please, believe me, we would never want any harm to come to Mr. Hollister. I would protect him with my life and I'm sure Consuela would do the same." Consuela nodded in agreement.

Nora said, "We understand. Detective Holliday is thinking out loud, evaluating all possibilities. It certainly appears from what you told us that the children had quite a motive to end Mr. Hollister's life. But you must understand that we only suspect foul play in this case as we have no concrete evidence, yet, that a murder, in fact, had been committed. The medical examiner wasn't sure if he had died of anaphylaxis or even if he ingested aspirin."

Hawk addressed both Benson and Consuela. "What was Mr. Hollister's condition? What was he dying from?"

Consuela said, "He had prostate cancer, a very aggressive form. He took it awfully hard when he found out. Told the doctor to do everything they could to save him. He was so insistent about more treatments, that his doctor ordered another series of chemo, but advised him it was probably too late."

Hawk asked, "I saw that he was taking seven pills per day. What were they for?"

The butler said, "I always made sure that the weekly pill box had the proper pills so that he wouldn't forget to take them. Let's see." He thought for a moment. "He had two blood pressure pills, a blood thinner, a pill for lowering cholesterol, vitamin D, vitamin K, and the latest one was a cancer med. I believe the name is bicalutamide."

Mortimer asked, "Did you notice that the cancer pill was very similar in appearance to an aspirin tablet?"

"Well, they do look similar, don't they? Do you think that the bicalutamide was replaced by an aspirin?"

"It's quite possible," Hawk said. "Would you by any chance know any of the people at the dinner that use aspirin?"

"Impossible to know. I'm sure maybe some of the ladies would carry it in their purses."

"Benson, you mentioned in the bedroom that all the children were upstairs while their father stayed in his office downstairs," Nora said.

"Yes. Here's where I think he made a grave mistake. He told them to all go upstairs to the rooms they grew up in and take their bits and pieces out. They all went up at the same time and stayed much longer than I thought they should have. It was at least an hour before the last person left."

"Who was the last to leave?" Nora asked.

Benson looked at Consuela, who was sitting quietly, biting her lips. "What do you think Consuela, was it Cynthia and her husband?"

"No, I think it was Darren and his girlfriend with a box full of stuff from his room."

Nora asked, "So who were the people present at the dinner?"

"They were George and Rhonda Hollister, Cynthia and Samuel Maxwell, James and Kay Hollister, Ashley Hollister, and Darren Hollister. Oh, yes, Darren brought his girlfriend, Tina Dionisio."

The detectives' eyes widened, particularly Nora's, when they heard the name of Tina Dionisio. *Surely, it must be another Tina,*

Nora thought. She asked Benson to describe the girlfriend and after he did, she was convinced that it was the same woman who she believed in a previous case was the main suspect in the murder of her lover's wife. She also recalled how Tina flirted with Hawk.

Suddenly, loud doorbell chimes startled everyone. "That must be one of the family," Benson said. He rose and walked to the door. When he returned, he informed the detectives that he asked Ashley, the youngest daughter, to wait in the family room. A moment later, the chimes rang out again. This time, the visitors were Cynthia Maxwell and her husband, Samuel. Benson seated them in the family room as well and told all three to wait.

Hawk said, "Consuela and Benson, thank you for your time. I think we have everything we need for now. We may be back for more questions later, though." He gave each of them his card and asked them to call if they think of anything else that might be helpful.

Benson led them to a sunny family room that opened onto a gourmet kitchen. The room was long and narrow, a classic green and cream Persian rug covered a large portion of the highly polished light oak floor. On top of the rug were an L-shaped couch and four matching chairs strategically arranged in front of a giant TV screen. Beyond the couch, large windows opened up to the beautifully landscaped yard.

Samuel stood as the three detectives walked in, the two women remained seated. Again, introductions were made and immediately Cynthia in a belligerent, arrogant manner, her arms crossed on her wide chest, barked, "What in the hell are you doing here? We were told that our father died in his sleep. So why are the police involved? Surely, you don't think that someone killed him?"

CHAPTER 5

CYNTHIA MAXWELL stood seemingly anxious to confront the detectives, arrows shooting out of her hazel eyes. Her contorted, snarling face reminded Nora of a vicious pit bull. With her hands propped on her wide hips, she lashed out, "So what happened here exactly? Benson told Ashley that Dad's body was already taken away for an autopsy. We don't want an autopsy on our father. Why in the hell was he removed so quickly before we even had a chance to see him? It just shows your bundling incompetence."

Nora responded, "Mrs. Maxwell, I know it's very difficult to lose your father and you are justifiably upset."

"Don't try to smooth talk us here. We're not fools. Cut out the bull crap and explain to us why you're here? Benson told Ashley that our father was found dead in his sleep. He was old and sick and old people die, you idiots."

Hawk said, "Mrs. Maxwell, after carefully studying the body, the medical examiner found evidence that causes us to believe that the death was suspicious in nature. We realize that you have many questions, and we don't have answers for you right now. We'll know more after the autopsy. So please bear with us and we promise to get back to each one of the family members with an explanation."

"You're looking to find a crime where there is none," Cynthia said, her voice still shrill. "You're probably bucking for a fat promotion. Come on, Sam, nothing for us to do here, let's leave." As they began walking out, Nora asked them for their full names and address. Her husband, Sam, provided that information. He apologized for his wife's behavior as Cynthia rushed out the front door, slamming it behind her.

Ashley remained seated at the edge of the long couch. She looked deflated and forlorn. Nora said, "This is very hard on you, isn't it?"

"Yes. I loved my father, but I admit I wasn't the most loving daughter. I realize that I didn't give him the time of day. I always sloughed him off. I thought that there's always going to be a next time that I could spend time with him, but now there will never be a next time." A tear or two streaked its way down her smooth cheek.

Hawk sat down next to her. "Ashley, we heard that the dinner last night was not pleasant for you and the others. Can you tell us what happened?" Nora sat down in the chair across from them. Mortimer remained standing with a piercing look at the poor girl.

"I came late as it seems I always do. At the dinner, my father was very bitter and angry at us for being neglectful children. He accused us of not caring for him, not visiting him, not spending time with him over Thanksgiving and Christmas." A few more tears from her hazel eyes snaked down her face.

"I know it's difficult, but please go on. What happened when you all went upstairs?"

"We all went into our rooms, got our stuff, and went home without being able to say goodbye to our father."

"I understand that you were up there for an hour. Why so long?"

"I can't tell you about the others, but I laid down on the bed and reminisced."

"Did you go into any other rooms, like for instance into George's or Darren's just to talk or reminisce with them?"

Ashley hesitated. Hawk and Nora could almost see her brain cells spinning around in her head trying to say what she thought she should. "I guess so. We all kind of went from room to room, talking to each other."

"What did you talk about?"

She looked squarely at Hawk. "Are you serious, man? We were just cut off from the trust and everyone was mad, and we talked about it."

Hawk continued questioning, "Oh…everyone was mad?"

"Well, duh! What do you think?"

"What did you decide to do about it?"

"I don't know what they decided. I went back to my room and laid down some more then I packed up what I wanted."

"Did you go into your dad's room?"

She hesitated again. "I might've." She blinked twice and adjusted her sitting position. A curl of her dyed blond hair fell across her cheek, her eyes red and puffy.

"Did anyone else go into your dad's room?"

Moving her right hand from her thigh and tucking it under her chin, she fidgeted as she answered, "I think everyone did."

"Now, Ashley, did you know whether your father was allergic to anything?"

"I'm not sure. Maybe peanuts?"

"You think peanuts?"

"Well, I think I remember my mother saying he was allergic to something. Usually, it's peanuts, isn't it?"

"Was he allergic to aspirin, perhaps?"

"Maybe. I don't know." She rapidly blinked several times, shifting her hand from underneath her chin to her left shoulder.

"Which one of your siblings or in-laws would be able to cause harm to your father?"

"I don't think any one of us would…well, maybe James."

"Oh, why do you say that?"

"I don't know, he always seemed to be a conniver to me."

"But he's your brother."

"Yeah, but we were never close. He always acted like my father or something. Always on my back about everything."

"But do you suspect that he would be capable of killing your father?"

She hesitated. "Who knows…maybe."

Nora asked, "Ashley, I heard about you all being terminated from the trust. It's too bad that you'll no longer get a monthly income from it."

"Oh, I believe we still would. Father said that he'd go see the lawyer next week to change anything."

"So, it is rather fortunate for you that he's dead."

"Listen, Detective Ricci, I guess it will work out after all, but I hope you don't have the impression that I wanted my father to die either before or after he changed the trust."

Nora continued, "And I suppose you all discussed that possibility upstairs when you were alone."

"What possibility is that?" Ashley suddenly squirmed.

"You know, if he were dead, your payments would continue."

"Of course not. I just don't believe that anyone of us, even James, could really kill our father."

Mortimer coughed and then asked, "Ashley, you all got together and decided to do away with your father, didn't you?"

Ashley stared at the man that stood looming over her. "No, no, no! We didn't all get together for anything. I told you; we would never kill him. Anyway, how would we have? He was locked away in his office downstairs and we were gone by the time he must've gone to bed. Listen, you make me so uncomfortable that I can't even think straight. I have to leave now."

She rose, snatched her worn Coach purse off the rose-colored stone coffee table, and ran out of the house."

The three detectives looked at each other. "That was interesting," Hawk said.

Mortimer commented, "They all did it. But how we're going to prove it, I don't know. It's a tough case."

CHAPTER 6

THE DOORBELL chimes rang out again. Benson walked from the library where he and Consuela patiently waited and opened the door to Chet Watkins from the crime lab. Hawk and Nora heard the forensic scientist's voice and met him in the hall. Nora said, "Thanks for coming so fast. I'm glad you brought your assistants. Let's go upstairs and I'll show you the room. We need a thorough search of the master bathroom and for sure bag the pill dispenser. Hopefully, you'll find something to help us with this case."

Before they went upstairs, Hawk jokingly said to Chet, "What happened to your khaki safari shirt that you wear? I've never seen you without one before. A plain polo shirt just doesn't go well with the image I have of you." They laughed.

Nora said, smiling, "Yeah, you looked like a real macho man before."

"Blame my wife. She said she was fed up seeing me in the safari look. So, she got me four of these golfing shirts, colors of Easter eggs. But I'll rebel and go back to the comfort of the ones with all the pockets. Anyway, I guess we'll start with getting prints of the people who live in this house. It's quite a grand place, isn't it?" Hawk and Nora nodded in agreement.

Standing next to them, Benson asked, "Why our fingerprints? Please believe me when we say that we didn't do it."

Oh, no, Benson," Nora said, "Taking your prints is standard procedure to differentiate which are yours from the others that might be found in the bathroom."

"I understand. I'll explain it to Consuela. And I'll be pleased to show these gentlemen the main bedroom, so you don't have to climb those stairs." He gave a sad smile. The first expression, other than a somber one, that they saw from him.

Each detective was deep in thought on the way back to the station. Finally, Nora burst out laughing, "I hope it wasn't the butler that did it. No one would believe us."

Mortimer said, "Well, it certainly might very well be him. He had certainly the opportunity and probably a great motive once we dig around a bit."

"What did you think of Ashley?" Hawk asked the two. "I think that she knows a lot more of what happened upstairs than she's letting on. We'll need to question her more in-depth."

Nora said, "I agree Clint. She's hiding something."

CHAPTER 7

WALKING INTO the Homicide unit, Orlinski stopped the trio by his desk as they walked by. "You should know that Captain Iona MacGregor wants to see you. Probably about a status report on the new case. She also wants to see Nancy and Harry." Nancy Salazar and Harry Ling were also homicide detectives in the unit. "Probably wants an update on the motel murder that those two are investigating."

"Geez, Orlinski," Nora said with a chuckle. "Do you always know everything about everything around here?"

"I make it my business," he chuckled back. "You better let Perez know you're back so that he'll inform MacGregor. I hear that she's in a nasty mood."

Nora muttered, "Great!"

"Oh, that's not good for me," Mortimer said. "She always finds fault with me. If it's not my clothes, then my mannerisms." He began to sneeze, once, twice, and finally stopped at four. He grabbed a tissue from a box on Orlinski's desk and pulled out a couple sheets, wiping his runny nose hard thus making it turn as red as Rudolph's. "This Denver dryness just doesn't agree with me," finding an excuse for his stress sneezes.

Hawk, Nora, and Orlinski exchanged glances, eyebrows raised. Hawk said, "I'll tell Perez we're here. Might as well get the show on the road."

After Hawk informed Perez, he went back to his desk at the back of the room. Nora was already at hers. Both were anxious to find time to not only finish the reports from the Ellis case they had solved earlier but now they had more to write with the new Hollister case. Unfortunately, they did not have much time to work on them again because Captain MacGregor pushed her way into the room, followed by Lieutenant Perez. "Okay, people, listen up!" MacGregor's loud voice boomed out. "Gather around."

She sat down on Orlinski's side chair as Perez remained standing at her side. Nora thought that she appeared tired with larger-than-usual bags under her eyes. Her short grayish hair, parted in the center, seemed wispy, and her uniform began to look tight. *She's gaining weight. That's not good, she's not a skinny woman to begin with.*

Right away, she gave an appraising look to Mortimer who had a habit of standing. "Sit down detective. And, my God, where did you find such an awful suit that you're wearing?"

"Oh, ah, Josephine bought it for me. I told her to get me something more stylish, but she said she couldn't find anything in my size at the thrift shops or consignment stores except for this one. You don't like it?"

"No, it's from the seventies. Get rid of it. You make enough money to go to a regular men's store to buy a decent suit. You detectives are not necessarily required to wear suits every day, but I want your clothes to look presentable and not embarrass this department. Do you understand, Detective Holliday?" *Gosh, she's tough on him,* Nora thought. *She shouldn't criticize him like that in front of everyone, although, she's right. He does look weird with his purplish suit and with the red suspenders and bowtie.*

Mortimer began sneezing. MacGregor squinted and turned her head to the side. "Yes, Captain, I'll get rid of this suit and will buy a new one. Thank you for your suggestion."

MacGregor seemed satisfied with that answer. "Okay, then, detectives Salazar and Ling. What's the status of the motel murder?"

Nancy replied, "Captain, we're pleased to report that Harry and I had solved it already."

"How's that?"

"A drunk friend of the victim did it. The so-called friend brought over a bottle of cheap vodka and after a while, the two got into a fight. The visitor pulled out a knife and stabbed him a couple times. It's one of those motels that caters to those down on their luck, the ones with disturbances we're called to all the time. While we were in the room, a neighboring tenant came by and told us who stabbed the man. Evidently, she was in the room with them but left because they were getting too drunk. She gave us his name, a photo off her phone, and where he could be found. Early this morning, he sat on a stool at a nearby sleazy bar already drinking."

"Yeah," Harry Ling broke into Nancy's narrative. "When we walked into the bar he said, 'What in the hell took you so long?' He confessed right there and said he was sorry. Said that he loses his temper when drunk."

Nancy said, "We took him into interrogation, read his rights, and afterward he signed a confession. Lieutenant Perez already reviewed it."

"Pretty lucky, detectives. Now what about this new case, the Hollister case?" She gazed straight at Hawk, then Nora. "I already had a tongue lashing from the decedent's daughter, Cynthia Maxwell. Said you had no reason to interfere in their family's funeral arrangements. Because of you, Hawk, Ricci, and Holliday, an autopsy will be performed. She was emphatic that the family doesn't want their father to undergo the knife and be cut up. She harped on the point that he was old and simply died in his sleep from natural causes."

She focused on Hawk. Taking the hint, he explained, "Captain, the three of us determined that the death was suspicious." Hawk then described the rumbunctious dinner the night before, and the threats Hollister received from his children because he threatened to cut them off from their monthly trust payments and most of their inheritance. "After dinner, because Hollister planned to sell the house, they were sent upstairs to get whatever stuff they had in their former rooms while Hollister closeted himself downstairs, locked in his study so no one would disturb him.

"The medical examiner had good reason to believe that he died of a severe allergic reaction. The butler told us that everyone knew Hollister was allergic to aspirin and one of the pills out of the seven he took each night looked remarkably like an aspirin and could've easily been switched."

Nora added, "We're waiting on word from Janeel, the ME; if she determines it to be murder."

MacGregor asked, "And you think that one of his kids did it?"

Mortimer spoke up, "Or maybe the butler or the housekeeper. Anyway, Captain, how much longer are we going to be tied up here? It was past noon and Josephine insisted that I come home for lunch today as she is making something very special. I think she said, 'Spinach rolls made of flaky gluten-free dough topped by vegan parmesan cheese.'"

Nancy looked at Nora, and her mouth dropped. Nora returned her glance, raising her eyebrows.

MacGregor's face turned red. Her voice raised, she shouted, "Holliday! you're unbelievable! I don't give a damn if your precious Josephine expects you or if she fixed that, in my opinion, awful meal. You'll leave when we're through here and not a second sooner. Understand? Tell your fiancé not to interfere in your work."

She took a deep breath, her chest heaving, and forced herself to calm down. Everyone was stunned and sat silently for a minute or so. Once MacGregor caught her breath, she queried, "Okay, Ricci and Hawk, what's your next step?"

Hawk looked at Nora. They really hadn't planned a next step yet, waiting for the autopsy results, but evidently, MacGregor wanted action right away. "We need to get individual statements from each of the people in the house the night before. Even though we don't have the autopsy results, we need to proceed with this case as if Hollister was murdered."

Nora said, "This is where Lieutenant Perez's team approach would be helpful. For example, we need to find out as much as we can about the people present. Clint and I will certainly interrogate each person, but it would be helpful if we had information on them as far as their background, bank statements, and a social media search before we interview potential suspects. Since there would be eleven of them, it'll take some time."

Orlinski said, "Well, you all know how much I love to do that kind of work. I'll be glad to start on it right away."

"I was about to suggest that," Perez said. Looking at Salazar and Ling, "I want you actively involved with this case since we have so many suspects. In other words, you all work together on this one."

"What about me?" Mortimer said, standing up. "Can I still work with Hawk and Ricci?"

MacGregor asked, "How good are you with the computer?"

"Oh, not good at all. I can write up a report, but I wouldn't know where to begin to search on social media."

MacGregor looked away from him, shut her eyes, and mumbled something inaudible. After shaking her head, she said, "All right folks, go grab some lunch and hit it hard this afternoon." Then a rare smile appeared on her face. "And Holliday, don't eat too much spinach, it'll make you green." Everyone but Mortimer laughed.

"Where do you want to go to lunch," Hawk asked Nora, not sure that she would go. He did not understand why, but the last few days, it seemed that she tried to distance herself from him. He had no clue as to her thoughts that more than ever she would like to be with him. But she needed to see some affection and more acknowledgment that he really likes her. She sensed that he did by the way he treated her, but somehow, he just didn't show it.

If Hawk could not commit to a serious relationship, then she would waste her time waiting for him regardless of how much she wanted him. Getting close to her mid-thirties, she desperately wanted to settle down with a husband and children. Besides, her mother was relentless in urging her to marry. She would not marry someone she didn't love and had turned down a couple of proposals.

With Hawk's lunch invitation, she decided to turn it down hoping that he would eventually realize that he missed her.

"Sorry, Clint, can't do lunch today. Maybe tomorrow."

CHAPTER 8

IT REALLY began to upset Hawk that Nora turned him down again. He thought that they were doing great together. She was unbelievably fun to be with. She was funny and highly intelligent and had an infectious laugh that made him happy. He could talk to her about anything. They seemed to fit so well together. *So, why the abrupt change in her attitude? She even asked if I'd go meet her family in Pueblo. I know she likes me, so why the brush-off?*

"Okay, Nora, no lunch together, but you promised me dinner and a massage to soothe my aching back and neck muscles that are still killing me." He was referring to his first case as a detective where to save himself from an execution with a gun pointed at him, he purposely drove the police cruiser into an embankment knocking the killer out. "You know, I'm still getting nightmares from that and all the close calls that we had."

Nora laughed with some bitterness. "You just don't give up, do you? Now you're playing the pity card."

"Of course. I want to be with you, Nora."

"Well, I'll let you know this afternoon, okay?" She snatched her purse, adjusted the skirt of her dark-gray suit, flung her long dark-brown hair to the side, and gave a gentle wave over her shoulder as she walked out the door.

As Hawk passed Orlinski's desk, the man stopped him, smiling mischievously, "Well, now is a good time for me to collect on that lunch you promised me for getting that info on the Ellis case. I'll collect that Polish vodka later. Besides, we need to get to know each other a little better."

"Sure, good idea. Where do you want to go?"

"I bet you have never had Polish food, have you?"

"No, but I'm game."

"Okay, let's go to one. Just a few blocks away. It's by no means a fancy place, but you'll love the food."

Orlinski drove his brand-new Toyota Rav. On the way there, he insisted on filling Hawk in on the latest gossip concerning Captain MacGregor. "She had a big fight with her husband, an antique store owner down on South Broadway. That made her mood foul. Took it out on poor Mortimer," Orlinski laughed. "I thought he'd have a stroke, he looked pissed, although I really couldn't tell. He always looks that way."

"How would you know that Stan? I mean about the fight."

"Oh, I have my ways." He laughed again. He took a quick glance at Hawk. "Okay, I talked to one of the robbery detectives over coffee this morning. She said that MacGregor ripped into her for nothing. A minute later, she apologized and blamed it on a nasty fight with her husband. I wish I knew what it was about. I bet it was over money."

"Stan, that's no big deal. Couples always argue and get upset, especially when money is concerned." *Holy cow! He's such a gossip.*

"Well maybe that's not a big deal but getting together for coffee with that cute detective was a big deal for me. I'm not you when it comes to women. I mean they fall all over you, don't they?" Hawk prepared to deny such a broad statement, but Orlinski kept on talking in his rapid style of dialogue.

"Actually, the reason I wanted to have lunch is so you could give me a few pointers. I'm thinking seriously of asking that detective out on a date. I'm really out of touch when it comes to the dating scene." He turned toward Hawk to see his reaction. Hawk hoped that he hid his look of surprise from Orlinski. "Oh, here we are, let's hope we can find a spot to park…oh, we're in luck, there's one."

The restaurant was an old two-story brick building on Colfax, painted in a beige color. Hawk surmised that the second floor was used as apartments. Upon entering through a brown entry door Hawk noticed an inviting, subdued atmosphere. His eyes were immediately focused on the antique, dark, wooden bar, and thought about all the drinks served over it for maybe a century. A large variety of liquor bottles and, most unusual, jars of vodka infused with vegetables, were artfully arranged on the old elaborate shelving at the back of the bar. A large flatscreen TV showing a hockey game was attached above.

The pleasant owner knew Orlinski and both he and Hawk were treated like royalty. They were seated at a high-top brown wooden table with matching wooden chairs. A pretty, slim waitress, dressed in black, brought menus and Orlinski suggested that Hawk take either the goulash or his favorite, Polish smoked sausage with potato pancakes, or fried potatoes and sauerkraut stew. Hawk chose the goulash. Each had water.

While the order was prepared, Orlinski said, "So, Clint. I was serious about getting some advice from you. I think I'm crazy about Monica. You know, I'm approaching fifty in a couple of years, and I feel that I missed out. Work from early morning to late at night had been my life. Monica is probably five years my junior, divorced with two kids. Clint, I want a family to come home to. I really like her and don't want to lose her. So, where do people go on dates these days? I suppose dinner. Do they still go to the movies?"

"Stan, I'm flattered that you're asking me for advice. I'm not sure I'm the man to give you any." He thought for a moment. To him, dating came naturally without much stress over where to take a girl. "Yes, dinners at restaurants. Maybe at each other's houses after you get to know each other better. You need to feel her out as to what she likes. Maybe she prefers a quiet evening together. Maybe she enjoys movies, concerts, symphonies, or dancing. Then does she like ballroom or rock? You just need to ask her."

"That's not good. I don't know how to dance."

"Well, if its pop music just move around and pretend that you know what you're doing. But Stan, you need to just ask her out, take her to a quiet restaurant and get to know each other a little better. After you do that, you can play it by ear."

"I'll do that. I'll invite her to a really nice place."

"It doesn't have to be necessarily expensive. Don't go overboard on the first date. Just someplace that's quiet where you can concentrate on each other."

The food came. Orlinski received a huge sausage plate while Hawk stared at a large soup bowl, wondering if he should chance it. He had goulash before but did not remember it being a soup. He swished it around and saw that it was filled with several chunks of beef hidden in the brown sauce or gravy. With the bowl, he was also served a plate with two potato pancakes sprinkled with green onions and side dishes of mashed beets, creamed cucumbers, and coleslaw. He took a taste of the soup while Orliniski watched for his reaction. "It's very good, similar to an old-fashioned stew that my grandma used to make, except this has a lot of paprika in it." He took another spoonful. "Stan, it's great, thanks."

"Try those potato pancakes."

Hawk took a bite, "They're wonderful. But I often had something similar growing up in Tyler, Texas. My grandparents on my mother's side were German. This food is remarkably like what I grew up with."

"I'm glad you like it. Was afraid that you wouldn't." Without pausing, Orlinski asked, "So are you and Nora serious about each other?"

Hawk had just stuffed some beef in his mouth and almost choked at that question. He felt blindsided. "Stan, where did that come from? I mean you changed the subject out of the blue."

"Clint, you gave me some good advice and now I want to give you some. "You're no spring chicken either. Don't become like me where you'll regret that you didn't get married and have a family. I've never done it, but it makes sense that if you jump around from one woman to the next, you'll never receive the satisfaction that your life is complete." *Who in the hell is this jerk that I barely know or knows me to give me such personal advice? Did I ask him to interfere in my life? I'm perfectly happy with my situation.*

"Stan, I'm not you. I'm not sure I want the commitment of a marriage at this time. What you think would make you happy doesn't necessarily mean that it's for me."

"Don't get mad. I know it's none of my business. But I see you and Nora together and can see how well you fit together. Don't lose her. She's a knockout, intelligent, and a great catch, but she won't wait forever. Someone else will come along and you'll be out of the picture."

Getting heated under the collar, Hawk wanted to punch Orlinski. He took some deep breaths, then said, "Stan, I know that you think that you're giving me great advice. It may be great advice, but I don't like people telling me what to do concerning my social life. One reason I live in Colorado, while the rest of the family is in Texas, is because they too had plans for me that I didn't agree with. So please, let's stay friends, but don't give me advice on my love life. It seems to me that you need to worry about yours at this moment." Hawk suddenly regretted his strong words. Orlinski looked disappointed. To soften his lashing out, he said, "And if you ever marry this Monica of yours, don't forget to invite me to your wedding. I have a feeling it won't be long in coming." Hawk laughed.

Orlinski laughed companionably. "You got it, Clint, but then you'll have to invite me to yours and whether you want to or not, that may not be long either." Hawk shook his head, still miffed at the man. *He's a real buttinsky. Mind your own business, man.*

Hawk paid for lunch and on the way back, neither one of them talked about women, families, or marriage. Instead, Hawk shifted the attention to the Hollister murder stating that they have a ton of witnesses to interview.

As they returned to the station, walking down the hall to the Homicide unit, a nice-looking thin woman, average height, with shoulder-length light-brown hair walked toward them. She wore a navy-blue business suit, and a light blue blouse with her jacket unbuttoned. A DPD shield was visible on her belt. Hawk saw that

Orlinski suddenly became animated, a wide smile on his face as she approached. The woman also grinned widely. "Hello, Monica," Orlinski said. "Ah, ah, did you have a nice lunch?"

"Oh, yes, Stan. I sat at my desk and had a peanut butter and jelly sandwich. Couldn't be finer than that, could it?" She said sarcastically. She then glanced over towards Hawk waiting to be introduced.

Orlinski got the hint and said, "Ah, Monica Pachek, this is Clint Hawk. Clint is a detective in our unit."

"Hello, Clint. I've heard about you. Everyone in the building heard of all the people trying to kill you. You're quite famous around here."

"It's a pleasure to meet you too, Monica. I really don't want that notoriety. But would you two excuse me, I need to get back." He told Monica once more that it was nice to meet her and went back to his desk wondering if Orlinski would in fact invite her out to that dinner.

CHAPTER 9

ENGROSSED AT her computer, Nora did not notice Hawk sneak up on her and playfully knock hard on her desk. Startled, she jerked. She batted him away in fun and laughed. "Man, I'm going to get even with you for that. When you least expect it, I'll get you." She laughed again. "So how was lunch?"

"I had lunch with Orlinski. Should I say more?" He chuckled. "No, actually, it wasn't bad."

"What did he have to say?"

"That he's in love and wants to get married."

"Smart man. It's about time."

Hawk thought he would shock her with the news, but she didn't seem fazed. He thought she would ask with whom, but she did not. So, he volunteered, "He met this detective over at Robbery and thinks that she's the one. Divorced, and has two kids. Instant family for him."

"Like I said, smart man. When's the wedding?"

"Don't rush it. He only had coffee with her, not even one date yet. There're out in the hall now setting it up. I hope."

"Well, if he knows what he wants, he should go for it and not dilly-dally around. I like a man who knows what he wants."

Hawk sensed that her conversation was really directed at him. The took a dig at him. But he was not about to commit himself to anything. "Yeah, good for him."

"Listen, Clint, I think we should interview Hollister's lawyer, Alan Windsor, about the will and trust for his kids. It would be good to know the status of that before we question them."

"You're absolutely right. I think we should do it right away."

"What about Mortimer? He's not back yet. Don't you think we better wait for him otherwise he'll complain about it again as he did in the Ellis case?"

Hawk rolled his eyes. "Well, he's late so we have an excuse. But, okay, let's wait another few minutes."

The door opened and Orlinski walked in, a Cheshire cat grin spread on his face. He threw a thumbs up to Hawk and sat down. A minute later, a medium-built man in a tan suit walked in, looked around for a moment, and with a wide smile made a beeline for Nora. She suddenly recognized him, stood up, and rushed to hug him. They embraced for much longer than Hawk liked. As a matter of fact, he hated it. The man was ruggedly handsome with slightly tanned skin and tawny hair. Nora turned toward Hawk and introduced the two, "Clint, I want you to meet my old partner from patrol, Seth Morgan."

Hawk stood, feeling awkward. Bubbling, Nora said, "I haven't seen Seth for years."

Hawk nodded and Nora turned her attention to Seth. "So, how's life been? How are Sherri and the kids doing?" Hawk mumbled that it was nice to meet him and sat down.

"She and the kids are fine, except that we're divorced for a year now. And you? Other than being shot at?"

Nora laughed, "Oh you heard about that."

"Oh yeah. Every cop knows about it." He glanced at Hawk. "Speaking of that is there any place where the three of us can talk privately?"

They sat down in one of the interrogation rooms and Seth sighed as he sat across from Hawk and Nora. "I'm here because I'm worried for you, Nora." Turning his attention to Hawk, he added, "And of course for your safety as well."

Suddenly looking concerned, she asked, "What is it, Seth?"

"I'm an investigator with the DA's office now and we got word from a correction officer about threats made by an inmate. I'm sure you can't forget, Devon O'Leary."

Nora's eyes widened. "Never. I still have nightmares about that creep. So, what about him?"

"It appears he boasted to another inmate that he'd arranged to get rid of the freakin' detectives that arrested him. Said you'd be dead meat before long. Said he's got a cousin that owes him one. Supposedly likes to kill people for the fun of it." Nora's heart fell to her feet. Hawk tensed up, clamping his jaw.

Hawk said, "Well Seth, that kinda ruins digestion right after lunch. Not something we wanted to hear." He tried to smile and act as if he was cool about it, but his stomach turned inside out. Nora placed her hand on his knee. Hawk could feel her hand quiver.

"We think he's just acting macho and blowing smoke. But just in case, we thought you should be on the lookout. All the corrupt cops you put away must hold a deep grudge, especially Bradford and O'Leary. As star witnesses in their upcoming trials, they'd do anything to make you disappear."

Obviously shaken, Hawk asked, "Any idea who this killer cousin is?"

"We made a quick search of who his cousins might be. He has a couple of female cousins that live in Kentucky—married women with a bunch of kids. Couldn't find any male cousins. Maybe he's just using that term to mean a close friend."

Nora asked, "Any idea how he could've contacted someone outside of the jail?"

"He had a girlfriend visit him. We reviewed a video and of course, no messages could be passed through the partition, but he did put up his hand against the glass and she seemed to study it before placing her hand over his as a sign of affection. It could be that he had a name and address scribbled on his palm, for her to contact. You know, we can't hear conversations and he held his hand to the side of the mouth so we couldn't lip read."

Hawk asked, "Did you follow up with the girlfriend?"

"That's just it. We think she gave a fake ID and we're not sure who she is or how to find her. I'll give you a still from the video for you to watch out for her."

Nora covered her eyes with her right hand, shook her head, and said, "Great. This is all we need after all we've been through."

Seth stretched his hand across the table and took her left hand, and gently squeezed it. "Sorry to be the bearer of bad news, especially after all this time that we hadn't seen each other." Hawk resented him holding her hand.

"We appreciate it, Seth," Nora said. "At least we'll know to watch our backs. Thanks."

Seth looked directly at Nora, ignoring Hawk, "If you need anything, anything at all, here's my card. Call me day or night. I'll be right over." Hawk decided that he didn't like this sleazeball at all.

Back at their desks, Nora asked, "So what do you think, Clint? Do we have a problem?"

Deep in thought, Hawk did not answer right away. Nora waited. "The worst thing that could happen to us is to dwell on it and let fear take over our lives. I'm not saying to ignore the possibility that there's someone out there, but for our sanity, we must live our normal lives as if we never heard the bad news, but watch our step."

"Do you think we should advise Perez and MacGregor?"

"Sure, since I'm sure they'll be informed anyway."

Hawk was right. Perez called Nora and asked her and Hawk to meet him in MacGregor's office. They were informed of the threat and assured the two detectives that the Department will be vigilant. MacGregor further said, "I think both of you need a vacation to a Caribbean Island or someplace far away for a couple of weeks. I'll authorize it right away."

Hawk said, "Thank you, Captain, and I'm speaking only for myself, but I want to see this thing through. I couldn't relax until the killer after us, if there is one, is caught."

"I totally agree," Nora said.

"Fine but be damn careful. Don't want to lose any of my detectives."

Walking back to their desks, Mortimer finally came back from lunch. He was more than an hour late. "Sorry, but after Josephine fed me lunch, I must've gotten food poisoning. I think I'm okay now."

"Oh, I'm sorry," Nora said. "Will you be able to work this afternoon?"

"Yeah, I'm fine now. Josephine gave me some herb concoction and said that it'll cure me. And it sure seems to work."

Hawk said, "In that case, let's get to work and take a trip to see Hollister's attorney, Alan Windsor."

CHAPTER 10

THE ATTORNEY'S OFFICE was in Golden, Colorado, a western suburb of Denver, bordered by the foothills of the Rocky Mountains that loomed over the Front Range of Colorado. As planned, Nora drove, encouraging Hawk to be on the lookout for any suspicious vehicles that may be following them. Seth Morgan's warning about a possible killer bore heavily on their minds. She took the Sixth Avenue freeway, which further west eventually connected to Interstate 70, the gateway to the many ski and quaint former mining towns.

Slouching in the back seat, Mortimer eyed the terrain with great interest. As usual, the early afternoon radiant sun illuminated the wall of mountains in the distance. The weather in August was hot but bearable. He liked the trip and felt like he was part of the team with the two detectives, his tall, lanky body relaxed. Never in this part of the metro area, he was anxious to see something new. "I wish Josephine would go places. There are so many interesting things to see around here. I'd love to go deep into those mountains. I've never been…and they're so close. But she just tells me it's expensive and foolish." He sighed. "Nora, where exactly are we going? I heard you say, Golden. Is that a separate town?"

The heavy traffic kept Nora's eyes glued to the road, but she managed to answer. "Yes, Golden is a separate municipality. I'd love to live there, but most places are out of my price range. Although, I don't have to live there to enjoy a slow walk along Clear Creek, get mesmerized by the swift turbulent water, or tube down the creek. Then stroll along Washington Avenue, gawk at the storefronts of the old town, eat ice cream, and afterward have dinner at El Dorado Mexican Restaurant. I love the food there."

Hawk asked, "You do that often?"

"Not as often as I'd like." Hawk nodded but did not say a word. *Who did she go with? Surely not by herself?*

Mortimer said, "Nora, you always know a lot of history of this area. What do you know of Golden?"

"Actually, there's a lot of history there. Golden was the first capital of Colorado. Before Colorado became a state in 1876, Golden was the capital of the provisional territory of Jefferson around 1860. Then it became the territory of Colorado with Golden still the capital because of its location between the small population of Denver at the time and the mining towns in the mountains which the merchants of Golden supplied. Later, as Denver grew, political forces moved the honor to Denver City, twelve miles east. Golden competed with Denver to be the major city of the State. Both communities realized that growth would come with a railroad spur out of Cheyenne. So, they began to compete to build the tracks. When it became apparent that Denver was winning, the Golden businessmen then turned their attention to a railroad to the mountain towns. I've read that because Denver's railroad made it to Cheyenne and connected to the east-west line, Denver grew to be the big city of the State."

Mortimer said, "That's interesting. Railroads certainly made big differences in settling areas of our country. Florida was mostly swamp land until Henry Flagler built a railroad running up and down the east coast. He built hotels and before long tourists began streaming in to get away from the cold winters up north…oh, wow, what's that beautiful building seeming to come out of nowhere standing by itself?"

Nora laughed, "That's the Taj Mahal."

"What? That's not the Taj Mahal. Isn't that supposed to be in India somewhere?"

Both Nora and Hawk laughed. "That's just what the locals call it. That's the Jefferson County Judicial Building. It's quite striking, isn't it?" Nora drove more northernly on Sixth planning to turn right onto 19th Street which would take her into the downtown Golden.

Hawk sat in silence for most of the trip. His mind was on O'Leary. He would not put it past him to find a way to get even with them even while incarcerated. *He probably has an even bigger grudge against Nora for how she was able to quickly subdue him and save my life from his planned ambush. She was spectacular with her proficient Taekwondo moves. He wouldn't forget that easily, especially a small-framed woman taking him down. Bradford also must be seething. They probably communicate in prison and scheme how to get to them. Get even and eliminate them as witnesses.* Hawk took the threat seriously.

He turned back to face Holliday. "Mortimer, there is something that you should know. You probably should ask Perez to assign you to work with other detectives for your own safety."

"Oh, no. My safety? Are you planning to kill me?" He looked serious with not a hint that he was joking.

Nora cracked up and Hawk smiled. "No, Mortimer we wouldn't want to kill you. Here's the problem. We were told that there may be a hit on us." He laid out what Seth Morgan told them and explained who Bradford and O'Leary were and why those corrupt cops were so dangerous. "Nora is driving because, as you might've noticed, I've been watching the cars behind us just in case. And we'll have to continue being overly careful until at least after the trial."

Mortimer sat silent digesting the information. "I'm in this with you and will take my chances. Don't want to work with anyone else unless I absolutely must. You're decent people and I feel you understand my shortcomings. I'm comfortable working with you. But I better not tell Josephine about this, or she'll have some politician that she knows, transfer me to another Division. I'm glad you told me. This way I can meditate on it."

Hawk made an appointment to see the lawyer at 2:<u>30 p.m.</u> and if they found the office right away, they should be on time. He was told that the office was a converted Victorian house in the Colorado School of Mines neighborhood. As Nora approached the university, Hawk thought about Marcie Turner who graduated as an engineer from there. From the moment he met Marcie, he had a crush on her, a blond with dazzling blue eyes, and a smile that disarmed. At least twice she asked him to move away with her to California and give up being a cop. She couldn't live with the fear of him not coming home, suggesting that he finish his Ph.D. and set up a psychologist practice. He worked hard to become a detective and giving that up was out of the question. He simply could not commit. Besides, he met Nora, and Marcie's attraction faded. *Why do I keep thinking about her so much?*

Now that his life was again in danger, a fleeting thought occurred to him that perhaps Marcie was right. How long would his luck last? He already escaped death four times. Nora said that he's like a cat with nine lives and he's got five to go. *But is this a way to live, constantly in fear?*

A gray-haired older woman sat behind a dark wooden desk. A large computer monitor shielded half of her face from view as they walked in. She scooted her chair to the side and with a pleasant smile asked in a raspy voice, "You must be the detectives from Denver. Please make yourselves comfortable for a few minutes. Mr. Windsor is in a conference, but he should be through soon."

They sat down on individual dark blue leather chairs with walnut armrests. A large stone fireplace faced them with a tall brass scale of justice on its mantle. To the right of the fireplace, hung a blown-up poster of Golden in the early days—wooden and stone buildings, horses pulling wagons as pedestrians dodged. Behind the secretary were shelves full of legal books. Above their chairs were two more posters of the area—one depicting the Buffalo Bill Museum, which is located at the top of Lookout Mountain, and another of the Coors Brewery. The floor was of stone tile with a large bear-skin rug lying in front of the fireplace. Hawk thought that if he ever did open an office, that's what he would like—a comfortable place to work in a home-style environment.

As they waited, they heard shouting behind the door to the attorney's office. Suddenly, the door swung open, and Cynthia Maxwell stormed out, followed by her husband. "I'm getting my own lawyer!" Cynthia yelled. "I have a right to a copy of the Trust and Will, you Jackass!" For a second, she seemed startled to see the detectives. She demanded, "And what are you doing here?" She did not wait for an answer, threw a middle finger at them, and rushed out the front door.

With his face flushed, Sam Maxwell apologized to Windsor and then to the detectives. "She's just not herself since her father died. Please pay no attention." They could tell that his wife's outburst left him embarrassed as he apologized again and, his shoulders stooped, left the office.

The incident with Cynthia obviously rattled Windsor. Nora felt sorry for the old man, probably in his early eighties, with deep wrinkles on his chiseled face and sagging shoulders. He wore a plaid, striped shirt, no tie, and western-style pants sporting a large silver and turquoise belt buckle. His short, balding white hair was meticulously combed. As he moved slowly past his assistant, he mumbled to her, "I don't need this crap at my age." Mustering a faint smile, he invited the detectives into his office.

Hawk was struck at the number of bookshelves on three of the four walls of the room, all crammed with law books. Behind his messy massive desk with files and papers scattered, certificates hung on both sides of the shaded window.

He pointed to the chairs. Nora and Hawk sat down, but Mortimer continued to stand. "Please sit down, sir," Windsor said. "I don't like people standing over me." Mortimer slowly complied. "I suppose you're inquiring about Hollister's last will?"

Hawk said, "Yes, we heard a conflicting story regarding that will. Do the children inherit anything?"

"I have a dilemma here whether I should answer that question. If Hollister were alive, I couldn't for sure. But now since he's deceased, my usual response is that you need to contact the personal representative of the estate and let him decide. But since I am the personal representative, I must make that decision." He chuckled.

"I got myself into a hornet's nest all because of my friendship with the decedent who begged me to handle the estate as the PR."

"PR?" Mortimer said.

"Yes, personal representative, but most people still say executor."

Nora said, "I can certainly understand you calling it a 'hornet's nest' judging by Cynthia Maxwell."

"Oh, you already met her. She's trouble, I know. What I don't understand is how a fine, decent, generous man like William Hollister could've raised such crummy kids. Except for James, they're all losers and parasites as far as I'm concerned."

Mortimer said, "James, you say. One of the daughters said that if anyone of them had killed their father it was James."

Windsor looked surprised. "Oh. That's interesting. James and his wife were the ones closest to their father. William used to tell me that it was James that visited, invited him, and all that good stuff. No, I don't buy that at all. Do you really think that Hollister was murdered?"

"We haven't determined that yet," Hawk said. "But if that turns out to be the case, any idea on who might've done it?"

"Oh, I wouldn't venture to guess. Cynthia certainly has a volatile temper, but so do most of the others. George is a lot like her. Devon is lush and if he's drunk, who knows what he'd do? And that Ashley is so spoiled, spends money like a drunken sailor so she's always out of funds. I'm worried how she'd survive without Daddy's help. William said that if she must earn her own way, she'll grow up quickly."

Nora said, "So what you're saying is that anyone of them could've done it."

Windsor added, "Or one of the spouses."

Nora continued, "We don't want to make you uncomfortable in divulging the contents of the will, so if we tell you of our understanding of the will, would you be able to just confirm."

Windsor nodded, then scratched the top of his head. "We heard that the butler and the housekeeper will get a certain amount. Then each of the children, except for James, will receive two-hundred thousand dollars. James will receive the balance or the bulk of a large estate. And the trust that paid the children a monthly distribution would be terminated."

Hawk said, "But this is what's confusing. At the dinner, the night before he died, Hollister said that he'd wait a week before he'd make that will that Detective Ricci described. If that's the case, then the trust would continue, and the children would inherit whatever was outside the trust. Yet, Benson the butler told us that the new will and the revocation of the trust had already been executed by Hollister before the dinner."

"Benson is right. William didn't trust his children and made the changes a month ago. He had a feeling that something might happen to him after he told them what to expect. I advised him against that gathering, but he felt he needed to express how much they disappointed him. So, except for some charitable contributions, Detective Ricci is correct. Since I heard from all the children, badgering me to divulge information about the will, I've set up the reading for early next week. Actually, I'd appreciate it if you would be present for that. You might find it informative, and frankly, I'd feel better about having you here. I think the meeting will be tumultuous and even nasty."

The detectives thanked Windsor for his candor and said their goodbyes. As they approached their vehicle, they saw a muddy dark grey Dodge Ram pickup spin its tires exiting the gravel parking lot with flying dirt and rocks. Encased in mud, the license plate was totally unreadable. Knowing that an assassin may be hunting them, paranoia set in as both Nora and Hawk suspiciously viewed the rapidly departing pickup.

"What was he doing in the lot?" Nora asked, her face troubled.

Hawk said, "Probably nothing." He thought for a moment. "Since we're nervous about it, I remember my first case where they put a tracker on my vehicle. It's a long shot, but I think I'll check out our vehicle just in case."

Nora and Hawk searched the undercarriage and the fenders of the Ford Interceptor. Mortimer searched as well. "Okay," Hawk pointed out, "here's the sucker. This small rectangular black box is the GPS tracker."

"Where did you find it?" Mortimer asked.

"Underneath the rear bumper."

"Oh God," Nora said. "The threat is real! Shit!"

CHAPTER 11

FINN O'LEARY was angry at himself for the way he departed from the lawyer's parking lot. He should have stayed cool and slowly exited the lot, rather than drawing attention to himself. Perhaps, he should have just shot them as they walked out, but there was too much traffic around and too many dorm windows from the School of Mines overlooking the office. At least, he was able to attach the tracker in time. *They'll never know it's there and in no way would they suspect that I'm out to get them; not yet anyway,* he thought. *How would they possibly know? When I peeled out, they'd just think it was some crazy teenager getting a kick out of spinning his wheels.*

O'Leary planned to make this a game, terrorizing them a little, before he brought them down. *I'll make this a cat-and-mouse game and they are the mice,* laughing savagely at the thought. A week ago, he was more than pleased to get a message from his cousin's girlfriend on a burner phone, one that he immediately destroyed afterward. As a favor, Devon O'Leary needed his help to eliminate a couple of cops in revenge and as witnesses in a forthcoming trial. He knew who to look out for as his girlfriend provided him with their names and photos. A piece of cake.

He owed his cousin. Years ago, when Finn was in the Irish Republican Army, Devon financed a cache of weapons for the IRA by smuggling them into Ireland using fishing boats that met in the middle of the Atlantic. That was the way he illegally entered the United States with the help of an Irish fisherman, an IRA sympathizer, who transported him to a waiting American fishing trawler that brought him to a Boston fishing dock. From there, he sneaked into the United States. All arranged by his cousin. Shortly, thereafter, the fishermen that were paid to transport him were all found shot to death in their boat. No witnesses.

Being skilled in weaponry and explosives, all gained through his experience with the IRA since his teen years, Finn soon developed a reputation as a phantom assassin among various mobs and other gangsters around the country that needed his services. He only dealt with them through ever-changing addresses on the dark web and cryptocurrency. Only his cousin, the cop, the criminal, that sat behind bars, knew that he was in this country and what he looked like. He never used his real name and always dealt in cash.

He operated under the radar, a stealth ability to avoid detection helped by the fact that he didn't officially exist in the United States. Committing many unsolved murders and bombings, Finn left investigators from several agencies such as the FBI, DEA, ATF, and state and local police agencies scratching their heads.

The more that Finn got away with his killings, the more emboldened he became. It was now a game to commit heinous crimes and get away scot-free. As an addiction, he needed a hit more and more often to keep the adrenalin of a kill going. A surge of power overtook him and enveloped him in a mantle of invincibility. Even if he didn't owe a favor to Devon, he would gladly have made it to Denver to kill two local detectives. *Too easy of a job. I have to have some fun with it, that's for sure.*

Hawk took the tracker with him inside the Ford. He knew that it needed to be dusted for prints in case the guy was sloppy, but he doubted there would be any. Nora's hands trembled as she pulled away from the lot. *Here we go again. Someone else is out there trying to kill us. God, please protect us, we sure seem to need your help lately.* Everyone sat silent for a few minutes, then Nora said, "Check the make and model of that stupid tracker. Perhaps we can hit a few stores to see if they remember who might have bought it."

"Probably a hundred stores and don't forget the internet," Hawk said. "You can get them at Best Buy, Walmart—"

"Okay, okay. Maybe that's not such a hot idea."

Mortimer said, "Any idea at all who it could be? Shouldn't be that difficult to track down a cousin, should it?"

Nora said, "That's what I plan to work on as soon as we get back. But do you still want to hang around with us, Mortimer? I have this bad feeling in my gut that it'll get nasty."

"Oh. Ah. I already told you I'm with you all the way. But I'm sure not going to tell Josephine about any of this. If I know her, she'll have a conniption fit. She thinks all we do is ride around all day and just talk to people. She really has no idea what we do. But to tell you the truth, I am worried. I've never been in any danger in Tampa as a detective. It's nerve-wracking." Mortimer sneezed several times; his nose began to run. Nora handed him a tissue out of her pocket.

"We don't like it either," Hawk said. "I have a pit in my stomach large enough to drive a Mac truck through, but we'll get him, don't worry."

Nora said, "You know though, this may give us an advantage. He doesn't know that we know about the tracker or that we can use it to smoke him out. Let him follow us or we can lead him to a place where he'd come to us. Of course, we have to be on our toes and make sure we see him first. Maybe, we could get one of the other detectives in a regular car to follow us at a distance as well and spot a tail on us. So, let's use the fingerprint kit and dust the tracker and leave it in the vehicle."

"Yeah, I like that," Hawk said. "Let him come to us."

Lieutenant Perez seemed sincerely upset after Hawk and Nora told him about the tracker they found in the Interceptor. He immediately called Captain MacGregor. She called for a meeting with the detectives and informed everyone of the threat to Hawk and Nora. She ordered Perez to put out a BOLO—Be on Lookout— for a dark grey muddied Dodge Ram pickup, although she cautioned that the man probably ditched it and grabbed another vehicle. "I want to hear of the colors, makes, and models of cars stolen in the last hour from anywhere in the Metro area, the mountain area, or anywhere else along the front range. Even Wyoming or Kansas. "Detective Ling, start working on it."

Nora told her of her plan to lay a trap for the killer. She thought about it for a moment, then nixed the plan. "We can't take a chance of getting any civilians hurt. And if we find an isolated spot to lure him to, he can't be that much of an idiot not to figure out what you're doing."

She looked around the room at each detective. "Instead, I want you all to focus on the relatives of Devon O'Leary. Even close associates. I'll authorize some overtime for tonight for that. Detective Orlinski, work on finding who this mysterious cousin might be. He probably has a criminal record, and you may start with the FBI database. Hell, even check Interpol, but I want a thorough search. Detective Salazar, please coordinate with Orlinski and work on it as well. And Holliday, you can go home as I'm sure your fiancé is anxiously waiting for you." She smirked as she looked at him. He sat straight up in his chair as though oblivious to the conversation, his head tilted toward the ceiling.

He sneezed, then said, "Oh. That would be good. Josephine said she'll prepare tofu hamburgers with wild rice. She did tell me not to be late."

"Well, there you go. Enjoy." MacGregor shook her head and rolled her eyes. "Now, detectives," looking at Hawk and Ricci, "what are your plans for tonight? You need to figure out how you'll remain safe."

Hawk looked at Nora. "I don't think that Nora should be alone tonight or maybe not even stay at her house."

"Oh, the big hero here," Nora chuckled. "What about you? Do you think you're invincible or something? Well, I don't want to disrupt my life for something that might or might not happen. I'll stay at home with a gun by my side." She glanced at Hawk. "Actually, Clint, why don't you move in with me for a couple of days." *Damn! Why did I say that? What happened to my plan to distance myself from him?*

Orlinski goes, "Oooo. Nice."

"No, Orlinski, Hawk would use my guest room. It'll be strictly professional."

Everyone laughed. Suddenly, a loud, ear-shattering boom shook the two-story building and rattled its windows. The detectives merged with the officers as they fought their way out of the station to find the cause of the explosion. Once outside, Hawk and Nora were absolutely devastated when they saw their Ford Interceptor as a smoldering, smelly hunk of charred metal. And to their horror, they saw Mortimer stretched out on his back on the asphalt of the parking lot only about fifty feet away from the blast.

CHAPTER 12

WITH A BLOOD-curdling sadistic laugh, Finn O'Leary gleefully enjoyed the destructive explosion of the bomb. *I'm so good at it!* He had an excellent vantage point in the back parking lot across the street from the police station. As planned, the explosive detonated perfectly using a remote-controlled trigger rigged on his burner phone. Not only was the targets' vehicle destroyed, but so were at least two or three others.

Always using his black nitrile gloves, he planted the bomb deep in the Ford's undercarriage while the detectives were in the attorney's office. At first, he was livid at his amateurish departure which attracted to himself. Soon, he rationalized that it added a sense of mystery to the game and would work out even better if, in fact, they suspected anything. *And if, by chance, they know someone is out to get them, then let them sweat.*

After he peeled out from the lot in Golden, he checked the small monitor that came with the tracker. O'Leary noticed that the detectives' vehicle had not moved for several minutes. Wondering why, he quickly drove around the block, parked his pickup away from view, and ran over to some bushes next to the dormitory building. He came just in time to see the well-dressed detective pull out the GPS unit that O'Leary thought he had hidden well. He hoped that the cops be satisfied with that and look no further. But then he thought, *why in the hell did they even search their vehicle? They must already know someone is out to get them.*

Sitting in a truck before he detonated the bomb at the police station, he watched a tall, goofy-looking detective walk out of the building, heading towards the police parking lot. He did not want to kill the poor guy since that was not part of the deal, so he set off the bomb earlier than planned. Nevertheless, the change in pressure caused by the blast wave knocked the lanky detective backward onto his ass, leaving him flat. He watched people run to the man.

Seeing enough, he knew he had to get out while the going was good before anyone noticed the truck. *That was a success. The first volley in the game. There's more to come before I put a bullet in Hawk's and Ricci's heads.*

He slowly drove away, but not before Nora spotted the truck and screamed, "There he is! There's the sonofabitch!"

O'Leary gunned the Ram, its 400 horsepower Hemi engine growled, ran a red light at Colfax, and flew down Washington Street. Nora shouted out to the patrol officers that stood gawking at the damage to the cars. "Now! NOW, GO!" But before they could clear a path wide enough to drive their vehicles through the debris strewn across the lot, she knew he'd be long gone. Instead, they radioed other patrol cars in the vicinity to locate him.

Perez had called an ambulance for Mortimer while Nora and Hawk rushed to his side. His eyes were shut, but they were relieved when they noticed his heavy breathing. "Mortimer, Mortimer are you okay?" Nora asked as she stroked his grayish hair.

Mortimer saw the crowd around him and he abruptly sat up, shook his head, and blew out a deep breath. Then he began a series of coughs. As he attempted to stand, one of the officers that formed a circle around him gave him a hand. "Wow. Holy moly, that was something. The noise. The heat. I never felt anything like that before. It's as if someone pushed me backward. Weird. If I were a few feet closer, I'd be gone."

"Did you hit your head on the pavement?" Perez asked.

"He put his hand to his ear and said, "I can't hear from noise. Speak up, Sir, I only see your mouth move."

"Did you hit your head," Perez shouted as he leaned closer to his ear."

He shook his head back and forth before he said, "No, I just stumbled backward as though someone pushed me. I caught myself, otherwise, I would've been knocked out, I'm sure. Don't worry, I'm all right. At least that's what I'll tell Josephine because she's not going to like this. That was a bomb that went off, right?"

"It sure was, Detective Holliday," MacGregor said. "Ah, here's the ambulance."

"I don't need an ambulance, Captain MacGregor. I'm perfectly fine."

"I want you checked out, anyway. You might've had a concussion from the blast wave."

"I don't need to. Believe me, I'm fine. Besides, Josephine will be waiting for me to come home in time for dinner. She said she's going to make those tofu hamburgers."

MacGregor laughed. "You're a character, Detective. Anyone ever tell you that?"

"Yes, many times. But I never did figure out whether that's good or bad."

"Well, maybe someday you will. I want at least the medics to check you over for a concussion. That's an order."

"Oh. Okay. If you put it that way."

MacGregor turned her attention to Hawk and Nora. Hawk had his arm around her trying to comfort her. She still had not stopped shaking. "Clint and Nora, I want you to go to a safe house for tonight. I'll have a security detail stationed in front and the back alley. You should be safe."

Hawk glanced at Nora. "What do you think?"

She remained silent for a long minute. "Captain, I'd rather not. We can't disrupt our lives because of some madman out there. The only thing I'd like right now is if Clint would agree to stay with me for a few days until we get that bastard. And get him we will. He won't outsmart us." Every one noticed her eyes well up.

"Geez, everyone is so stubborn around here. Holliday doesn't want to go to the hospital to get checked out. You don't want to go to a safe house for your safety. What am I supposed to do with you people? Okay. Go home. I'll still have someone stationed in front and back of your house, Ricci. Detective Hawk, go home to get whatever you need for a few days and hightail it to Nora's. If you're up to it, tomorrow I want you to work on the Hollister case." She looked around at the detectives still standing around on the lot. "The rest of you concentrate all your efforts on the SOB that did this."

At the ambulance, after he was checked for a concussion, Holliday gingerly walked to his vintage Oldsmobile automobile and drove home to Josephine. Nora decided to leave her Ford Escape in the lot for the night and accompanied Hawk to his house in his Jeep. She came in with him, and as he gathered his stuff she flopped down on the couch. As she lay staring at the ceiling, she flung her arm over her eyes and forcibly exhaled. "Clint," she called out to him upstairs. "What's going on with me?"

Clint came over to the upper landing of the staircase. "Whatcha mean?"

"I mean. I always thought that I was a tough girl. Capable of all kinds of crap. You're the psychologist. Does stress compound on itself, making you feel incapable and useless?"

Hawk walked down. He sat at the edge of the sofa after she moved her legs. He took her feet and placed them on top of his legs. "Yeah. As far as I know, stress or let's say, fear, compounds on top of itself and begins to play with our psyche." Nora rubbed her forehead, shaking her head. Hawk continued after a brief period of silence. "But my dad always told me that grief, fear, and pain just make us stronger. That's what we have to focus on now. You and I are stronger now. We can take it."

Nora said, softly, "You think so, do you? I don't feel that way right now. I want to run away. Run away and hide." She opened her eyes and looked hard at Hawk. "And I want you to run away with me. Escape to a place where there is no fear or stress."

Hawk chuckled. "Sounds wonderful, but—."

"I know, 'but.' Wishful thinking, right?"

"Right. Such a place doesn't exist. Fear and stress are part of life. We must learn to cope with it. As my pappy in Texas used to say, 'Be strong, tough.' And that's what we must be, Nora, strong as steel and tough as my grandma's beef jerky."

She forced a weak laugh. "Okay. That's the pep talk I needed to hear. Go get your stuff and I'll make you a fantastic frozen dinner from Costco and give you a massage that I promised for your poor aching back and neck. Then you'll have to tell me about your hard-as-nails family." She laughed again, this time more naturally. "Come on, Clint, laugh with me and we'll both feel better." She made a silly face crossing her eyes and both laughed like idiots until tears ran down their cheeks, releasing so much bottled-up stress. Suddenly the world didn't seem as bleak.

As they approached Nora's house, they spotted the police cruiser. They waved at the officer as Nora retrieved the garage door opener out of her black leather purse. Inside, Hawk hung up a couple of suits and dress shirts in the closet, threw some socks and underwear in a dresser drawer, and showered while Nora shoved a lasagna in the oven. She made a mixed garden salad and uncorked a bottle of red wine. As promised, after a quiet dinner, she gave Clint the massage he bugged her about for the past several days. He almost fell asleep, and Nora's eyes began to droop. The massage was short, and she promised a much better one when she wasn't as tired.

They took some coffee and some cake, that Nora defrosted, to the officers who guarded the house. Afterwards, exhausted from the events of the day, including the strain of fear of death, they each retired to bed early. Hawk plunged into bed and was out cold. Nora tossed and turned for a couple of hours before deep sleep overwhelmed her.

Early in the morning, Hawk woke up first. He headed for the kitchen to put on a pot of coffee when he noticed the front door deadbolt unlocked. *Nora must've gone out.* As he passed by the dining table, he noticed a green sheet of paper with bold type. Picking it up, his heart fell to his knees, his head began to throb. The note read, "Didn't do it this night, but tomorrow or maybe the day after will be your last day. Prepare. Top of the morning to you."

Hawk ran out to the patrol cruiser. The officer's head was askew as he slouched in his seat. Hawk felt the pulse in the man's neck, a nasty bruise marred his left temple. "Tom, Tom, wake up. Come on Tom, come to." He shook him gently. Tom finally rolled his eyes open, squinting, groggy, and unable to focus. He placed his hand over the bruised area.

"I must've been knocked out."

"Looks like it. Remember anything?"

"Stupid. I left the door unlocked. Out of nowhere, some guy swung it open and as I turned to see who it was, he whacked me. Musta whacked me out immediately. Sorry Hawk. I flubbed up."

At that moment, Nora ran out. "Clint, what's going on?"

"Call 911, we need an ambulance." Nora ran back to get her phone. After calling for help, she ran back out. Hawk was afraid to tell her of the note but knew he would have to. And she would soon discover what happened to Officer Tom Washington.

Running back outside again, she saw how pale Hawk looked, and surmised it would not be a good morning. Hawk relayed the story to her. "But there's something you'll need to see when we go in," he told her. The neighbors began to gather, and Hawk asked them if they had seen or heard anything in the middle of the night. No one saw or heard anything. After telling them that everything was all right and no need to worry, several went back to their homes. A few stayed and persisted with questions. Nora didn't know what to tell them but promised to get back to them later.

After Tom was taken away by the ambulance, Hawk and Nora hurried back into the house. She read the note and her hands started to tremble. Collapsing into the nearest chair, she cupped her head with both hands, then rubbed her temples. Hawk thought that she'd get hysterical, but instead, she calmly said. "We'll get the bastard. I think he flubbed up already with his arrogance. Inadvertently, he gave us a huge clue. He's Irish, probably with the last name of O'Leary like his murderous scumbag cousin."

Hawk said, "You deduced all that from that note? Was it the 'top of the morning' that did it?"

"Exactly, and it's interesting that he used green paper, isn't it? When MacGregor told Orlinski to check Interpol, I thought she was kidding. But I think we should start there as soon as we get back to the station or, hopefully, Orlinski had already done it. Also, we need to dust for prints, just in case."

Hawk said. "The door handle, too. It was unlocked. I bet picking a lock is no problem for the psycho."

"Do you think that he's out there right now staking out the house?"

"I wouldn't put it past him. Actually, I hope we pick up a tail so we know what he's driving."

"First let's check out your Jeep. If he had free rein of the house, he might've planted a bomb or another tracker."

CHAPTER 13

A THOROUGH SEARCH revealed no bomb or tracker. As they drove back to the station, Hawk glanced incessantly in the rearview mirrors while Nora strained her neck poring over the surrounding traffic. Nora said, "Unless he's that good, I don't see anything suspicious, do you?"

"No, not really. I saw a white Ford pickup that kept the same distance behind me and changed lanes every time that I did, but that was way back, and I hadn't seen it since."

As soon as they walked into the Homicide unit, Orlinski, Salazar, and Ling rose up and approached them, "What in the hell happened to you this morning," Orlinski asked, looking more concerned than usual. "MacGregor and Perez are having quite a pow-wow about you two in Perez's office. They even shut the blinds. I could hear a little of the conversation. MacGregor wants you to leave town, and take vacation days, and Perez thinks that you need to bring the guy in before you could go on with your lives."

"Great," Hawk mumbled. "They'll probably send us off to Timbuktu."

Nora said, "Orlinski, did you take up MacGregor's suggestion that you contact Interpol."

Orlinski began to laugh, then he noted Nora's stern face. "You're serious, aren't you?"

"Yes, I have this gut feeling about checking with them."

"Well, let's hope, because I haven't been able to find any relatives of O'Leary other than a sister in West Virginia."

Nancy said, "Yeah, I've looked through all the social sites like Facebook, Twitter, and Instagram; no luck. O'Leary isn't on anything. The sister, a single mom, though, has pictures all over. It appears that she is expecting her fifth child. There is no mention of any relatives at all."

Harry said, "I doubt if she's after you then." He chuckled. Nora didn't think it was funny.

Orlinski sat back down and immediately started punching the keyboard. Without looking up from the monitor, he asked Nora, "What makes you think that we need to check the European Central National Bureau?"

Nora explained the green note. "See if they have any information on any O'Learys."

Orlinski kept clicking on the keyboard. In the meantime, Harry Ling told them of the stolen vehicles since last night in the areas that MacGregor asked him to search. "There were three Honda's—two Civics and one Accord. Also, it was a big night for pickups—four Ford F-150s, one Dodge Ram, and one Chevrolet Silverado. In the metro area, only the Civic and two of the F-150s were taken."

Hawk said. "Gangbangers really like those Hondas, but what about the two Ford pickups. What colors were they?"

"Let me check." Harry flipped through his sheets. "One was tan and the other white."

"Where was the white one taken?"

"It was stolen from a grocery store parking lot on Downing."

Nora asked, "Whatcha thinking Clint?"

"I'm thinking that after the explosion, he took off down Washington. He had to get rid of the muddy Dodge as soon as he could knowing that the cops were looking for that vehicle. So, he must've ditched the pickup probably before he got to the interstate. Downing is just a few blocks away. I bet if the patrol units drive up and down some alleys in the area around Washington and I-25 and between Washington and Downing, they would find the Dodge tucked away, maybe next to a fence. He could have easily walked to that store's parking lot and slithered away with that white truck."

Harry said, "Sounds reasonable to me. I'll get patrol to search for it."

"Bingo." Orlinski exclaimed, "There is a Finn O'Leary wanted for bombings and for a list of murders in several countries in

Europe—Ireland, UK, Belgium. They'd been searching for him for a decade. He was involved with the IRA and considered extremely dangerous. But they lost complete track of him five years ago."

Nora asked, "Any photos of him."

Orlinski kept searching. "Okay, I found an old one. It's at least ten years old. A mugshot. I'm printing it out now."

The detectives gawked at the round-faced, long-nosed man with coal-black hair and eyes. A distinctive scar ran down the right side of his thin-lipped small mouth. Nora said, "We need to get it to our sketch artist, Pete, to see if he could sketch what O'Leary would look like ten years older. How old is he now, Orlinski?"

Orlinski looked it up. "He's fifty-three right now. I'll check his immigration status."

Perez stood off to the side and listened. After remaining quiet, he said, "Good work. I want that photo sent out to every officer and detective in the Department. And Hawk, why do you think he may be driving a white Ford pickup?"

"Morning, Lieutenant." Perez nodded. "On our way here, I thought for a while that a white Ford pickup was tailing us. But just as I began to get concerned about it, the driver changed lanes, rather suddenly, I might add, and made a left turn onto First Avenue, so I gave up on that idea. But, it could've been him now that I hear that a white F-150 was stolen."

"All right. We'll take it from here. I want you and Ricci to start working on the Hollister case. MacGregor is getting heat from the press. We need some answers fast. I tried to get you another vehicle, but instead, I heard some of the most colorful swearings from the motor pool. The guy reminded me that every vehicle you were assigned had been damaged and as far as they're concerned, you'll never get another one."

Hawk protested, "But none of that damage was my fault."

"Don't worry about it. I'll let them cool off a day or two and try again. In the meantime, drive your personal vehicle and keep track of your mileage. By the way, where is Mortimer this morning?"

Orlinski said, "Oh, he called and said that he's got a terrible headache. I told him to go see a doctor, but he said that Josephine is giving him some herbs that will take care of it. He'll be in this afternoon."

After making an appointment, Nora and Hawk set out in Hawk's Jeep Grand Cherokee to the Washington Park area to interview James and Kay Hollister. Their nerves were still frayed with the thought of someone out to kill them so they continued to carefully screen for vehicles that might be shadowing them. Hawk said, "You know, Nora, if O'Leary is our guy, he knows where you live, where we work. He doesn't need to follow us. He could wait for us as we get to your place or wait for us in the parking lot as we get out of the car."

"Don't you think I know that? That's why we need to be one-up on him. Let him come to us, but we have to be prepared."

"And how do you propose that?" Hawk asked.

"He's obviously good at disappearing and that's why he operates under the cover of night. Since he likes bombs, we need to borrow a bomb-sniffing dog to sniff out if any that had been planted in or around the house or the car."

"You think that's what he'll use?"

"Actually, no. He's a sadist who wants to get the thrill of watching us suffer before he kills us. He'd have to return to the house. I think that's what he'll do. He'll wait for us to fall asleep then enter the house again, wake us and get a high from scaring the bejesus out of us."

"Nora, do you really believe that he thinks we're idiots and wouldn't be prepared for him?"

"That's exactly it. He'll think that we'd never imagine that he would do the same thing two nights in a row. But, why not? He's arrogant enough. It could very well be tonight." Nora tried to appear tough and not afraid as she discussed this with Clint, but deep inside she was a wreck. And Clint sensed it.

As they passed by the beautifully landscaped Washington Park with the cool glistening lake, she craved freedom from stress. The thought that today or tomorrow could be her last day on this beautiful earth sent a sharp pain to her temple. Oh, how much she wanted to just lay in the sun, carefree, by the soothing water. No matter how she tried to calm herself, the fear of death enveloped her whole being. She glanced at Hawk, her hero, and tried to calm herself with the notion that together, one way or another, they'll twist themselves out of danger.

After remaining silent and focusing on Nora's comment that O'Leary would be arrogant enough to enter their house at night again, Hawk decided that enough is enough. O'Leary is already achieving what he wanted simply by injecting fear into their minds. "Nora, get that SOB out of your mind. We'll nab him. Don't let him play mind games with you. Let's concentrate on what we're paid to do. We're on Garfield Street and that big house on the left is where James and Kay live."

CHAPTER 14

JAMES AND KAY HOLLISTER invited Hawk and Nora into their newly built home. As was typical around older parts of Denver, the old bungalows were scraped off, and larger, impressive houses rose in their place. As the detectives followed the couple past the stained glass and metal door and into the expansive tiled foyer, they smelled the newness of the place—fresh paint, and new carpets. Everything looked bright with the floor-to-ceiling open windows that faced them. They were escorted into the home office located to the right of the entryway.

They were asked to sit down next to a cherrywood desk. James Hollister walked around the desk and sat behind it. Kay Hollister sat off to the side. Behind James, a matching credenza was topped with bookshelves. One of the shelves contained books of biographical works of historical figures, another had novels and yet another had travel books, mostly of Peru. The rest of the shelves were filled with travel souvenirs, again mostly of South America.

Nora was the first to speak. "Thank you for seeing us, Mr. and Mrs. Hollister. We know it's a very difficult time for you and talking to us would be the last thing you'd want to do. We are deeply sorry for your loss. It must've been a shock to you to hear of your father's death."

James cleared his throat and swallowed twice, then cleared his throat again. "It is extremely difficult. I was very close to my father. I believe that Kay was too."

"Of course, I was. I loved the man."

With a sad expression, Nora continued, "I understand. I can't imagine losing my father."

James said, his voice breaking, "Thank you for that." He lowered his eyes, staring at the shiny desktop for a moment. He again cleared his throat, "I understand that you don't believe that he died a natural death?"

Nora said, "We're not sure yet until after the autopsy, but his death does seem suspicious."

"I can't imagine any one of us would be evil enough to murder him. Benson believes that someone slipped my father an aspirin by substituting it for another similar med." He stopped talking as he looked away and sucked in a deep breath, his wide chest heaving. Rubbing his eyes with the back of his hand, he spoke again, his head still turned away from the detectives. "Oh, God! I'm sorry, but it's been hard on me. I'm going to miss him so." Kay stood and slipped over to her husband and wrapped her chubby arm around his shoulders. "Was it really the aspirin that he died from?"

Hawk answered, "It very well might be."

Kay asked, "Then Benson was right."

"Perhaps."

"How would someone do that?" James asked, his eyes narrowed, his forehead scrunched. "I mean, my father and Benson were so careful with prescriptions."

"Mr. Hollister," Nora queried, "Obviously, you knew that your father was allergic to aspirin, how about the rest of the family?"

"Detective Ricci, everyone in the family knew about that. My father almost died from an anaphylapsis—"

"That's anaphylaxis shock, honey," Kay said.

"Yes, whatever she said. He was a few seconds from dying according to the nurse in the E.R. This happened about ten years or so ago and he was extremely careful to avoid anything with aspirin such as Aleve, Advil, and all that stuff."

Kay said, "We just can't understand how William could've ingested an aspirin, even by mistake. As Jimmy said, Benson always made sure that the man never took any pills that contained aspirin such as Advil, Aleve, and stuff like that."

Nora asked, "Do you think Benson would contrive to switch the meds on purpose?"

Neither answered immediately. They seemed to be mulling it over. Finally, James answered, "Gads, I hope not. He has been so loyal. But I'll tell you what. Money is money and I'm sure he knew that he'd be inheriting a big chunk."

Nora asked, "Would that reasoning also apply to the housekeeper, Consuela Rivera?"

"Well yes, I suppose. But, I would never believe she'd do such a thing. She is so quiet, harmless, really, and seemed to care a lot for my father." He thought a moment, "No, I wouldn't suspect her at all."

Hawk studied the short, overweight man in his early forties that sat across from him. James Hollister had a pale moon face and a prominent double chin, narrow brown eyes, and shaved head. He wore a faded red Nike T-shirt and tan cargo shorts. His wife, also squat, and about the same age, had large green eyes and short blonde hair. She also wore tan shorts and a T-shirt with the Phish band logo plastered on her buxom chest.

Hawk asked, "Do you really think the butler would be capable?"

James thought for a moment, "Nah, I don't think he would. But you never know, do you?"

Hawk said, "That's exactly it. We just don't know at this point. Assuming that Benson didn't do it, perhaps you and Kay could help us with who you think would be capable."

Kay returned to her seat and said, "If it wasn't Benson, then I can't imagine anyone of the kids that could actually kill their father. I mean, sure, George has a nasty, arrogant streak. He likes to argue and lost his temper on the golf course a few times. He got so steamed that he shoved a player down to the ground, but, jeez, murdering his father would be hard to believe. Now, Cynthia, she's somethin' else. She's got a temper, that woman does. I don't even want to look at her, afraid that she'll bite my head off. If anyone of the kids did it, I'd say she could of." Kay stopped and glanced at her husband. Hawk noticed the disapproving look that he gave her.

Nora asked Kay, "What about the other children? I believe there is also Darren and Ashley."

She took a quick glance at her husband. "Well, Darren is an alcoholic as far as I'm concerned. But I don't think he would kill anyone. He's too busy screwing around with all sorts of bimbos. Like the one, he brought to dinner. And Ashley is a spoiled party girl, half stoned, whose head is usually up in the clouds and wouldn't be serious or smart enough to even come up with a plan to kill a spider."

"Kay," James said, "You're being a little unfair to that woman that Darren brought with him. She looked classy for a change, and I couldn't believe that he found someone that good-looking to go out with him. He must've impressed her with how much money he has or will inherit."

"Well, I don't know why you think she's so classy. Just a gold digger that's all. But I sure noticed you gawking at her all night."

James was about to counter when Nora decided they were getting off track. "What do either of you know about that woman? We were told her name was Tina Dionisio."

James said, "Not much. I bet, though, that Kay is right. She must've been after Darren's money to put up with him."

"Oh, why's that?" Nora asked.

Kay was anxious to answer. "She just didn't have that honest look about her. Actually, the more I think about it, she could very well have done it. Darren might've told her about Dad's allergy, and she heard how little he'd receive if the trust was terminated, and the will was changed. She had the opportunity, that's for sure. I mean, Darren was showing her the whole upstairs like a realtor or somethin' and I saw them in William's bedroom."

"Who else did you see go into that room?" Nora asked.

"Everybody went throughout the whole upstairs like a big scavenger hunt, searching for things to take. I mean they were mad, and I saw people grabbing stuff not only out of their former rooms, but even out of William's."

Hawk asked, "Who and what?"

"Oh, let's see. I saw Rhonda go through his dresser drawer and snatch a silver belt buckle. When she saw that I saw, she said, 'Oh, it was ours to begin with,' and stormed out of the room."

Hawk continued. "Do you get along with Rhonda?"

"Hell no. She acts so high and mighty. She looks down on me and Jimmy. Isn't that right, honey?"

James cleared his throat. "Yeah, they all do actually. You see, they're all well-educated, but I wasn't much of a student and barely made it through high school. Didn't want to go to college so I took the money from the trust and spent a year in South America. There I picked up some kind of parasite that disabled me for a while. When I came back—" He hesitated and cocked his head towards the window. "Dad made me go to work somewhere, even though I was well set with my monthly trust payments. I thought I'd like something where I'd be with people. I'm a real people person. A friend of Dad's had a bar downtown and offered me a job as a bartender. I loved the job and the people. It was a lot of fun, like going to a party every night."

He glanced at Kay. "That's where we met. Kay was also a bartender there. We clicked and have the best marriage of anyone that I know. I look at my siblings who keep their noses high in the air, so high that they don't see the real world, and for the most part, their marriages are in disarray. But I'll tell you what. We've always been the happiest of the bunch. And that includes their greedy spouses."

Kay said, "And do you know what? We're the only ones that cared for William. We were there at his beck and call. He was a lonely man the last few years and we felt so sorry for him. I even called George and Cynthia and asked them to at least visit their lonely father. You think they would? More or less told me to mind my own damn business. That's the kind of people they are."

"And what about Darren and Ashley?" Nora asked. "Did you ask them to visit their father?"

"No. With them, I knew it would be no use. Darren is too much of a playboy who wouldn't give his old man the time of day. Ashley is so wrapped up with whatever she's doin' and is totally irresponsible. A real airhead. Probably from using drugs."

"Now, honey," James said. "We don't actually know that. Just suspect it."

"She sure seemed high to me the rare times that I saw her. Anyway, the only times either one of them would come to visit Dad was when they were out of money. As soon as they got what they wanted, a quick 'Thanks Dad, you're the greatest' a hug, maybe, and they'd vanish without even sitting down with him just to chitchat."

Hawk asked, addressing James, "What about the spouses? Any of them could've murdered William?"

"As Kay said, Rhonda has an overly aggressive streak. Samuel Maxwell is very mild and courteous. I like him. Don't think he'd kill anyone. Of course, Darren and Ashley aren't married." He looked at Kay, "But honey, I don't think that Tina was all that bad. I watched her and she was uncomfortable at the dinner. I think she wanted to jump out of her skin. She didn't want to go upstairs, but Darren almost dragged her up there."

"Well, that's not how I see it. She gawked at everything in the house, sizing everything up thinking what she'll get out of hooking stupid Darren. I don't trust her at all." *I don't trust her Tina either,* Nora thought back at meeting her and suspecting her as the murderess in the prior Ellis case. *She's everywhere where there is money. And people die around her.* "And Jimmy, stop thinking and talking about that bitch. I don't want to hear it."

Nora and Hawk could not help but chuckle. It was so obvious that Kay was jealous of Tina. But Nora was still interested in pursuing the subject. "Kay, you said that Darren could've told Tina about an aspirin allergy. When would that have been, you think?" Hawk glanced at Nora, knowing that she'd love to nail Tina.

Kay answered, "Who knows what that woman knew? Darren, especially if he had a drink or two, was a huge blabbermouth."

James said, "Yeah, he sure was. I remember Dad getting on him for telling people about his business. Dad was sorta a private man and didn't like strangers knowing how he made his fortune in the stock market. He was a little like Warren Buffet and just knew what and when to buy and when to sell."

Kay added, "Yeah, and Darren could've very well told her about an aspirin allergy when they were in William's bathroom with all those pills out in full view on the vanity."

"Oh, come on, honey. You're really stretching it. Why would they even discuss it? Makes no sense."

"Well, I wouldn't put it past him. Darren wouldn't carry aspirin with him, but Tina might've in that fancy alligator leather purse of hers. You know, we women usually carry aspirin for headaches and cramps."

Hawk asked, "You mentioned a trust and a will. I assume that since William Hollister is dead and he didn't have a chance to revoke the trust and make out a new will, everything remains the same for all of you?"

James and Kay exchanged glances. James said, "My father confided in us over dinner one evening, about three weeks ago, that he had already terminated the trust and that I'll be inheriting the bulk of the estate, once he passes."

"And, why would he do that?"

"As I said, my dad and I were very close. He would come into the bar, sit at the counter, and watch me work. He always ordered a club soda with two twists of lime. He would sit there for a couple of hours nursing that one drink. Damn, I'll miss him." James began to sob.

Kay handed him a tissue and took over the conversation. "We knew about it. You see this beautiful house?" Both detectives nodded. "Well, he gave us the down payment, co-signed on the loan, and told us not to worry. That we'll have plenty of money, probably within a year, to pay off the mortgage. That's when he told us about the inheritance we'd receive."

Hawk asked, "And none of the others knew anything about it?"

Kay said, "No. When would they even know about it since they never bothered to communicate with him?"

"Who is your mortgage company?"

James and Kay again exchanged glances. Hawk noticed both sets of eyes narrow. James finally answered, "It's Brickton Mortgage Depot. Are there any more questions? I think we were very cooperative with you, but I'm exhausted. The stress of losing my dear father is too much for me to take."

Nora said, "We understand and certainly appreciate your time. I do have one quick question. Are you both still employed at the bar?"

Kay said, "No, we quit last week."

The detectives thanked them and as they approached Hawk's Jeep, their hearts sank when they spotted a green piece of paper tucked under the driver's windshield wiper. A tight band of fear encircled their insides as they carefully approached the car. They knew who had left the note. Hawk's hand was steady as he read, "Enjoy your life while you can. Maybe today or maybe tomorrow will be your last day."

CHAPTER 15

AFTER SCANNING the street and the surrounding area for any sign of O'Leary or any suspicious vehicle, Nora rushed back to the Hollisters to check their ring doorbell video. Hawk headed across the street to the neighbors. Both came back, disappointed that their cameras only covered the area up to the sidewalk, Hawk's Jeep not visible.

As they left for the station, Hawk blew out a deep breath, punching the steering wheel with the side of his fist. "Damn! That bastard is getting under my skin! I'm madder than a wet hen! Damn! We need to catch that SOB!"

Feeling the same, Nora rotated her neck like a radar beam on the lookout for O'Leary. "He's got to be out there, laughing at us."

"Not for long. We'll get him." Hawk placed his right hand on Nora's knee. "Don't worry. We'll get the turd."

She forced a smile. "We better or my parents won't like it at all." The half-smile faded quickly as she told Clint to take some deep breaths. "Your mind can't think straight if you're so wound up."

After finally settling down somewhat, she sunk into the back of her seat leaned her head into the headrest, and shut her eyes. Both Hawk and she remained silent for a few minutes, each deep in their thoughts. Nora spoke up first, "We really need to concentrate on the Hollister case, but with that psycho out there, it's sure hard, isn't it?"

"I know. Let's get our wretched minds off the sonofabitch." Hawk glanced at Nora who had just turned to look out the back. "What did you think of James and Kay?"

Nora said, "Okay, let's talk. Something just doesn't feel right about them. Did you notice the wall of photos in the office?"

"Yes, what about the photos?"

"From what I could tell, all the photos were of Kay's family. One photo of Kay and James together, the rest of what I think are her parents and siblings or friends. None of James's parents or siblings or anything."

"What are you saying?"

"I'm saying that if James was that close to his father, you'd think there'd be at least one photo of him or his parents. It's probably no big deal. Then, I noticed without much prodding from us, quickly they were to give us suspects. First Benson, then Cynthia, then Darren and Tina. And then, as to how close and how much they loved the father, they talked up a storm, volunteering information on how good they were. Remember, we were taught that if a person is truthful, his answers are usually short and direct. If untruthful, the person goes into a long-detailed narrative."

"Yeah. I've noticed that. Do you think they might be guilty?"

Nora thought about it before answering. "I just don't know. Maybe. But I'd like to see how the other interviews go. Darren is next right?"

Hawk answered, "Yup. And I now remember why his address is so familiar. His condo is in the same building as that of Tina Dionisio. That's probably how they met."

"Okay, if Tina is involved, then I hope she and Darren conspired to kill the old man." Nora laughed. "Of course, you know I'm kidding."

"You really don't like her, do you?"

"No. I agree with Kay. She's a gold-digger." But I do have a question for you, Clint. Why do you like to interview people at their place rather than having them come into the station?"

"Two reasons. I think it's best if we see how they live, sorta look around the place, at photos, just like you mentioned with James. Then, I believe that if the person is in their own environment, they're more relaxed, not so much on guard, and may say things that we'd not even think of asking."

"Makes sense. Okay tiger, go get them."

A moment later, Hawk received a call from Lieutenant Perez. "How far are you from the station?"

"Not too far. Why?"

"Come by and pick up Holliday. He's real antsy. Driving me crazy. Said he should be there with you."

"Lieutenant, he should know that we found another green note from O'Leary threatening us again. Josephine will not appreciate him assigned to us if we could get shot at or blown up at any moment."

"God! I think that MacGregor is right. You two need to get out of town and pronto."

"We'll get him, Lieutenant. We both want to stay and see that it gets done."

"Stubborn, aren't you? Anyway, back to Holliday, I told him that he may not want to be around you because of the danger from O'Leary. I gave him a case to do, but he insists on being with you. Said he can help protect you. Maybe he's got a point. Come get him."

"Okay, copy that."

"Hawk, you and Ricci be careful out there."

CHAPTER 16

AFTER MORTIMER squeezed into the Jeep Cherokee, the three detectives headed for LODO—Lower Downtown—area of Denver. Suddenly, Mortimer sneezed piercingly. Both; Hawk and Nora jumped in their seats. They thought it was a gunshot. Nora's heart raced. But Mortimer didn't think anything of it, just blew his nose into a very used handkerchief.

"Bless you, Mortimer. That startled me."

"Oh, sorry, Nora. Josephine always says that my sneezes are too loud." *No kidding,* Hawk thought.

Mortimer continued, "I'm glad we're together. I'm used to working with you. Although Josephine doesn't like the idea. But I put my foot down for a change and told her that's police business and I walked out. Not sure of the reception I'll get when I come home."

Hawk laughed, "In other words, you told her how the cow eats the cabbage."

Mortimer scratched the top of his head. "Cabbage? Cow? I just don't understand what that means."

"Oh, it's just an expression my grandfather always used when he told somebody that's how it is whether the other person liked it or not." Mortimer still looked perplexed.

Nora said, "We don't want to cause any problems between you and your fiancé."

"Don't worry about Josephine. She was getting just too bossy. I guess the bomb going off almost in my face set her off. Oh, Detective Salazar asked me to tell you that a vehicle was stolen from Washington Park early this morning. It was…" Mortimer closed his eyes, lifting his head trying to remember. "Oh, it was a 2020 Honda Ridgeline."

"What color was it?" Hawk asked, his ears perking up.

"Oh, yes, it was dark grey."

"It can't be, but I've seen a Honda pickup that's been behind us since we left the station and I see it behind us now."

Nora and Mortimer abruptly twisted their necks and glanced in the back. "I don't see it," Nora said. "Where is it?"

Hawk checked the driver's side mirror. "Huh. I can't see it now. Must be a false alarm." He glanced at Nora, grinning. "Never mind." She lightly punched him on his shoulder. "Did you make that up, just to make me jump through the roof?" Nora looked serious, in no mood to joke around.

"No, seriously, I saw it. But it must've turned."

"Lots of old brick buildings around here," Mortimer said as Hawk spotted a space to park across the street from Darren Hollister's condo. "That one there looks like an ancient factory of some kind," pointing at a five-story building.

Hawk chuckled. "It must've been at one time, but lots of these old places are now converted to condos or lofts. That's where Darren lives, and Tina Dionisio has a condo there as well."

Nora glanced at Hawk. "You would certainly remember well where Tina lives, wouldn't you?"

"You're not a little jealous, are you?"

"Not at all, but I do know that if she had a chance, she'd have her hooks into you before you knew what hit you. So don't give her the opportunity. And this time, when you interview her, I'm going with you." Hawk laughed. Mortimer had a puzzled look on his face. Evidently, he had forgotten that after the three of them interviewed her in the last case, the Ellis case, she called Hawk and said she had further information and asked him to her condo alone. Nora did not forget and refreshed his memory.

Nora buzzed Darren's condo as they stood in the pre-entry. They heard the front door unlock and headed for the elevator. But as they approached, Hawk and Nora remembered that Mortimer had claustrophobia and elevators made him physically sick. Mortimer studied the elevator, and just by gazing at the door, beads of sweat rolled down his forehead, his breathing shallow. Hawk said,

"Darren's condo is only on the fourth floor. Why don't we walk up? It'll be a good exercise." Nora had already proceeded to the stairs.

"Oh, thank you. Josephine thinks I should see a shrink about that. I've seen them before when I was much younger. They didn't do a damn bit of good."

As they rounded the landing on the second floor, Mortimer began to fight for breath. They stopped and rested for a minute. "This thin mountain air," he said, still breathing hard. "I can't get used to it. Josephine says that I should be all right in a couple more weeks. To tell you the truth, I miss the sea level of Tampa."

Nora said, "You'll be fine. Have some patience, that's all."

They finally made it up to the fourth floor, found the condo, and introduced themselves to Darren after he opened the door. He was of medium height, in his early thirties, with balding dark brown hair, an oval fleshy face, unshaven, and a noticeable paunch. He wore flip-flops, short shorts, and a T-shirt with a BMW logo. With a toothy smile and a moderate odor of alcohol on his breath, he welcomed them in and asked them to sit down in front of a huge, granite, stone fireplace. The furniture was simple. Two matching sofas, that Nora recognized from Pottery Barn, sat across from each other perpendicular to the fireplace. A water-stained, walnut coffee table stood in between. On the far wall, behind one of the sofas, an ornately carved Asian chest was the most impressive piece of furniture in the place.

Hawk noted that the condo itself was different from Tina's. Tina had the top floor with extra tall ceilings and tall arched windows. *A loft within a loft*, he remembered. Darren's was more like a typical apartment even though it also had ten-foot ceilings. The most outstanding features were the exposed extra-large round red heating and cooling ducts in contrast to the black ceiling.

Mortimer remained standing as the others sat down. Darren took a good look at the tall, gaunt individual with an elongated face whose head sported a one-inch butch cut. He laughed to himself at the man's old-fashioned, ill-fitted, suit. "Hey, man, sit, won't you? I want my guests to be comfortable."

"No thanks. I'd rather stand."

"Okay bro, whatever."

Darren then focused all his attention on Nora. She felt his abraisal and his roving, lustful, dark-brown eyes. She pulled her dark gray skirt to make sure her knees were covered and tugged on her lavender blouse, pulling it higher to her chin. "You know, I don't mean to stare, but you look so much like my hot new girlfriend, a little more beautiful perhaps." Nora first blushed then became angry. While at her job, she strived to be as professional as possible and felt that the sexist remark was totally inappropriate and demeaning. However, she did not let the comment, that she was more beautiful than Tina, slip by and hoped that Hawk caught it. She glanced at Hawk and saw him scowl at Darren then he glanced back at Nora and winked.

Darren plopped down next to Nora and spoke. "Where are my manners? I need to offer you something to drink. Scotch, whisky, beer, anything?" He leered at Nora. She stood and sat down next to Hawk. Both turned down his offer of a drink. Darren next looked up at Mortimer. "What about you, ace? You look like you need a good stiff drink to loosen up."

Looking startled, Mortimer said, "Oh. No. I never touch the stuff. Josephine says that it's bad for you. She once took a class on alcohol, and you shouldn't be drinking. Especially before noon. It'll rot your liver."

Darren laughed. "Who in the hell is Josephine and why should I listen to her, bro? Are you bustin' my chops, man? Anyway, if you don't want anything, it's no sweat off my back. I need a drink, though, before you all grill me. He looked at Nora, would you excuse me, beautiful?"

"It's Detective Ricci, Mr. Hollister."

"Sooory, Detective. Have it your way." Shuffling to the Asian chest, Darren lifted the lid. Inside was a cabinet designed for liquor bottles. A panel at the front folded down and formed a bar. They heard him throw a couple of ice cubes into a tumbler, then pour himself at least three fingers of Scotch.

Nora said, "We're here as you know because of the death of your father. We're very sorry for your loss. I realize that it's so hard to lose a parent." Making his way back to the sofas he said, "Yeah, thanks for your condolences. It is a great loss. My father was a very generous man." He looked at Hawk. "All right, you have questions. Shoot."

At that instant, Mortimer let out one of his explosive sneezes that sounded like a gun going off. It startled Hawk and Nora. Darren jumped and spilled some of his liquor onto the geometric multicolored rug.

"Wow, man," Darren said cranking his neck toward Mortimer. "That really scared the crap out of me, man. Put a muffler on that." He thought of something and said, "Wow, I now remember that Tina described you and laughed that she almost believed it when she was told that you're a human lie detector." He suddenly burst out in uncontrollable laughter. That was pretty dumb of her actually."

Mortimer said, "Sorry about the loud sneeze. But don't laugh so hard because I can tell when people lie."

"Yeah, sure, dude. You can fool Tina maybe, but not me. I'm too smart for that."

Hawk asked. "Did you tell Tina that we'd be interviewing you today?"

"Yeah. I told her that you folks would be over this morning. She remembered the names. She warned me that if you bring a really tall dude that insists on standing, then watch out." He then addressed Nora. "She doesn't like you much. Probably thinks you're too good-looking now, that I see you." He then looked at Hawk for really the first time. "She seems to think you're great, though. Should I be jealous?"

Hawk said, annoyed, "Listen, Mr. Hollister, we're not here to socialize. We have an important job of finding out what happened to your father."

"I understand. I'm sorry. Maybe I had a little too much to drink already. Tina is trying to get me to cut down. Hard to, though. I've been drinking more since my dad died." He remained silent for a minute. His eyes drooped. "Quite frankly, I must admit I wasn't all that close to my parents. My mom was a little Hitler, a real dictator, always punishing us kids for something or other. I remember the time-outs when I spent many hours in my room when I was small, not allowed to leave."

"What about your father?" Hawk asked.

"I guess he was better. Sort of afraid of my mother though. He never stood up for me. Then when I got older, he was always on my back for drinking, chasing women, you name it. I really didn't want to go to college, but he forced me. He said, he made a big mistake with James, and he was going to make sure I get a degree of some kind." He thought for another minute, his eyes closing again. "I guess, he wasn't all that bad. He got me out of a few scraps—a shoplifting charge, a couple of DUIs."

Hawk said, "Sounds like a good father to me. He was there for you. Didn't he set up a trust so that you kids would be well set?"

"I guess. He was okay until out of the blue he decided to take the money away from us. The trust really wasn't all that much, a mere five thousand a month. That wasn't enough to support my active lifestyle, but it helped."

Nora asked, "What are you busy with? Do you work anywhere?"

Darren laughed. "You think I'm a bum, don't you? Well, I'm not. I got my degree all right. It's in marketing. I'm a sales rep for a plumbing manufacturer and get commissions for orders. Love the job. Don't have to work too hard...it gives me time to play. And it's the playing that takes bunches of greenbacks."

"And how are your commissions?" Nora asked.

"Not too bad. Could do better I suppose, if I spent more time on it. But you know life is too short. Got to make hay while the sun shines as my dad used to say when I was a kid."

Mortimer said, "You appear to be a lazy man to me."

Everyone turned toward him. Darren answered, "Yeah, well. That's the way I am, bro. My parents tried to mold me into work dynamos like themselves, but I didn't see it."

Hawk said, "You didn't see it because your parents or your dad provided for you."

Darren closed his eyes and lowered his head. He took a huge sip of Scotch. After a short silence, he mumbled, "I suppose so. I admit that I'm spoiled."

Nora asked, "And once you heard that your dad was terminating the trust and you'll be left out in the cold, you had to do something about it before he acted to take the money away from you."

Darren drained the glass of alcohol. "Not me. I heard from Cynthia that someone substituted an aspirin for one of his pills. I suppose whoever did it, did me a favor."

"Now who would've done it?" Hawk asked.

"That's a good question bro. I suppose that's your job to prove who done it."

Hawk continued, "Did you see anyone go into your father's bedroom or bathroom that night?"

"We all did, kinda. As a last remembrance of the room that we, as kids, used to play in. It brought back fond memories. Tina loved the room and the bathroom and said that she wished she had something like it. I think she said that she could put her whole condo into the bedroom."

Suddenly Mortimer blurted out, "You're the one that killed your father because he was going to cut you off the trust and any inheritance."

Darren turned abruptly toward him, and his eyes widened. "Man, you don't drink, but boy you're sure on somethin' bro. I wouldn't mind having a puff of that stuff."

Mortimer's statement didn't just surprise Hawk and Nora, it also annoyed them. This was the third time that he had been assigned to them that he made such an accusation out of the blue without any indication that the suspect might've done it. *What's he trying to accomplish with a statement like that without first getting all the information from the suspect,* Hawk thought as he glanced at Nora with raised eyebrows. Nevertheless, they carefully watched Darren's body language to see how he reacted to the accusation. He appeared calm, almost as if sedated. They couldn't get a good read maybe because the alcohol dulled his senses. He closed his eyes and swayed a bit.

"What do you mean by that?" Mortimer asked, his full lips protruding. "I don't understand."

Darren shook his head. "I see what Tina meant. You're crazy, man."

Mortimer continued, "And it was you and Tina that conspired to kill him."

Finally, Hawk noticed a twitch in Darren's eye. He rolled his fingers into a fist. "Tina and I had nothing to do with my father's death. Actually, I must've loved him because I feel so sad that he's gone."

Nora said, "If you didn't do it. Who could've done such a thing?"

Darren smiled, then laughed. Don't you know that it's always the butler? But then, everyone in our family could've done it. We're all a bunch of brats with no scruples. All we wanted from the old man was his money. And as you noticed, I said 'we.'"

Nora asked, "But there must be someone that you suspect if you didn't do it."

He laughed. "Look, I have no idea. I know that George and Rhonda were ready to kill him right there at the dinner table. I saw the loathing in their eyes. Then there's Cynthia with her out-of-control temper. You'll find out, darlin', when you talk to her. Better bring that big guy with you." He pointed at Mortimer with a shaky finger. Then laughed. "Hey, come on guys, give me a break, I need to take a nap."

Hawk said, "One more question. Did you know that your father was allergic to aspirin?"

"Sure."

Did you tell Tina that when the two of you were in your father's bathroom?" Darren's eye twitched again.

"No, of course not. Why would I?"

Hawk said, "Well, for one, you suggested to Tina when you saw the pill box, that it would be easy to kill your dad by switching a med that looked like an aspirin with the real thing. That's when Tina told you she had an aspirin in her purse. It was easy. An easy murder that no one would figure out, or so you hoped."

Darren's hands tightened their grip on the cocktail glass he was holding. The veins on his temples throbbed. He took in a deep breath, then said, "You're as crazy as this big fellow here. You must be smokin' the same thing."

Nora asked, "And did Tina have aspirin in her purse?"

He looked straight at Nora. His eyes narrowed. "You all need to leave. Now! Get out!"

As the detectives walked past the elevator to the staircase, Hawk and Nora both spotted a green half-sheet of paper taped next to the elevator. They knew that someone had just entered the elevator because it was on its way down. Hawk sprang forward toward the stairs, in hopes of beating the elevator down. Nora followed him. They missed whoever it was. As they ran out the front door, they saw a man in a black jogging suit and a green baseball cap, jump into a dark-grey Honda Ridgeline, and take off down Blake Street. Nora had the note in her hand. Their hearts pounded as they read, "Remember it might be tonight or maybe tomorrow. See you soon."

CHAPTER 17

A FEW MINUTES later, Mortimer sauntered out of the building, carrying three green half-sheets of paper. He joined Hawk and Nora as they stood on the sidewalk in front of the place, still trying to recover their breaths. They spotted the sheets Mortimer held as he said, "I was coming down the stairs. On the third floor, I noticed a similar piece of paper taped to the wall next to the elevator. I found sheets on the second and first floors, all next to the elevator. I bet there's one on the fifth floor also. Maybe, I should've gone up to that floor to look. The guy obviously didn't know what floor we were on, only the building."

Nora said, "That O'Leary is absolutely crazy. He really took a chance going up and down the building. Let me run up to the fifth floor and grab the sheet if there's one. Who knows, maybe that one would have some prints?"

Nora managed to slip into the building just as a man walked out. While she took the elevator up to the fifth floor, Hawk called Perez telling him about the green notes and asked him to get a BOLO out immediately for a dark-grey Honda pickup. Showing sincere concern for their safety, Perez told him that he would do it immediately and advised them again to watch their backs.

A few minutes later, Nora reappeared with another green sheet. She looked squarely at Hawk, "What should we do? I'm still shaking. You look sorta calm. Evidently, I'm not as brave as you and that really bothers me."

Hawk sidled closer to her and gave her a bear hug. "We'll get him," he whispered. "Those bits of paper just show us how arrogant he is. Look at the chance he's taking by following us, spending all that time putting up those stupid sheets. We're shaken up right now. But I know you're strong and tough. Look how you handled Devon O'Leary and those two goons that tried to kill Marcie and you.

You're the bravest woman I've ever met. That's why you're my bodyguard." Hawk chuckled.

"Some bodyguard I'm turning out to be." She tried to return the laugh but couldn't. "Then, I saw a direct threat and I acted on it. Now we're dealing with this psychological shit that this son of a bitch is throwing at us. It's the unknown that bothers me."

"If you let the creep shake you up like that, then he's winning. Because he's so arrogant, he'll make mistakes and we'll get him."

Nora looked at the troubled face of the man she came to love. This time she gave him a toothy smile. "Clint, you're the greatest. I actually feel a lot calmer. I guess I needed your assurance and that powerful bear hug of yours." This time, she chuckled.

Mortimer said, "Hey. It's close to noon. I better hurry home for lunch. Josephine doesn't like to wait and gets angry if I come too late. Could you take me to the station right away?"

Nora suggested, "Mortimer, why don't you call her that you have to interview more witnesses? I'll buy you lunch."

"Oh. But I told you before that if you and Hawk keep buying me lunches, I'll have to reciprocate someday, and it may be too expensive. Josephine wouldn't approve."

"Don't worry about it. You won't owe me. Just call her."

"Well, since you're buying, I'll do that. Besides, she was making a vegan chili which, frankly, I hate. I really could use some real meat, like a hamburger."

Hawk and Nora looked at each other. Hawk shook his head in disbelief.

In the Jeep, Hawk and Nora decided on a fast-food place. Hawk remembered the Burger King on Colfax and headed that way. Meanwhile, they overheard Mortimer tell his fiancé that he was not able to join her for lunch as duty called. They also heard some rapid squawking from the other end of the call. Finally, Mortimer said, "Josephine, I can't help it. We have to interview another witness right away. I'll see you tonight. Please don't be mad…no, you do not have to call anyone to complain."

Nora asked, "Complain to whom?"

Mortimer shook his head and blew out a hard breath. He blinked his eyes several times then looked at Nora. "Oh. Yes. She tells me that she knows well some upper-up in one of the Divisions, but she won't tell me who it is. Frankly, I think that's how I got this job." Hawk and Nora were surprised but remained silent.

At the Burger King, Mortimer asked for two giant Whoppers containing two hamburger patties in a bun and a large Pepsi while Nora and Hawk each ordered a Junior Whopper, one patty in a smaller bun. Neither felt like eating much. Hawk barely finished his while Nora just took a couple of bites and left it in the container. Mortimer, on the other hand, gobbled up both hamburgers with such relish, refilled his Pepsi twice, and sat back in the chair, his head back, his eyes closed. He looked satiated but when he opened his eyes again, he noticed that Nora left a good portion of her hamburger. "Nora, are you going to finish that?"

"No, I'm too tense."

"May I have it then?" Amazed, she nodded. "You know. It feels so good just to eat the hamburgers. I'm so tired of garbanzo beans and that kind of stuff. Never heard of garbanzo beans or tofu until I moved in with Josephine. She keeps telling me that they're healthy and I'll get used to it. Maybe I will, but right now this is a slice of heaven."

Nora and Clint laughed. Mortimer looked puzzled. "Did I say something funny?"

Nora remembered that the man admitted that he just didn't understand jokes or funny situations. "We laughed because the thought of a hamburger as a slice of heaven just sounded funny at the moment."

Hawk sat there listening to their banter with a smile on his lips. He glanced at his Tag Huer watch, "It's getting late. Are we ready to go? We've got a lot of work to do."

At that moment, Nora's cell rang. It was Lieutenant Perez. After she clicked off, Nora said, "We better hurry back. MacGregor wants to see us as soon as we get there."

Perez joined the three detectives as they entered the captain's office. Motioning for them to sit, MacGregor set aside an autopsy report, sucked in a deep breath, and blew it out. "That's a report from Janeel Thompson. She determined that Hollister died from aspirin anaphylaxis. So, it is murder. But the reason you're here is because I don't like my detectives threatened." Hawk and Nora caught the sharp tone of her voice. "I don't like that he, whoever he is, knows your every move, and I don't like that you're sitting ducks out there. He could've taken you out at any time. What are you going to do about it?"

Nora glanced at Hawk, her eyes wide. Hawk cleared his throat and swallowed. "We think he's going to try to get to us tonight, probably early in the morning. We have a plan, but it would be helpful if we could have a bomb-sniffing dog at Nora's place and a signal detector for a GPS tracker. I believe that my car and probably Nora's have one hidden somewhere deep in the undercarriage. Otherwise, how is it so easy for him to track us?"

"Okay, I'll make the arrangements."

Hawk said, "The dog would be a good precaution, but Nora and I talked, and we don't think O'Leary would use a bomb. It's personal with him. He'll need to see the fear on our faces before he squeezes the trigger. I'm sure of it."

MacGregor said, "I have a better solution. Leave. Fly somewhere."

Nora said, "And then what, Captain? I mean, ah, we have to come back eventually and either he'll wait for us or come back another time when we least expect it. He's on a mission for his cousin, that I'm sure about."

"All right. I see your point. I'll have some officers stationed in your house tonight."

Hawk suggested, "O'Leary is no dummy. A sociopath, yes, but no dummy. He'll be very careful to make sure the coast is clear. He'll make sure that Nora and I are alone, tucked away for the night, before he'll make a move. But we'll be prepared to take care of him if he comes after us tonight."

MacGregor sat silent for a long minute. "All right, then. I'll trust you to protect yourselves." Addressing Mortimer, who appeared to be dozing off, slumped on the couch, she queried, "Detective Holliday, will you be there at Detective Ricci's house tonight?"

Startled, Mortimer immediately sat up. "Oh. Ah. Ah." Then a loud sneeze followed. "If I need to be, certainly. I just must make arrangements with Josephine."

Nora said, "That's all right, Captain. Hawk and I will handle it fine."

"All right, then. Lieutenant, would you see if all the detectives are in? I want an update on the Hollister case."

CHAPTER 18

ALL WERE accounted for as MacGregor and Perez joined the detectives. MacGregor was first to speak, "Detective Orlinski, what are you working on in the Hollister murder?"

Orlinski rolled his chair further from the desk and turned to face the group. "After receiving a call from Hawk regarding the name of James Hollister's mortgage company and a review of the assessor's website, I've found out that James and Kay purchased the property about three months ago, and no payments had been made on the mortgage. Period. As a matter of fact, the company sent a letter to both James and the decedent that unless the payments are up to date, they'll begin foreclosure proceedings."

Nora said, "But they just moved in."

Orlinski said, "Yeah, I don't know what held them up. Probably something to do with the father. Anyway, to go on, the bank isn't too worried now because, evidently, there was a mortgage life policy on the life of the father that paid off the mortgage on the two-million-dollar house in the event of his death. James sure lucked out, getting an expensive place like that paid off."

Hawk said, "They're really making out with the death of William." He addressed Nora, "Didn't one of the sisters say that they'd suspect James and Kay in the murder?"

"Yeah, it was Ashley. Said he was a conniver."

MacGregor said, "All right. So, James and Kay are possible suspects. What about Ashley?"

Hawk said, "So far, I don't think we can rule anyone out. Ashley is a spoiled brat who relied totally on her father's money to survive. I suppose when she found out that the gravy train would come to an end, she might've been desperate enough to kill. We'll go back and interview her once again. I think, if she knows anything, she'd be the first one to break. Although she acts dumber than a box of rocks, it may be an act and she may be sharper than she appears."

Detective Nancy Salazar said, "I got some information on Darren Hollister. He was fired from his sales job a couple of months ago. They didn't tell me why. He owes the company advances that they made for prospective sales. Last communication from him was that he'll come into a lot of money and will pay every penny of it back."

Mortimer said, "Lost his job because of drinking, I'm sure. Josephine is surely correct when she says that drinking is not only expensive but will lead to ruin."

"Good point, Detective," Perez chimed in. "I hope you stay away from it."

"Oh. Yes, of course. I gave up whatever beer I enjoyed after I met my fiancé."

"Do you have anything else to contribute here, Detective Holliday?" MacGregor asked, seemingly annoyed.

"Oh. I think that Darren and his girlfriend, Tina, did it."

Hawk and Nora glanced at each other, surprised by his comment. Perez asked, "And why do you think that?"

"He's an alcoholic. Always needs money to support his habit. His answers to Clint and Nora's questions were flippant. In other words, he acted as though he wasn't bothered by those questions at all. However, I watched his hands as I stood over him. He was nervous. Every time he didn't like the question, he'd take a drink of Scotch and try hard not to let it bother him. Then there's his girlfriend, Tina. We hadn't interviewed her yet, but I remember her from the last case. She'll do anything for money. I'm sure she thinks she found a sucker in Darren. I'll run it past Josephine, and I bet she'll agree."

You could almost hear MacGregor growl at the mention of Josephine. "Detective Holliday, Josephine is not a detective, and maybe you shouldn't be discussing your cases with her."

"Oh, but she has good insight. Besides, she doesn't leave me alone until I tell her about every detail of my day. She finds it entertaining." He looked at Hawk. "Of course, I won't tell her anything about those delicious hamburgers I had for lunch."

MacGregor said, "It's none of my business, but I think you have a problem with your fiancé, and you don't know it."

"Oh, I'll have to think on that."

Perez asked Detective Harry Ling, "Did you find out anything about George and Rhonda Hollister?"

"Yes. I went to their country club just to talk to folks out there about them. It amazed me how much they are disliked. They all said that both are arrogant, and George has an uncontrollable temper. The staff absolutely hates them since they treat them like dirt. Boss them around, demean them, and if they tipped them, it was never more than ten percent. A member of the club told me that George likes the poker games in the back room. I first had to assure him that I was with Homicide and have nothing to do with gambling before he opened up to me. Said that George owes 'a ton of money to various members' and they were putting pressure on him to pay up or else they'll try to expel him from the club."

Nora asked, "Would that be a big deal for them?"

"Oh yeah. Sounds like a huge deal because that's like their second home. They spend a lot of time at their country club."

Hawk asked, "What's their source of income?'

"George works as an accountant. Has a solo office at DTC—Denver Tech Center. Makes pretty good income, about a quarter mill a year. But his bank accounts are empty. Spends too much on rent for a prestigious office. He's behind one month on his mortgage payment on his three-million-dollar house. He deposits five thousand every month from the trust and spends more than that each month on club dues, food and drink and that kind of stuff." Ling looked around the room. "I guess it costs a lot to keep up with the Joneses." He cackled. "I'm glad I don't have to worry about it."

MacGregor said, "Another child of William Hollister that had a strong motive. They probably all were relying on the funds from the trust and a sizable inheritance once the father dies, to maintain their lavish lifestyles. Who worked on info on the two daughters?"

"I did," Nancy said. As far as Cynthia and her husband, Samuel Maxwell, are concerned, they seem to be better off than the others, although they need that money from the trust to make it. They recently purchased a home in Vail. That's after selling their jewelry business in Arvada and their million-dollar home in Wheatridge, which was free and clear. They paid a million as a down payment on the house in Vail and financed the rest."

"How much is that house worth?" Nora asked, knowing that property in Vail was sky high.

"Hold on to your hat, Nora. They bought that house for five million dollars. Way out of their league as far as I'm concerned. From what I can see, they barely have enough money coming in to make the twenty-three thousand monthly payment. I think they were relying on the trust payment for their living expenses. They really bit off more than they can chew."

MacGregor thought about it, "Yeah, but they can always sell the place if they had to. Do you think they have a strong motive to kill the father?"

Harry said, "I think so. That's probably Cynthia's dreamhouse, and she doesn't want to lose it, even if she has to kill her father to keep it."

There was a lull in the conversation, so Nancy continued, "As far as Ashley is concerned, she seems to be a mess. Hasn't worked since college and relies solely on the trust payment. She rents a small apartment in the Highlands area and, according to the neighbors, parties all the time. They suspect her of being a druggie. The landlady said that she has sketchy live-in boyfriends that seem to come and go, disturbing the neighbors. She sounded pretty fed up with the girl and was ready to evict her. Calls her totally irresponsible and a real birdbrain."

Perez asked, "Nancy, in your opinion, could she have killed her father?"

"If she's desperate enough, yeah, I'd say she could've. But I'd sure like to interview her before I have a feel for it."

"I'll leave the interviewing up to Hawk and Ricci," Perez said.

"And me," Mortimer chimed in.

"We'll see," Perez was committal.

MacGregor said, "Okay, so, any other suspects?" She looked straight at Nora.

"There's the butler, Benson, and Consuela, the housekeeper. I doubt that they could've done it. They seemed awfully loyal to William Hollister. Consuela couldn't even talk. Her voice was shaky, and she cried the whole time we were there."

Orlinski laughed, "That's who you need to watch out for. Loyal is only as loyal goes. There's money involved. I understand that the old man announced to everyone that they'd be getting a sizeable chunk of his estate, isn't that right?"

Hawk said. "That's right. We haven't ruled anyone out yet. Hell, everyone has a dog in the fight with this murder."

Perez laughed, "More Texas humor, Hawk?" The detective smiled back.

Nora said, "The funeral and the reading of the will are scheduled for next week. The lawyer, Alan Windsor, asked us to attend because he fears there'll be a fight. I think we should go to both events."

MacGregor said, "That's a good idea. I want you there for sure. You may learn something. But before that, I want you to interview Cynthia Maxwell and Ashley again."

Hawk said, "For Cynthia, we'll have to go to Vail, two hours away. We still have time this afternoon to see Ashley if we catch her at her apartment."

Mortimer butted in, "I need to go with them since I've been with them for all the others."

MacGregor frowned and then smiled. "Yeah, go with them, but you'd better check with Josephine first." Everyone laughed, but Mortimer didn't see the humor and thought that she was serious about that. "Oh. Okay. I don't understand what's so funny, but I'll do just that and get her permission to see the suspects. Actually, I'm excited about a trip to Vail. I've looked on the map and it's right in the mountains. I asked Josephine to go on a trip there a couple of times, but she says that it's just too expensive. So, this will be a treat for me." He thought a minute while all the others were holding back their laughter. "Oh. We'll have to eat on the way, right? Do I have to pay for that myself, or is there an expense account?"

Nancy couldn't hold it any longer. She burst out in a robust laugh, joined by everyone else.

Mortimer looked around and saw everyone laughing. Perplexed, he asked, "Did I say something funny again? People always tell me that I'm funny, but I don't understand what they mean."

Nancy said, "No, what you said is not funny. It's just the way you phrased it."

"Oh. I still don't understand."

Perez interrupted, "Okay, people. We have work to do. And Holliday, the department will pay your expenses for lunch. Just give me a receipt. And don't buy any steaks or lobster tails, okay?"

"Oh, would a couple of hamburgers be all right?"

"Geez," Perez grunted. "Everyone, get busy."

And with that, Hawk, Ricci and Holliday exited the station and made their way to Ashley's apartment, hoping to find her at home.

CHAPTER 19

FINN O'LEARY dragged himself into his lonely motel room where he was registered under the fake name of Jason Winters. He missed his latest girlfriend, back in Boston, yearning to fall into bed with her. The motel was a dive along West Colfax Avenue frequented by prostitutes, drug addicts and winos. The run-down, depressing room sported an ancient TV that took up most of the space on a scratched laminated dresser. An old, many times washed bedspread covered the sagging mattress.

He could afford much better, but in a cheap motel, he could get lost among other denizens. The last job he did for a mobster paid one hundred thousand in cash, and he had a chunk of it with him stored in at least two locations. The job for the New York mobster was a piece of pie as far as he was concerned. He staked out a bar in the Hell's Kitchen area of Manhattan and waited for the victim to walk out the door.

Knowing that most people follow the same daily routine, he studied the man's habits for a week and knew approximately the time he'd leave the bar on that particular day. Parking a stolen vehicle across the street from the bar, he held the Glock 45 pistol in his right hand and his left finger on the window button to lower the tinted side glass when the time came. The man and his girlfriend walked out laughing. An excellent marksman, O'Leary collected his fee.

O'Leary stole another car just in case he was spotted in the Honda pickup. Adept at being able to steal any vehicle within twenty seconds, he never needed to purchase one. If he thought he'd use it for a few days, he snatched plates off another vehicle of the same color, make and model. This time he took a grey, older Kia Forte sedan and parked it in the back of the motel lot between two old pickup trucks.

Exhausted from being out all night and morning in his attempt to intimidate his new victims, Clint Hawk and Nora Ricci, he shoved aside the bedraggled bedspread exposing a thin yellowing bed sheet. He collapsed onto the squeaky and bumpy mattress. He lay supine, his eyes staring at the gray ceiling. The air-conditioning unit under the window growled and whined as if in agonizing pain.

O'Leary wasn't pleased with himself. Somehow, he blew it. For all these years that he'd been illegally in the United States, he never experienced the anxiety in which he found himself this time. Something wasn't right. Nobody knew who he was. No one suspected that he was the Finn O'Leary, the ruthless killer that disappeared from Europe. He knew that Interpol was actively searching for him. But he wasn't worried until now. He had this gut feeling that they, they being the people he was to kill, somehow figured out who he was. This meant that so did the Denver Police Department, and therefore, so did Interpol.

He made a big mistake by readily complying with his cousin's request to put the fear of God into them before he killed them. He liked the idea of a game, to play with their psyche, to frighten and keep them on edge. The green sheets he used proved that he knew where they were at all times and that he could get to them at any time. He believed that they would be forced into hiding, and he would make sure he'd know where they were. Instead, here they went on with their jobs as if there was no threat against them. He should not have played any games but got them in the first instance when they walked out of the law office in Golden. Then they would not know that anyone was out there gunning for them. He chastised himself for missing an excellent opportunity when they casually walked out the front door. It would have been over. He could have caught the next plane out and no one would be the wiser. I am a fool for listening to Devon. *My cousin was always the stupid one. At least that's what all the relatives in Ireland used to say. And I'm probably just as stupid for going along. Bollocks!!!*

Too wound up to sleep, O'Leary switched on the TV. It took time to warm up the tube, but when it did, the first thing Finn saw was his mug plastered on the screen with a request from the police to call them if he's seen. There was a caution for the public not to approach since Finn O'Leary is armed and extremely dangerous. The photo was taken at least a decade ago. O'Leary had aged, but he was still identifiable. *Shit! I was right. They know who's after them. But how? No one else ever figured it out, and I had the best of them chasing me all over Europe. I got to kill them as soon as possible and get out of here. Damn! Damn! Damn! My cover is blown. I need to get out of this country. Brazil, that's where everyone goes.*

O'Leary began formulating a plan as he lay on the squeaky bed. He thought that he would have some time before the crotchety old manager of the motel watched TV and put two and two together. Now he needed the rest. It will be a long night, but he was too hyped up to sleep. He would have to kill them, then make it back to New York. There he knows someone that will forge another passport for him and someone else that has a seaworthy sailboat. If he pays him enough, he will sail all the way close to the shores of Brazil. *To avoid customs and immigration, I'll take a dinghy to some secluded beach and walk ashore as if I belong there.* But that photo of him would be broadcast all over the country. He would have to buy some disguises such as fake beards, mustaches, eyebrows, fake noses, different caps, hoodies, makeup, whatever it'll take.

Now that he formulated a plan of escape, his thoughts shifted to the detectives. He had to take care of business tonight at the latest. If he must, he would kill them in open daylight since they know who is after them anyway. But he would prefer the cover of darkness. They would be at that woman's house. He was not sure if Clint Hawk was shacking up with her or whether he was there for protection. He doubted that they would go somewhere else for the night. They would again have police presence guarding the house. But they may not even expect him to return to the house since it would be foolish of him to do so. Nevertheless, they would be prepared. *But if I follow them to a spot where I can get off two quick shots and escape, that may be even better.*

After racking his brain on how best to kill them, O'Leary jumped out of bed with a solution. He hastened to the bathroom and pulled out an envelope of cash that he had hidden. Then he grabbed his suitcase and threw in his toiletries—his clothes were never unpacked. He ran out the door, threw the suitcase in the back seat and pulled out of the parking lot. He had shopping to do and two people to kill.

CHAPTER 20

HEADING TOWARD Ashley Hollister's apartment building, Nora drove Hawk's Jeep while he vigilantly watched for any vehicles that might be trailing. From the police station, Nora proceeded south on Washington, then west on Speer Boulevard. On Speer, they passed two local television stations, Denver Convention Center, the theater district, several cranes erecting more skyscrapers and Elitch Gardens Amusement Park. Nora sighed as she viewed a carefree world of the park, so far removed from her daily stress. Thousands of kids out for the summer, enjoying the Ferris wheel and all the other rides spinning energetically under brilliant blue cloudless skies. *I'd give anything to be out there right now,* Nora dreamed. They traveled over I-25 and turned north onto Federal Boulevard into the once Italian district of Denver.

Nora said, "This area sure brings up old memories. My grandfather's brother and his family used to live in the area. Father's family came from around Florence, while my mom's came from Sicily. And while my grandfather ended up in Pueblo working in the big CF&I Steel Plant, his brother came to work on the railroads in Denver. He and his wife bought a house not far from here with a big lot where they grew vegetables. We had many good times, eating the old country food and playing with cousins."

"Are there still many Italians that live here?" Mortimer asked.

"No, they're scattered all over the metro area. I guess most of them moved to Arvada and Lakewood. This area is now so hot that these old houses that you could buy for twelve to twenty-five thousand about twenty years ago, now go for a million or more. It's crazy. You missed the boat, Clint. If you had bought up here when you first came to Denver, you'd be really well off right now."

"That's always the case. If only. Then, I couldn't afford a pot to pee in."

Mortimer cleared his throat. "What makes this area so special? Just some old houses with new ones thrown in between here and there."

Nora continued, "That's what attracts the millennials right now. The older, the better. Plus, there's a lot of restaurants and boutiques that you could walk to. Actually, there's a pedestrian bridge over I-25 in the lower Highlands area of Denver, or LOHI as the locals call it. That bridge takes you close to the Union Station downtown, where there's more action. It's a cool area and I wouldn't mind living here at all. Funny that I didn't think that much of it when my relatives lived here. And neither did they since they moved away."

Ashley's apartment house looked new with the contemporary boxy architecture. It stood among the small brick houses on either side and across from it, which were built in the 1920's or earlier. A house a few doors down was an old two-story Victorian—a real painted lady—with its colorful trim that emphasized the six gables and the arched front windows.

The three detectives walked up to the second floor. After knocking several times, Ashley finally opened the door, a skeptical look on her worried face. "I remember you. You're the detectives investigating my father's death."

Hawk said, "Yes, for sure. We have a few more questions for you. May we come in?" All three took a measure of her. She looked completely different from the first time they saw her when her hair was beautifully styled, and her clothes looked neat and stylish. Now, she appeared disheveled, wearing baggy pajama pants and a stained gray sweatshirt.

"Oh, Detective. I'd love to visit, but I need to get dressed since I have an appointment with this sweet Vietnamese woman to do my nails." She stuck out a hand at Hawk. "See, they're absolutely frightful. And I've got a really important date with a guy that I think I really like. By the way, sorry for the way I look, but I wasn't expecting you."

Nora said, "It'll only take a few minutes. It's still early in the afternoon."

"I just can't. I got to go. Sorry." She began to close the door, but Hawk shoved his foot over the threshold.

"Ashley, since we're here, we need to talk. I'm sure it'll be more pleasant here than an interview room at the station."

"You mean you'd arrest me?"

"Not an arrest. But since you are a person of interest, as are all your siblings, we would take you in for questioning."

Ashley's fake smile faded, and her eyes narrowed. Hawk saw a mean look in them that he hadn't noticed before. After pursing her lips and hesitating for a moment, she finally allowed them to enter. There wasn't much to the tiny apartment—a U-shaped tiny kitchen with a stack of dirty dishes in the sink, two red barstools underneath the front counter, a cramped living room and an open door to the bedroom, her unmade bed visible. The place had four narrow unpainted wooden chairs, a small dark veneered dinette table cluttered with paper, a plate with a half-eaten piece of ground beef patty that looked like it's been there for a while, a dirty fork off to the side and a coffee mug. A three-cushion sofa sat behind a coffee table decorated by an empty wine bottle, two crushed beer cans and two paper cups. *Gads!* Nora thought, *she's messy and her furniture is so bad, Goodwill wouldn't take it. What does she do with the money she's supposed to receive?*

Ashley pulled out three of the chairs from underneath the dinette, turned them toward the couch, and asked them to sit down. Nora and Hawk sat on the sofa and Ashley on one of the chairs. Mortimer remained standing off to her side. She patted down a chair and asked him to sit. He still stood. She addressed Nora, "This man makes me nervous. He's standing over me and glaring down at me. Would you please ask him to sit?" All three detectives observed her hands shaking before she placed one hand over the other and tightly held them into a ball.

After Nora asked Mortimer to sit down, Ashley calmed. Frankly, it also made Nora nervous when he stood over her. It was unsettling. She could not figure out whether he did it on purpose or whether he just liked standing. After some silence with all three detectives' eyes fixed on her, Ashley spoke with a little raspiness in her voice. She sniffled again, a habit that they had noticed when they first walked in. "I don't understand what you want from me. I told you everything I knew about my father's death when we were in his house."

Hawk said, "There's just a few more questions, Ashley. You mentioned that James would be most likely to kill your father. Why exactly do you feel that way?"

"And I told you that he's a conniver."

"Yes, but what do you mean by that?"

Without thinking, she blurted out, "I can't believe you'd ask such a stupid question. Good looking, maybe even gorgeous, but dumb as an ox."

"Oh," Hawk said, unfazed by her insult. "And why is that?"

"I learned in middle school what a conniver is."

Hawk continued, "Would you enlighten me?"

"Geez, you're somethin'. Someone that plots to get what he wants. He always was my sneakiest brother. A big cheater." She paused and stared at Hawk. "Okay, you want to hear what I know of James, I'll tell you. He did everything he could to become Daddy's favorite by always hanging around him, inviting him out, poisoning him against all of us. He and that wicked wife of his brainwashed Dad into believing that we didn't love him. But we all did in our own way. Why do you think that Daddy was going to leave everything to him? He made him change the trust and the will so that he was the most to benefit. A lawyer friend that I ran into in a bar said that James must've used undue influence on my father."

Nora said, "If he was going to inherit almost everything, then why murder your dad?"

"The rest of us talked about it. George found out that he was going to lose that new house of his. And he thinks that Daddy balked at helping him out any more than he already had. He's always done it before, but he musta said that he won't help any more with the house. And get this, George said that the mortgage had life insurance on Daddy's life. So, if he died, James would have a paid off house. He just couldn't wait for Daddy to die a natural death."

Nora said, "But if he had waited, he'd inherit a ton of money."

"Yeah. That's something we can't figure out."

Mortimer asked, his head raised, his eyes closed, "What about you, young lady?"

Looking at Mortimer, she said, "What about me?'

"Didn't you need your father to die before he had a chance to terminate the trust and change the will?"

"No. How can you say that? That's so mean. You think I would kill my father for the money? I loved my Daddy."

Mortimer continued, "Oh. How would you support yourself without his help? You don't work, do you?"

"No, not now. I didn't have to, before. I'll just find myself a job, that's all."

Nora queried, "What kind of a job?"

Irritated, Ashley's face went sour. "I'm not a total loser. I do have a college degree in art history. And I'm sure that I could find work in an art museum or a gallery somewhere. I'll survive, don't worry about me. I may even get married to a rich dude that's been hounding me lately. He's a nerd, but he's got a ton of money from a software business, and he loves me."

Hawk said, "I'll be happy for you if that's the case. But going back to what you told us back at the house, you said that you went into your dad's bedroom." She nodded; her eyes narrowed. "Were you there by yourself?"

After a long pause, she said, "No, I went in there together with Darren and Tina. She really loved that huge room."

"Were the three of you together in the bathroom?"

Another pause. "Yes, because Tina was so excited at how large and fancy it looked that Darren and I went to join her."

"Did you notice the pill box?"

"You mean that black box that has all the medications for the day that my dad was supposed to take?"

"Yes."

"Yeah. Actually, I remember that Tina pointed it out and commented that it's identical to the one that her grandmother has. She said, 'Just shows you, rich or poor, you still have the same problems when it comes to health.'"

Hawk continued, "Did she say anything else?"

Asley lifted her head and closed her eyes. "Yeah. She said, 'Even the pills look like the kind my grandmother takes, except for those that look like plain aspirin.'"

Hawk and Nora exchanged glances. Hawk asked, "And then what was said?"

"Nothing, really. I think that Darren mentioned that it better not be aspirin. That it would kill dad because of his severe allergy to it."

Nora said, "But yesterday, you couldn't recall what your father was allergic to."

"I guess I forgot."

"Then what happened?"

"Nothing. I left them in the bathroom and went to my former room."

"Did you go back afterward to your dad's room?"

"Yeah. I went back and checked out all the rooms so that I'd remember them for all time. I was very sad. I was even crying."

Nora continued, "Was anyone in your dad's room at that time?"

"Yeah. George and Rhonda were just coming out of the bathroom as I walked in. George was nasty to me and asked me in a gruff voice, 'What the hell are you doing here?' I turned around quickly and left."

Hawk asked, "Do you think that they might've switched the meds?"

"Oh. I never thought of it. I doubt that they would, but I never liked my older brother. He was always mean to me. There's a big age difference, and we were never close, so who knows what's in his stupid, arrogant mind."

Nora asked, "Were you ever by yourself in the bathroom that evening?"

"Nope. You can't pin this on me. I would never have harmed my daddy." Tears welled up in her blue eyes, giving them a glistening shine.

Nora asked Hawk and Holliday whether they had anything else to add. Hawk said that he was ready to go, but Mortimer stared at the ceiling. "Mortimer, do you have any questions of Ashley?"

"Oh. I guess not."

Ashley asked, "Am I off the hook? Do you still think that I'm a suspect?"

Hawk said, "We're still investigating, and unfortunately, we're unable to clear anyone at this time."

"Oh, God! The nightmare continues."

"But Ashley, I must tell you," Hawk said, "That your information today was very helpful, and we appreciate it. Thank you. If you think of anything else that we need to know, here's my card. Please call me."

As the three left Ashley's apartment, Hawk's cell blurted out the *Bad to the Bones* tune. "Hello, Detective Hawk. This is attorney Alan Windsor. I thought that you should know that my place was broken into over lunch. I believe it concerns the Hollister case, and you should come by."

CHAPTER 21

TINA DIONISIO knocked hard on Darren's door twice, the second time harder, with no answer. Becoming concerned, she used the key that he had given her previously. Darren lay asleep on the sofa, curled in a fetal position. She called out his name but to no avail. Shaking him vigorously until he opened his eyes. He blinked a few times, then rubbed the back of his hand over his face. It took a moment to recognize Tina standing over him.

"What happened?" Darren slurred.

"What do you mean what happened? You obviously fell asleep from drinking too much again. Don't you know that booze will kill you?"

Darren tried to shake the sleep from his head and swallowed hard, then coughed lightly. "Yeah, that's what Josephine also says."

"Josephine! Who in the hell is Josephine?"

"Damn, if I know. That's bizarre. Where did that come from?" He closed his eyes as his head swayed toward the back of the couch. "Oh, I know. That tall, skinny and really weird detective you told me about said that Josephine said that alcohol will kill. But I have no clue who she is."

"I think you drank a little too much, baby. I'll make you some strong coffee. After all, I have to keep you healthy." Tina walked a few steps over to the sink for water and poured into a fancy gourmet coffee maker.

"Will you keep me as healthy as this, Josephine?" Darren broke out in an uncontrollable fit of laughter. He could hear Tina chuckle in the background.

After draining the large mug of strong black coffee, Darren felt better. He still, though, had a horrific headache. "I need an aspirin. My head feels like it'll split wide open."

"Oh, I'll get you one out of my purse."

A few minutes later, Tina asked, "Are you able to tell me what happened with the detectives?"

"Yeah, I guess so, although I don't remember much." He paused. "Let's see, that woman detective was a real knockout." He laughed as Tina slapped his shoulder."

"Ouch! That was a little hard."

"You'll survive. So, what questions did they ask you?"

After another long pause, "They wanted to know about my relationship with my parents, I think. Then they asked about the trust and the will. I think I told them that I have a great job and that the trust payments are helpful, but I can do without them. I really can't remember what I said, Tina."

"Okay, then what?"

"Then they asked me about who could've killed dad. And I told them it was their job to find out. One of the questions I remember was whether I saw anyone go into dad's bathroom."

"What did you say to that?" Tina suddenly looked troubled.

"Well, ah, I had to say that you and I went into the room."

"Oh, no! You didn't."

"Well, yeah. Other people saw us in there. I couldn't lie about that. Then, that crazy detective accused us of conspiring together to kill dad."

"Oh, God! What did you say?"

"I denied it, of course."

"How vigorously did you deny it?"

"I made sure that they knew that we didn't do it. Actually, I kinda threw suspicion onto George and Cynthia. Let the hound dogs loose on them." He chuckled, then grabbed his head. "Ouch!"

"Any other discussion about me?"

"Ah, they asked about Dad's aspirin allergy and wanted to know if I told you about it that evening. They also asked if you had aspirin in your purse." Her face paled.

Tina hissed, "Oh, God! What did you say?"

"That's when I kicked them out. I didn't even see them leave. I musta passed out."

"Listen, Darren. Next time follow my advice and get a lawyer before answering any questions. I'm counting on you to get that inheritance you're entitled to. As I told you, I need your account to keep my new position with the investment bank. You promised me that I could be your financial advisor. I need to bring in at least two million in investments in the next six months or I can kiss my job goodbye. I need to replace the half mil per year that I lost when Ellis fired me."

"I know, darlin'. There shouldn't be a problem. My share of dad's estate would be close to that alone. Anyway, I need a drink. This whole experience was too much."

"No, Darren, that's the last thing you need. We must keep our heads clear."

CHAPTER 22

AS THE DETECTIVES piled into Hawk's Jeep, they carefully looked around, trying to remember the cars in the vicinity in case one of them began to follow. Nora sat behind the wheel again, and from his passenger seat, Hawk could scrutinize the vehicles on the road. As Nora left the parking spot, he noticed a grey, older model Kia Forte pull out a minute later. He decided to keep an eye on that vehicle.

"We need to go to Golden again right now, "Hawk said. "That call I received a couple of minutes ago was from the Hollister's attorney. Evidently his office was burglarized while they were out this afternoon, and Windsor thinks it's got something to do with the Hollister murder."

Nora said, "Really? That's interesting. Sure, let's go. Mortimer, would you call Perez and tell him where we're going?"

"Oh." He cleared his throat, then coughed mildly. "I understand we're going back to the law office where we were before, correct?"

"Yes, exactly."

"Oh. Okay. Glad to do it. And then I'll call Josephine and tell her as well because we might be late for dinner."

Hawk and Nora exchanged glances with furtive smiles. Mortimer made the calls, then said, "Lieutenant Perez said that we're outside of our jurisdiction so don't step on any toes with the Golden Police Department. Oh, yeah, he said to watch ourselves."

As Hawk twisted to check behind them, he asked in jest, "And what did Josephine say?"

"Oh, she wasn't too happy, I think. She likes it when I come home between 5:30 and 6 o'clock. Told me to hurry back because she is making a new Indian dish."

Nora asked, "Did she tell you what it is?"

"Oh. I believe she said a biryani made with vegetables and chickpeas. A few times, I complained to her that we eat a lot of garbanzo beans, so now she calls them chickpeas as if I don't know the difference." He paused. "I have an idea. Maybe we can stop and get another hamburger before going back to the station."

Nora glanced at Hawk for his reaction to Mortimer wanting to eat again, but Hawk seemed concerned with what he saw behind them. "We'll see, Mortimer, how the day goes," she said. Then asked Hawk, "What's wrong?"

"Probably nothing. That little grey Kia has been holding a steady distance behind us since we left. Why don't you slow down, and let's see if it'll pass us?"

Nora said, "We haven't yet received that tracker detector that you requested. Too bad. Do you think that he has another tracker under this car?"

"Looks like it."

Finn O'Leary knew that he had to get out of Colorado and disappear. He had already disguised himself with a fake gray beard and a gray mustache. The photo that they showed on TV was taken at least ten years ago and portrayed him with long black hair. He found a small barber shop and asked that his hair be cut short and dyed gray to match the beard and mustache. As he entered, he glanced at the television and saw that it was tuned to a sports channel and not the news, which made him breathe easier.

He had this job to do as a favor to his cousin and was kicking himself for waiting this long. *It's Devon's problem, not mine. I'll just do the job, shoot them and take off. Better not take any chances by going to the house tonight—unless I have to."*

Because of the hidden GPS tracker, O'Leary found his prey's Jeep on 28th Street in Highlands. He waited for them to return to the vehicle so that he could follow, looking for a good opportunity to get rid of them. Even the big lanky guy. As he followed the Jeep, he noticed that they slowed considerably, and he was catching up. He had a decision to make. If he also slowed, they'll know for sure that they're being followed. He decided to pass them when he was able in the heavy Sixth Avenue freeway rush-hour traffic. As he passed, he turned his head slightly away from them, hoping that they did not get a good look at him. With the tracker, he was not worried about losing them.

He exited at Indiana Street and pulled off to the side, watching their progress on the screen. The detectives turned into Golden, and he realized that they were heading to that same law office where he had first picked them up earlier with the tracker. He remembered the building across the street where he hid and watched them as they found one of the trackers. That was a trick he used in the past. If anyone looks, make one easy to find, but always plant two, one deeper in the undercarriage.

As he drove toward Golden, he began formulating a plan. O'Leary wondered if he would be able to get off two shots with his semiautomatic pistol—a bullet in the head for the good-looking guy and one for that gorgeous brunette. He would not worry about the goofy one. He decided that the idea would work. Get them by surprise before they can even reach for their holsters.

That was the plan. He would shoot them before they knew what hit them, run back to the car and take off easterly toward Kansas. In some small town, he would steal another vehicle and make his escape back to New York.

That was the plan until he arrived at the scene.

Change of plans.

The place was crawling with cops. Something happened in the law office. *Okay, okay, don't panic. I got to come up with another strategy or stay with the original plan.* As O'Leary returned to the car, he thought whether he should still hang around and continue to follow them and look for that perfect spot to execute his plan. But he was taking too much of a chance this way. So, he decided on his original plan remembering how easy it was to enter that woman detective's house and leaving a note. *She probably didn't even notice that I took a couple of bananas from the counter.*

He'd steal another commonly used vehicle, change plates and head to her house. He had to get there before they came home or before police cruisers arrived as protection. He would park the car in the next block and sneak into the house, making sure no one sees him. He was good at that. He would find a good hiding place, perhaps in the basement, maybe a crawl space under the house. Small in stature, limber and nibble, he knew he could fit into a large box if he had to. Then, after they go to sleep, he'll take care of business. *And if they're up waiting for me, which they probably will, I'd surprise them from within, making them sweat. I'll put the fear of God in them, that's for sure. I'll make them pee their pants before I pull the trigger.*

Devon would be happy, and I won't owe him a damn thing after this.

Satisfied with his plan, he cruelly laughed out loud as he sped toward Nora's house.

CHAPTER 23

DETECTIVE LAURA Kiplinger of the Golden Police Department met the three detectives as they walked into the Windsor Law offices. She was a tall, slender, striking woman in her mid-thirties with long fire red hair that framed her freckled oval face. She spotted the badges. After introductions, she said, her voice mellow, "Mr. Windsor told me you'd be stopping by. He thinks what happened here is related to your murder investigation in Denver." She looked at Hawk as she spoke, sidling closer to him. Nora noticed and immediately took a dislike to her. She knew that Clint seemed to be a female magnet, but she couldn't get used to it. It was mainly because she felt insecure as to how exactly Hawk felt about her. He seemed to run hot and cold with her.

Nora stepped closer to Hawk, deciding to take control. "How exactly is a burglary related to our case?"

Turning her attention to Nora, Detective Kiplinger said, "I'll let you talk to the attorney about it."

Nora persisted, "Could you tell us what happened here exactly?"

She smiled. "Of course. It was the paralegal's birthday. She's eighty-one today and still working. Awesome, isn't it? She glanced at Hawk and smiled. "Anyway, Mr. Windsor took her and some of her friends out to a long lunch to celebrate. They didn't arm the security system, thinking they'd be back sooner than they were. You know, he's over eighty himself. I hope I'll be in the condition those two are in when I'm eighty."

"So, what happened?" Nora asked with impatience in her voice.

Nora caught the sharp tone when Kiplinger explained, "Someone kicked in the back door and went into Mr. Windsor's office there." Pointing to the open door, the same one they had walked through before.

Mortimer asked with a light cough, "Ah, what was taken?"

"That's just it. Nothing but a copy of a will that's involved in your case. I'm sure he'll tell you all about it. Strange."

"Oh, what's strange?" Hawk asked.

Kiplinger said, chuckling, "Well, if I went to the trouble of breaking down a door to burglarize a place, I'd take some of these beautiful items that are just in this front room. I sure would love to snuggle up with someone on that bear rug in front of my fireplace." She glanced at Hawk, smiling sweetly.

Nora knew exactly what she was getting at. *That bitch!*

Hawk smiled back, then said, "Shall we go talk to Mr. Windsor now?"

"Sure. My investigation is over." Glancing at all three detectives this time, she said, "I'll send you my report if you like."

Hawk acknowledged, "That'll be great. On the other hand, before you go, may we look at the back door?"

"No problem. I'll join you."

Walking around the building to the backyard, Hawk noticed sneaker footprints in the moist dirt leading up to the rear door. Another one was on the old door itself, the impression left when the person kicked it open. The frame around the door appeared neglected and should have been replaced long ago. It was brittle and didn't take much force to split, rip the rotten door jamb and spring the door open. He took several photos with his iPhone of the footprints, door and frame. He asked Kiplinger, "Did your crime lab people take molds of those prints in the soil."

"I'm sure they did," Kiplinger said. "And, of course, they looked for prints. Didn't find any other than those of the lawyer and his paralegal."

"We have a real expert in sneaker soles. Would you send a copy of the molds to Chet Watkins at our crime lab? And if your people didn't take any molds, would you mind if Chet comes out and does it?"

"No problem. I'll let you know. Just give me your card."

Hawk thanked her. Nora watched her shake his hand while her other hand lingered on his arm. "I'll call you if anything comes up."

Nora had enough of her and began walking to the lawyer's office. She heard Mortimer say to Kiplinger, "That'll be most helpful. Thank you." *Yeah, thanks a lot.*

Attorney Windsor stood up from behind his desk to greet them as they walked in. "It's a little chaotic here now, especially since I gave my paralegal, Faye, the rest of the afternoon off after the police took her prints. It's so disturbing when someone violates your private space. It's the first time it happened in the thirty years that I've been in this building."

Nora said, "I know from experience how traumatic it is. We're so sorry."

"Aw. It could've been much worse, that's for sure."

Hawk asked, "Mr. Windsor, what was taken?"

"The only thing that I can see is a copy of William Hollister's will."

Nora queried, "Just a copy?"

"Yes. Of course, you need the original to probate an estate and, lucky for me, I kept the original at Mr. Hollister's request. I ordinarily don't do that, but I made an exception in his case."

Hawk asked, "And they didn't find the original?"

"No. I have a safety deposit box at a bank where I keep important original documents. Good thing. If that original had disappeared, there might've been a big problem."

Mortimer sucked in a deep breath through his whistling nose. "It must've been one of the kids or their spouses, don't you think?"

"I would assume so. Who else would want it?"

Hawk asked, "How do you know that they took the copy? Perhaps it's mislaid somewhere."

"Oh, Faye is meticulous with the files and what's filed in them. The file drawer that contained Hollister's file wasn't shut all the way when I came back for lunch. When I pulled it open, I noticed that the Hollister file wasn't in its proper spot in the cabinet."

“How would you know that?” Nora asked.

“By Faye’s numbering system. The file was out of sequence and the tab was about a quarter of an inch higher than the others. So, I pulled it out. Going through it, I noticed that the new, updated will copy was missing. A copy of the old will remained.”

“What does that tell you?” Mortimer asked.

“It tells me that now someone knows what’s in the will and who is getting what. I assume that if it was one of the children that took it, he or she would inform the others, except for maybe James, who is inheriting most of the estate.”

Hawk said, “This case is getting more complicated. That’s for sure.”

“As you know, I plan to have the reading of the will next week. I hope you’re still intending to attend.”

“We’ll be here,” Nora said. Then she thought of O’Leary out there trying to kill them. She suddenly felt a huge pit in her stomach as she said, a slight tremor in her voice, “At least, I sincerely hope so.”

CHAPTER 24

LATE AFTERNOON approached too quickly. Nora dreaded going back to her house. She wished she and Clint could just keep driving, far away from Denver, and hide in some secluded spot until O'Leary was found. It all seemed surreal knowing that they had to hurry to her home—her cozy home—to lay a trap for the psycho. She should feel safe in her own sanctuary. Then a chilling thought entered her mind—*what if we're already too late, and it's not us setting a trap for him, but he's the one laying the trap?*

Her breath caught in her throat, and her heart felt as though it was at 200 beats a minute. She gritted her teeth as she glanced at Clint, who sat twisted to the side, watching the traffic behind them. His expressive face betrayed a deep concern. Noticing his clenched jaw, she thought, h*e's sweating this as much as I am. Just as scared but tries to hide it and put on a brave front.* As she studied Clint, she thought, *he's really sweet in his attempts to minimize the danger. Wants to lower my anxiety. Too bad it's not working.*

In a way, Nora felt sorry for Hawk. Here he was, just beginning his career as a detective, but so far, he had had no break from constant danger. It began with his as a fellow detective, Devin O'Leary, another cold-blooded killer and the cousin of Finn, tried to kill him on several occasions. In addition to that, there were other life-threatening incidents.

Then, a little later, she shuddered at the thought of how close they came to death by a fatal bullet by the hand of the boss of the crooked cops, a case that they solved. That incident took place at her house, no less. *So much for wishing for a perfect sanctuary.*

In another case, Hawk again was shot at, narrowly escaping. Since then, Hawk complained to Nora of his nightmares that kept him awake. He would wake up drenched in sweat. *This encounter and threat from Finn O'Leary would make his nightmares worse. Like pouring salt over a wound.* She felt sorry for him. And then she felt sorry for herself for once again being in danger, possibly about to be killed, and once again in what should be her safe, peaceful home.

Nora's thoughts were broken when Mortimer asked, "I guess it's too late to stop and get a hamburger. I'll buy one for myself."

Hawk glanced at his TAG Heuer watch, a gift from his parents. "Mortimer, if we stop now, you'll be late for dinner with Josephine. Won't she be pissed off?"

Mortimer sneezed. "Oh, I guess so. It's best if she's not mad at me." His voice sounded disappointed. "More garbanzo beans it is."

Nora and Clint felt bad for Mortimer. They never met his fiancé, but through Mortimer, it was as though they knew her. She didn't sound like the right fit for him.

Nora said, "If we survive until Sunday, why don't you and Josephine come over for dinner at my house? I'll prepare a vegan meal for her and a meat dish for us." She glanced at Hawk and laughed as she drove, "That includes you too, big boy."

Mortimer said, "Oh, no. Josephine would never go to anyone's house, especially for dinner. She'll never admit it to you, but it'll cost money to get there." He thought a moment, "Then she'll feel obliged to invite you back, and that's more expense and a lot of bother. Besides, I couldn't eat meat in front of her."

"Well, maybe a little later she'll agree to a visit."

Hawk said, "Well, Mortimer, we're almost at the station, and you'll only be a few minutes late. Josephine should be happy about that. Maybe even give you a big kiss out of joy."

Mortimer sneezed and rubbed his forefinger under his nose. "That would be nice, but we don't do much of that." Both Nora and Clint tried to hide their smirks.

After Nora parked, Mortimer strode to his old Oldsmobile 88, still sporting Florida plates. The other two walked into the Detective Unit and were immediately confronted by Lieutenant Perez, who appeared sincerely worried. "Are you sure you want to go back to your place, Nora? I'd feel much better if you stay somewhere else. Why not Clint's place?"

Nora glanced at Hawk. "How do you feel about that?"

Hawk said, "I think that would only prolong the agony. It's not difficult to find out where I live. I mean, the two hired killers from the Ellis case found me quickly enough to take potshots at me. If we're not at Nora's tonight, he'll probably head to my place. If we go to a hotel, he'll gun us down at the station. Perhaps try to blow up all of us. No, I think we stay the course."

Nora said, "I agree."

Perez said, "In that case, I'm coming with you. Better with three of us in the house."

Hawk said, "Thank you so much for your kind offer. But for all we know, he may have a heat detector and know that there are three people in the house and suspect that we're expecting him. I have great confidence in Nora. Look how she single-handedly took down Devon O'Leary, and later the two hired killers. She's amazing, and between the two of us, we'll handle it. After all, Nora told me that she's my bodyguard."

Nora flushed from the compliment. She sidled over to Hawk and put an arm around his waist, pulling him toward her. "And, Lieutenant, he's my bodyguard. Seriously, we'll be back to work tomorrow. We can't die tonight. We have the Hollister case to solve." She forced a chuckle. No one returned her laugh.

"All right then. But I'll be monitoring everything, and in case anything happens, I'll be right there. Oh, yes, here's the signal detector that you requested. Keep it. It's a gift. I bought it for you over lunch." Both Nora and Hawk protested that it shouldn't be a gift. But Perez held up his hand for them to remain quiet. "It didn't cost that much. Maybe I can get MacGregor to reimburse me someday. But as far as the bomb-sniffing dog, the handler will probably come late, if at all. Evidently, the dog is being used at an airport freight warehouse this evening."

On the way to Nora's, Hawk pulled over to a UPS store. "Why are we here?"

"I need some bubble wrap."

"What for?"

"It makes a lot of noise when someone steps on it."

Nora said, "But we don't want to scare him off. We must end this."

"I was thinking—"

Nora laughed, "Oh, you were actually thinking? How novel." She continued to laugh, almost hysterically, releasing some of the tension. As laughter is contagious, Hawk couldn't help but laugh along. Both had a good belly laugh. If anyone had walked by in the parking lot, hearing and seeing them, they would think that there were two crazy people.

After they settled down, Nora said, "Okay, what were you thinking?"

"We'll place sheets of bubble wrap not by the doors but in strategic spots close to where we'll be. Or we may not use it at all. We'll see."

"Okay, makes sense, I guess."

After Hawk came back, he slid behind the wheel and said, "Nora, I'm starving. Let's get something. I'll tell you what. Let's go to a nice place and have a great meal. No wine or drinks, though. Gotta keep our heads straight."

"You can eat at a time like this?"

"You bet I can," Hawk said. "Come on. You'll be into it once you begin eating."

"Okay, if you insist, you silver-tongued devil."

"What do you suggest?"

"Clint, it's your show. Pick out anything. I really don't think I could eat a thing. I'd rather, though, that it be quick."

"Well, in that case, let's go to French Press on twelfth and Madison. It'll be quick, and they have a variety of food. Plus, a good cup of coffee will keep us alert. Besides, we really need to keep up our strength.”

Hawk liked the cozy atmosphere of the restaurant with its wood-simulated tile floor, old, refurbished brick wall on the left and wood paneling on the right. The tables with shiny walnut tops were surrounded by dark blue wooden chairs. The place had a comfortable appeal with its many chandeliers. They ordered at the counter. Nora had a cheese and ham crepe, while Hawk requested a French dip sandwich. Both ordered coffee.

Sitting silently across from each other, Nora stretched her hands out toward him. Hawk took the thin, gentle fingers into his. “Gads, they’re cold as ice. I’m so sorry that we have to sweat it tonight. You’re really worried about it, aren’t you?”

“Aren’t you?”

Hawk closed his eyes and clamped down on his square jaw. “Of course I am. My insides are shaking at the thought. On the other hand, I have a gut feeling that we’ll get O’Leary tonight.” Nora blew out a breath. A twinkle in her eye appeared as she smiled, “Okay, my hero, we’ll go to work and do our job. Although, I think I need to call my parents, grandmother and brother and tell them that I love them.” She looked hard at Clint, “I know nothing about your family. I assume your parents are doing well. Are all your grandparents alive? Any siblings?”

Hawk laughed. “Yes, I’m lucky. I have all my grandparents, and I have two sisters. They’re all in Texas. I talk to them all the time, especially my dad.” He sighed before he sucked in a deep breath and blew it out. “Probably not a bad idea to call all of them tonight.”

“What does your father do?”

“He’s a petroleum engineer. Has a firm with a couple of partners. My Mom is a stay-at-home mom. My grandparents are retired. My paternal grandfather was a rancher, and my mom’s dad was a cop with the Dallas PD. As a matter of fact, my parents plan to come out for a visit this winter. They're all into skiing. I'd like you to meet them."

Nora smiled. "I'd love to." *I wonder how he'll introduce me. A girlfriend? I wish it were a fiancé.*

The food was served, and just as Hawk thought, Nora plowed right into the crepe with enthusiasm. He enjoyed his sandwich as well with the flavorful dip.

Hawk paid for the meal, and both returned to the Jeep, dreading what lay ahead. Hawk turned on the signal detector, and it showed, indeed, a GPS tracking device on the vehicle. "Well, I guess he'll know when we're at the house.'

Nora said, "I wish we had a tracking device on that creep."

"Would've been nice, that's for sure."

When Hawk turned right onto Colorado Boulevard toward the house, his cell rang. It was an unknown Denver number to him. Nora's eyes were on him. Placing it on speaker, he answered.

"Hello, Detective Hawk, this is Tina Dionisio. I'd like to talk to you tonight. Can we meet?"

"Not tonight. I'm in a tough spot. What's this all about, Tina?"

"I'd like to be helpful with your investigation. I can tell you what I saw."

"It'll have to wait till tomorrow. Can you come to the station?"

"I'd rather not. If a client happens to see me, it won't be good for my image if I walk in or out of a station."

"In that case, I'll give you a call and arrange a meeting."

"Alone. Right?"

"No, I have to come with my partner."

"No, alone. Or else I won't cooperate."

Hawk glanced at Nora. She nodded for him to go alone. "All right, but not at your condo. Let's meet at the Milk Market. I'll call you when I'm available."

Tina reluctantly agreed. After Hawk clicked off, Nora said, "I bet she won't tell us any more than we already know. She's certainly not going to admit to anything. Watch out for her, Clint. She's up to something."

Hawk kept driving and the closer they came to Nora's house, the pit in both of their stomachs grew into a Grand Canyon.

CHAPTER 25

AN HOUR HAD passed since Finn O'Leary sneaked into Nora's house. To his delight, it was easier than he thought. As planned, he left a stolen silver Nissan Altima a block away. Before that, he made a stop at a dollar store and picked up a clipboard and paper. Pulling out from his backpack an extra-large baseball cap, he covered most of his forehead and part of the ears. Years ago, he stole official commercial patches portraying various agencies and private companies and attached one to his cap and one to his yellow vest as if he was on official business of some kind. He unpeeled a small fake half-moon tattoo, the type that kids like to play with, and pressed the sticky side to his cheekbone. His reasoning was that if anyone took a good look at him, they would describe a man with a tattoo on his cheek.

Donning a fake full beard, extra-large dark sunglasses with wrap-around frames and a bushy mustache, he took off carrying the clipboard, hoping that if anyone saw him, they would think he was only doing his job. And better yet, if they thought he was selling something, they would stay away and pretend they weren't home.

He brazenly walked up to several doors on the way to Nora's, to homes that had their shades drawn shut, and only pretended to knock or ring the doorbell. He imagined that if he did that, if anyone were watching, they'd assume he was peddling door-to-door.

Nora lived on a very quiet street. It looked deserted. Just the way O'Leary hoped. After briefly staking out the neighborhood and seeing that most of the residents were away at work during the day, he knew that he had at least one-half hour before they started returning.

As he came up to Nora's house, he took a quick glance around and still did not see a soul, not even any kids out, but he expected that soon the cops would arrive to guard the place. His original plan was to enter through the back door, especially if the police were there already or snoopy neighbors were out. Since he had not seen anyone, only an occasional car that drove past, he decided to use his professional lock-picking tool to unlock the door. He proceeded to do that, blocking the view from the street with his body and the large vest. Not opening the door yet, he waited on the small porch, acting as if someone else from the inside had opened it. He dramatically nodded his head and made hand gestures as though he was invited in.

Inside the house, O'Leary searched for a perfect place to conceal himself once the detectives arrived. As he walked about the house, a rare sensation struck him. Deep down, he had this uneasy, heavy feeling. His heart pounded. *What the hell? Am I nervous? What's going on? This is a piece of cake. I'll stow away, and when they least expect it, I'll surprise them, put a scare into them, and shoot them with my silencer. No one will hear. I'll quickly exit to the rear, jump over the back neighbor's fence, and sneak to the other block before anyone knows they're dead."* The internal pep talk, however, did not quash that sinking feeling that it may not go as easily as he thinks. *Man, Cousin Devin will owe me big for this.*

Not finding a decent place to hide on the main level of the small house, O'Leary made his way down into the basement. He hated basements. If he were to be discovered, he had no way out. *But I won't be discovered. I have the luck of the Irish with me. It'll be all right.*

The basement was full of clear plastic bins—Christmas and Easter decorations, one containing a nativity scene. A large plaster turkey sat on top of one of the bins. Looking around further, he saw more bins containing Halloween decorations and blankets. An ugly statue of a witch stood in the corner. Next were statues of Santa Claus and two reindeer. On the other wall were racks of hanging clothes. The rest of the disorganized space was taken up by old furniture, skis, tennis rackets and a set of golf clubs.

O'Leary's eyes next fell upon an old soft recliner stored beneath the stairs. As he walked toward it, he realized that he could hide behind it in the dark spot of the dimly lit basement. He liked the idea that he would have eyes on whoever spotted him and could take the person down with his gun. That chair then became a resting spot until such time that he heard the detectives come home.

After what seemed like an eternity, his muscles tightened as he heard the detectives slowly enter through the garage door. He was ready for them. He waited long enough and was prepared no matter how long it took to catch them unawares. He wanted them to settle, get comfortable, and set the guns down, hopefully a distance away. Then as they relaxed or made it into their beds, he would surprise them when they least expected it. He would make them sweat, scare the hell out of them, watch them plead for their lives, then shoot them. He chuckled as he heard their footsteps on the squeaking floor above.

CHAPTER 26

THE READING of the will was scheduled for next week, and James and Kay Hollister could barely wait. They knew that once the will was probated, they would be multi-millionaires. They sat together on the taupe leather couch in their great room. Success was in their sights and both sat smiling ear to ear. James raised his hand in the air and Kay tapped it for another "high five," at least the twentieth since the detectives left the day before.

"We did it," James crowed. "We did it. Now we have a house free and clear and soon will be filthy rich."

"I know, it's so wonderful to think about. But Jimmy, they say, 'Don't count your chickens before they hatch.'"

"Aw, you're a worry wort. Nothing will go wrong. We knew how to get my father to give almost everything to us. We did it, and actually, I enjoyed spending all that time with him. I will truly miss him."

James noticed early on how his siblings seemed to avoid their father. He didn't quite understand why. William was a generous soul who was generally there for them as they were growing up. But he seemed to be a burden to his brothers and sisters, especially since they all acted so high and mighty. James wondered if they were ashamed of their father, just as they were of him. Both were kept out of their perceived "high society." William was more like James. He was not a good student, did not like school either, and after high school, he went to work flipping hamburgers at Wendy's. Being a hard and conscientious worker, he advanced rapidly. He became a crew chief, then an assistant manager and finally the manager of the store. From there, he became the district manager and started earning "big bucks," as his dad used to say, and he began dabbling in stocks.

William's big break, though, came when he married into money. James' maternal grandfather gave the married couple one-million dollars as a wedding gift. Being very astute and just plain lucky, he quit his job at the corporation and invested most of the gift money. He was lucky. Within five years, his investments doubled. Another five years, and he more than doubled it again. From there, he built up considerable wealth, more than he ever dreamed was possible for a man without a college degree. The richer he became, the more he bestowed on his children, only to be disappointed when the money made them soft, spoiled, and arrogant.

James saw his father's frustration, and he played on that frustration. He made sure that he and his wife became the favorites, at the same time dropping hints of how mistreated he was by his siblings. And James and Kay did everything in their power to stay by him, to call once or twice a day, to take him out, invite him to parties. They knew that he greatly appreciated their attention, and they became closer each day.

"What are you thinkin' about, sittin' there so quiet and frowning?" Kay asked. "Just a minute ago you were high-five'n me with a great big grin on your mug."

"I've been thinking about dad. It's great to get the money and all, but he's gone, and I'll miss him."

"I know what you mean. I already miss the old codger. But I've been thinkin' a lot about somethin' else."

"What?"

"How the others will react. They ain't going to take us gettin' the money sittin' down. I think we'll be knee-deep in lawsuits, or even worse."

"What do you mean, 'worse'?"

"Come on. Grow up. Our lives may be in danger."

"Aw, you've been watching too many of those crime shows. I doubt that anyone of them would kill us for the money."

"Are you crazy? Your dad was murdered. I want you to get a bodyguard tomorrow."

"Come on, Kay. You're blowing this out of all proportion."

"James Hollister, do it. Tomorrow."

"Okay, okay. But let's wait till after the reading and see how they're reacting."

"How do you think they'll react? Congratulate us?"

CHAPTER 27

HAWK AND RICCI cautiously entered the house, guns drawn. They thought that there would be a small chance that the sadistic killer could already be inside waiting for their return. Tonight, they took no chances. After all, they had plenty of threats that this night might very well be the fateful night. Nora began a thorough search of the premises with Clint a few steps behind, covering her. Relieved that no one jumped out of a closet or from under the beds, they began the descent down the basement steps. Again, Nora went first, and on the upper level, Hawk backed her up. After she scanned the area, looking carefully, she stopped at the recliner chair underneath the steps. She thought of looking behind it, but it seemed almost impossible for someone to hide in that narrow corner space between the chair and the wall."

"We're clear," Nora said as the two detectives made their way up. Walking into the kitchen, Nora asked, "Are you still hungry? Would you like anything more to eat? My fridge is pretty empty, but I do have some luncheon meat, some great Italian bread, and, of course, I have a ton of frozen food."

"No thanks, Nora. I'm good. But I'd like something to drink. Remember, no alcohol."

"Of course. How about a tall glass of Pellegrino?" Hawk indicated his approval with thumbs up.

In the meantime, Hawk went back into the garage and came back with the roll of bubble wrap.

Nora eyed the wrap. "I don't think we need it until we start conking out later. Let's sit on the sofa." They walked listlessly past the dining table to the living room section of the L-shaped room. The dining set stood in the short and narrow part of the "L." Neither one was in a talkative mood. This might be the last night for them on earth, and they felt the weight of it all, the beginnings of a headache seemingly affecting them both.

Both took off their suit jackets. Nora hung her beige blazer in her bedroom closet while Clint hung his on the back of the dining room chair. He removed the set of handcuffs and his holstered weapon and placed them on the coffee table, then quickly withdrew his gun and placed it by his thigh with the safety off. Nora left her belt with the cuffs and holster in the bedroom but carried the weapon back with her. Before she sat down, Nora asked, her voice almost a whisper. "How about a little TV?"

"Better not," Hawk said, voice low as well. "We need it quiet in here. We need to listen carefully."

Nora looked out the window and saw the patrol car parked in front. "I'll leave the drapes open."

Hawk agreed. "Come sit," patting down the cushion next to him.

Nora tried to manage a half-smile. "Okay, hotshot, what shall we do?"

"Let's talk. I've been meaning to ask you about your family. You mentioned your grandmother and your parents. Who else is in your family?"

In an exceptionally low voice, leaning her head back against the sofa and staring at the ceiling, Nora said, "I have a brother, Gino. He's very successful. He bought out my grandparent's place of 160 acres with a bunch of water rights. Then he bought some more acreage here and there and now has fertile land all the way up and down the Arkansas River basin from Pueblo to Lamar. He grows everything from chili to cantaloupes to alfalfa to a variety of vegetables. He's very busy and constantly needs help. As a matter of fact, he wants me to join him, make me a partner and run the office part of it."

"Impressive. Would you want to do it?"

She turned her head toward him. "The way I feel right this minute," she hesitated. "I'd rather do anything else than this. But this is what I wanted to do. It's crazy to constantly place our lives in danger."

Hawk tried to continue the conversation while alertly listening to possible strange noises. "So, those grandparents, are they your mother's parents?"

"No. They're my dad's. My mother's parents both died a few years ago from cancer. I miss them so much. They were so sweet and loving. Of course, so are my paternal grandparents as well."

"So, which grandmother was it that taught you all those wonderful Italian dishes?"

"That was my maternal grandmother." She paused. "I really miss my family and hadn't had a chance to drive down to see them in a while. Pausing again, she said. "If we survive this, I'd like you to go with me to Pueblo, just for a ride. I'll give you the fifty-cent tour, and then we can stop by my parents' house for dinner."

She noticed Hawk's eyebrows arch. "Clint, it doesn't mean anything with you going for the ninety-minute ride. Just as a friend, that's all, to keep me company."

"Yeah, I think I'd like that—spending a day with you." He chuckled. "Of course, I'm lucky that I spend every day with you at work, but this would be different, that's for sure."

"Okay, it's a date then. Let's just survive the psycho." Nora smiled her full, natural smile, the first one that Hawk had seen all day. He smiled back, and Nora leaned in and kissed his cheek. He then leaned into her and kissed her on the lips.

Nora whispered, "That was sweet. I liked it."

From there, the conversation turned to gossip about MacGregor, Perez, and the other detectives. After that, they got into some serious discussions about the middle east, its history going all the way back to the days of Babylon. They talked about how the boundaries were formed after the second world war and how it has caused so much unrest now. Before they knew it, an hour or more had passed. They began to feel the fatigue of the stressful day. Nora stood and said, "Have to go to the bathroom, throw some cold water on my face to keep me awake. Be right back. Maybe we should make a pot of coffee?"

After she left, Hawk rested his head against the high back of the sofa and stretched his legs onto the coffee table. He shut his eyes. Nora emerged from the bathroom and teased Hawk that he was asleep, then in a low voice said, "Bummer! I forgot something. I'll be right back."

Nora quickly dashed off.

Suddenly, Hawk thought that he heard a creaking sound coming from the basement. He straightened and gripped his pistol.

CHAPTER 28

FINN O'LEARY exhaled from relief when the two detectives made their way upstairs. Holding his breath when Nora peered seemingly straight at him, his finger was curled around the trigger, ready to fire. Luckily, she did not see him in the dark corner underneath the stairs. If she had, it would have been surely his end, shot by Hawk after he blasted Nora. He was grateful for the contortionist exercises that he learned while still in Ireland. He had practiced the movements and trained his muscles to remain limber, and it certainly became a lifesaver now as he scrunched further into the corner.

After the detectives made their way upstairs, he intently listened to their footsteps above and knew that his victims stopped for a few minutes in the kitchen. He heard one of them open the faucet, probably for a glass of water. A few minutes later, the footsteps led to the living room area of the house. At that point, he felt safe and forced himself out of the confined space. It took a minute to crawl out, surprising himself when he let out a grunt. It was a mistake, and he couldn't believe his negligence. He remained crouched in silence, waiting for any reaction to his groan. Hearing nothing, he proceeded to free himself. The stiffness, the numbness was overwhelming, but he managed to pull himself further into the basement where he could stand and stretch his muscles.

Angry at himself for coming up with what he now believed was a dumb plan, he wiggled his legs and arms, massaging the muscles. *I'm losing it. When I was younger, I wouldn't have gone through this crap. I would've shot them the moment they walked into the house. It would've been done, and I'd be out of here.* He was again mad at his cousin, Devon, who insisted that he terrorize them before killing them. *Okay, I promised, but how would he ever know if I did it or not? I just need to go up there right now and do it. They wouldn't be expecting me if I popped up from the basement and shot them before they'd have a chance to react. On the other hand, if they're not together, I might only get one and the other would get me. I'll have to think on it some more.*

O'Leary yawned hard, realizing that he hadn't had any good sleep in days. He needed to get this over with and get out. The more he waited for the right moment to surprise them, the more restless and aggravated he became. He paced back and forth within the four walls of the basement like a caged animal. *It's too early. They're still on alert upstairs. I need to wait a little longer for them to drop their guard.* He eyed the old leather recliner and decided to wait it out in comfort. *I can't fall asleep. They might come downstairs.* No matter how hard he tried to stay awake in the quiet basement, he caught himself dozing off, then slapping himself on the face to keep awake.

After suffering for at least an hour, fighting his urge to sleep, he looked at his florescent-dialed watch and decided no matter whether it was right or not, he was going to do it now. His patience had run out. Listening carefully to any sounds from upstairs, he heard muffled voices. *They're together, good.*

Still listening, he heard the voices cease, and footsteps on the creaky floor led toward the bedrooms and bathroom. He heard a door close and water run down into the sewer line running between the joists and across the unfinished ceiling a few feet away. Knowing that they were now separated, he had to wait and avoid being surprised by the second person suddenly coming out of the hallway. *As soon as they are together again. So that I can see them both, I'll quickly fire off two shots and get the hell out. No, no, hell. That's too easy. Devon wants me to make them sweat first. Shit!*

So, he waited for when he thought that the two were together and settled before springing the surprise of their lifetimes.

CHAPTER 29

THAT EVENING, an emergency meeting was called by George and Rhonda Hollister at their house. Present were all the siblings and their spouses except for James and Kay. Being the oldest and the bossiest, George took charge and demanded that they sit down, pointing to his magnificent Italian custom designed table that was embedded with colorful quartz crystals throughout the high gloss of the snakewood. Ten snakewood chairs with high backs covered with maroon fabric circled the round table.

Before each person, was a Waterford crystal glass of wine and a matching, but larger, goblet of water. After they were seated, Darren immediately took a swig of the wine and asked, "Hey, bro, where's James?"

George stood and said, "James wasn't invited, and you'll understand why in a minute." He peered at them, cleared his throat, took a mouthful of wine, and spoke. "Okay. Here's the deal." He cleared his throat a couple more times, and puffed out his cheeks. "Someone left a large envelope on our doorstep. Had no name or return address on it. You can't believe my surprise when I found a copy of Dad's last will inside."

His dull grey eyes looked at each one of them to see a reaction. Seeing the expected expressions of surprise, he continued. "Now, none of you are going to like this, but it seems that our dear departed father lied to us. He told us that he would wait a week before he terminated the trust and changed the will."

"What?" Sam blurted out. "He didn't wait?"

"No, Sam. He did not. It seems he signed the will a few weeks before he invited us."

"Oh God!" Ashley said. "What am I supposed to do now? You mean, we're not getting anything?"

Everyone began talking at once. George called out in his deep booming voice, "Now settle down. Let's be civilized." He waited for everyone to stop jabbering. "No, as he said at that dastardly dinner, we're each getting another two-hundred thousand. Benson is getting half a mil, and Consuela, who as far as Rhonda and I are concerned, was as reliable as a broken clock, will receive three-hundred thousand. I can't believe it! Neither one of them deserves that much money. This whole thing incenses me to the point where I want to hang myself or someone else."

"That means that James is getting everything else," Cynthia screamed, her voice shrill. She stood, placed her hands on her round hips and stared at George, breathing hard. "I'll help you hang them. I'll start with James, then Benson, then Consuela, who I always hated. All three bastards screwed us out of our inheritance."

Darren looked at his older brother, "So how did you get this will? And bro, how about some more wine here?"

George shot him an annoyed look. "Weren't you listening, broooo?" mocking his brother, "Someone left it on my porch."

Cynthia asked, "Now, who could that be?"

"Hell, if I know. All I know is that when I came home from work, I noticed a large manila envelope sitting upright by the front door."

Sam said, "That's the strangest thing. Who would be interested in the will other than us here? If it was one of us, then why didn't they set up the meeting and bring a copy? Why all this cloak and dagger stuff? Don't you have cameras around your house?"

Rhonda said, "No, George will spend thousands on frivolous things, but when it comes to something for the home, he's a real tightwad. It took me forever to talk him into at least getting a security system, and then he doesn't even want to pay a monthly monitoring fee. It's a fight every month."

George turned red in the face. "Rhonda shut up. You know money is tight right now. Don't air our dirty laundry in front of the family." Rhonda blew out a hard breath, sat back angrily in her chair, crossed her arms over her chest and slid her chair back away from the table. She shot George a look that could kill.

Darren laughed. "Oh, my big brother, remember what they say, 'When poverty comes in through the door, love flies out the window.'" He laughed some more, but no one joined in.

"And you shut up, too, you drunken bastard!" George yelled out, veins on his forehead popping out.

Darren lifted his arms in a show of submission, "Okay, okay, man. But how about some more wine?"

Ashley said, "Darren, you had enough. This is a crisis we're going through, and you're not taking it seriously."

"I'm not going to dwell on something I have no control over," Darren said, chuckling. "There isn't much that any of us have any say in at this point. We just have to take our lumps and live with it."

"Bull crap," Cynthia shouted out. Her darkened pupils looked like they could bore a hole through him. "There's plenty we can do. We'll sue. Our father was unduly influenced by those people, especially by James' and Kay's con game. Hell, pretending that they actually cared for the old man."

"Yes, that's what I told the police," Ashley said. "I told them that he's a conniver."

George raised his hands, "Stop with this legal crap. I talked to my lawyer, and he said that if a will was made out because of fraud or incompetence or because of undue influence, then it could be set aside. But, and this a big but, we must prove it, and that is difficult to do. I believe that dad's doctor and lawyer will both testify that he was in his right mind and knew exactly what he was doing."

Sam asked, "Then what you're saying is that there is nothing we can do?"

"No. Unless for some reason, James were to die within thirty days of dad's death, then his share would go to the four of us, but that's highly unlikely."

Everyone sat up and leaned their elbows on the table. "How's that?" Cynthia asked. The same question was on everyone else's mind.

George picked up the copy and read, "For the purposes of this Will, a beneficiary shall be deemed to have predeceased me if such beneficiary dies within thirty days after the date of my death."

"Huh," Darren said. "Well maybe James will die of overeating." He laughed again.

Ashley said, "Huh, nothing, Darren. I know what you're thinking." She looked around the room, "Maybe all of you are thinking. But get that thought out of your minds. No one here could ever do such a horrible thing, let alone to our brother."

Darren laughed again. "Listen sis, don't be so damn naive. We're all vultures here."

"Speak for yourself, you idiot," Rhonda said.

CHAPTER 30

FINN O'LEARY keenly listened for footsteps indicating that one of the detectives had returned from the bedroom area. He wanted them together in one spot. He had enough of the basement. Now was the time. *Time to kill the bastards and head out of Denver and back to New York and on to Brazil.*

He inspected his Walther PPQ M2 pistol, the same one that his hero, James Bond, used in his movies. He was obsessed with the character. He admired how the writer portrayed Bond as a man that could escape seemingly the most precarious situations. And the notion that James Bond had a "License to kill," kill at will, if necessary, made him feel empowered to believe that he also had justification to kill when necessary. O'Leary then checked the Osprey silencer, making sure that it was securely fastened to the Walther. Knowing that silencers did not muff most of the noise of a gunshot, he still thought that it would be quiet enough so that the cops, wasting their time, sitting on their asses in the car on the street, wouldn't hear. Nevertheless, one way or the other, he had to escape from the house in an instant after he fired the weapon.

When he first searched for a place to hide, as he went downstairs, O'Leary noticed that three threads in the center of the stairs leading into the basement had a bad creak. Going up and down a few times, trying to find a spot on the threads that did not creak, he noted that the outside edges were solid, but he'd have to step exactly at a certain spot on the thread. He made a mental note to himself where to step to avoid the squeak.

Deciding to wait at the top of the stairs until the detectives were together for their big surprise, he began his ascent to the upper floor, his pistol in his hand. After taking the first two steps, he wiped off the sweat that formed a mustache above his upper lip, his eyes wide and unblinking. On the third step, he noticed his stomach doing flip-flops, and he did not quite know why. *This is simple. I just go up, scare the bejesus out of them, then shoot them. I've been in worse situations. I can't be scared, can I? That's crap.*

On the fourth step, O'Leary's breathing became heavy, and he continued wondering if his body was telling him that it might be a trap. He discounted the feeling as just sudden nerves. *I must be getting old. Well, as soon as I get to Brazil, I'll live a life of luxury.* He remembered that he would have to be extra careful on the next three steps. He stepped to the very edge of the thread on one, then to the opposite edge of the other and to his dismay, the step creaked. *Shit! It wasn't too loud. I doubt if they heard it upstairs. If so, they'll probably believe it was only the house settling.*

He slowly trudged on. On the next step, he made it without creaks or squeaks. On the step after that, one that he did not expect, he heard another creak. O'Leary stopped instantly, blowing out a breath, waiting to hear if there was any reaction from the detectives above. Hearing nothing, he moved to the top of the stairs and waited for the two detectives to join each other. His pistol ready to go.

CHAPTER 31

HEARING THE second creak from what he thought might be the basement steps, Hawk quickly got up, suddenly on sudden alert. *He's creeping up the stairs*, he thought. A cold shiver ran throughout his body. His heart fell into his stomach.

Positioning himself next to the kitchen, he heard the floorboard squeak as O'Leary crept toward him. The man abruptly stopped short of the living area when he did not see the detectives. After a minute of hesitation, he slowly took a couple more steps into the carpeted living room. Out of the corner of his eye, O'Leary spotted Hawk. Before he could react, Hawk lunged at him, tackling him to the floor. Hawk was on top, but O'Leary struck Hawk with his gun, stunning the detective enough to drop his weapon and allow O'Leary to roll him over and pin him down with his powerful broad shoulders, rendering Hawk's arms useless. Hawk tried to kick him off, but the killer had his knee on his groin and at the same time, clamped his large, powerful left hand over Hawk's throat, cutting off the air to his lungs.

Hawk struggled, punching him where he could and trying to buck the man off. O'Leary was shorter and smaller than Hawk, but he was all brawn, all muscle, surprising Hawk with his seemingly inhuman strength. He pressed and squeezed Hawk's body with the torque of a bulldozer and, at the same time, not letting go of the pistol.

Hawk had never felt such sheer strength as from a man that had him pinned down to the floor, rendering him useless. He was a bear, a gorilla, an ox, a combination of all three. No matter how he squirmed and attempted to inflict harm, he could not shake the monster off. Nor could he breathe.

At that moment, Nora walked out of the hallway. Her breathing became rapid when she spotted Hawk in trouble. A gray-haired man's body was sprawled all over Hawk, and held him by the throat, a gun still in his hand. Her heart banged against her chest, beating as fast as that of a hummingbird. At first, her body was tied into knots as the scene rapidly was playing out in front of her eyes. She suddenly remembered that she left her weapon on the bathroom counter but realized that she had no time to retrieve it. She had to go to Hawk's aid now. Without hesitation, she flew toward the men, disregarding that O'Leary had a gun.

Out of the corner of his eye, Hawk caught Nora flying toward them and saw O'Leary's gun aimed at her, his index finger closing in on the trigger. He had to react quickly to save her. *Now!* Mustering all the strength that he could manage, he again drove the limited movement of his fist into the O'Leary's side, this time evidently hitting a sensitive spot and at the same time pushed to buck him off. He felt the vise over his throat tighten. Unable to throw the load off him, he managed, though, to move the man a fraction, enough to disrupt his aim at Nora. Hawk felt relief that the slug missed Nora since he heard the bullet enter the large picture window.

At the same moment, Hawk barely noticed Nora's foot slam into O'Leary's head. "Sonofabitch," the killer yelled, but the grip on Hawk's throat didn't subside, and he knew that in a few more seconds, he'll be unable to hold out. *This is it. This is how I die.*

With her quick Taekwondo moves, Nora jumped up and as she came down, her right leg struck O'Leary's wrist knocking the weapon out of his hand. Then she spun around and, with her right foot, bashed him on the temple. It did not seem to faze him. She twisted around again and came down hard with her left foot striking the Adam's apple of his neck. Only then did he let go of Hawk's throat as he fell back, sucking in as much air as he could, his chest heaving. With Nora's help, Hawk pushed O'Leary aside while Hawk also gasped for air, forcing himself to stand. Hawk stood up with a hand from Nora.

Only stunned by Nora's kick, it did not take long for O'Leary to dive for his gun, lying a few feet away. Nora did not hesitate to kick him with all the force a slim, delicate woman could gather and strike him on the side of his head, then spun around and wallop him as he staggered back. O'Leary should have been knocked out, but he managed to spring to his feet. Hawk threw a punch with his right fist into O'Leary's solar plexus, followed by a left hook underneath his chin. O'Leary fell to the floor, out cold.

Nora saw the shadows of the officers who were guarding them run toward the house. She quickly opened the door, fearing they would kick it in. Still breathing hard, she told the confused cops, "We got him. Take the bastard away."

O'Leary came to as they were trying to cuff him. He shook his head to clear his mind, then, when he realized what the officers were doing, like a raging bull, he stood up and shoved them away, hard enough that one fell to the floor while the other staggered back. Hawk and Nora quickly went into action. Nora struck him behind his knee with her foot while Hawk hammered his face and underneath the chin. As O'Leary fell back, he hit his head hard on the edge of the tabletop, causing a bleeding gash on the back of his head.

With his throat raw, barely able to talk, Hawk advised the officers to double cuff him and place him in leg irons. "He's a strong sonofabitch. He could pull one pair apart."

When O'Leary finally came to, his nose and back of his head bloody, he was escorted out, battling all the way. As he was being shoved into the back seat of the cruiser, he glared at Nora and Hawk. With fury and anger, he shouted out, "There's no jail that can hold me. I'll be back to get you both." He laughed as though it didn't bother him—a fiendish laugh, like the ones portrayed by villains in horror movies. Chills ran up and down both Nora and Clint. They took his threat seriously.

After they re-entered the house, Nora had so much nervous energy built up that she began straightening up the furniture left in disarray from the fight. Then she went into the garage and came back with a roll of duct tape and used a piece of it to cover the hole and crack in the picture window.

She sighed and said through gritted teeth, "That prick nearly killed us, and on top of it all, I have to replace this glass. I wonder if there's some victim's compensation that I could get?" She puffed up her cheeks and blew out a hard breath. Glancing at Hawk, she noticed him collapsed on the couch, one leg up on the armrest and the other hanging down. Chuckling, she said, "You're a funny sight, my dear." She started to laugh, but Hawk was in no mood to laugh. His body hurt all over, especially his neck.

As they settled down with a couple of beers to unwind, Nora asked, "Why didn't you use your weapon? You had a clear shot at him, and he had a gun in his hand."

"I didn't want to mess up your nice home with blood all over the place." He sat there thinking, then said, "I guess the adage that 'you can't judge a book by its cover' is appropriate here."

"What do you mean?"

"I was totally mistaken about him. I'm bigger, in good shape, and I believed that I could easily take him. I really don't know where his strength came from. He must work out constantly. I bet he could bench press five-hundred pounds. Anyway, your house is not all bloodied up, and we don't have a police shooting to deal with."

"That's so considerate of you, but next time shoot the douchebag and don't ask any questions."

"Let's hope there'll never be a next time."

Nora said, "Oh God! Let's pray not. Clint, stay the night. My nerves are raw." She looked at him with pleading eyes. "I really need some company right now."

CHAPTER 32

NORA AND Clint sat on the sofa, holding hands, Nora's head on his shoulder. At 11:25 o'clock, Hawk's phone rang out the *Bad to the Bone* tune. Both jerked as the quiet was abruptly interrupted as both had just begun dozing off.

"Don't answer it," Nora said. "I can't hear any more bad news."

Hawk let it play a little longer. Then he saw that Detective Nancy Salazar was calling. He reluctantly answered and placed the call on speaker. "Hello, Clint, I'm sorry to disturb you so late, but I thought you'd like to know that two of our suspects in the Hollister case were gunned down about an hour ago."

Hawk sat up, as did Nora. "Who, where and how?"

"James and Kay were shot in front of the bar that they used to work in. It looks like a drive-by shooting. We'll check the cameras in the area tomorrow. Perez wants you and Nora to take the lead on those murders as well. By the way, I couldn't believe what Perez told me. You and Nora captured the long-wanted Finn O'Leary. Good work. But how are you two doing?"

"Still shaken up. Sorry, I can't come in to investigate the scene right now. But you and Harry are top notch."

"Thanks. Just tell Perez that. I sometimes get a feeling that he doesn't trust us to do a good job."

"Oh, I don't think so, Nancy. He knows the quality of your work. He's throwing this case at us because it's all connected to the father's murder."

"I guess so. Any idea how Nora is holding up? Perez didn't go into any details. He said that he'll discuss it at length at a meeting tomorrow. Betcha guys had a really tough night with that sonofabitch."

"Nora and I are both a little raw right now. I don't think we could even drag ourselves to our beds, let alone the crime scene. We're both totally exhausted physically and especially mentally."

"You poor things. Always seem to be under the gun. Anyway, get some needed rest, and we'll see you tomorrow."

As soon as Hawk punched off, Perez called. Nora grunted, and Hawk answered. "Sorry to disturb you. You weren't sleeping, were you?"

"No, it's okay, Lieutenant."

"I want to tell you to sleep in and come in around 2 o'clock tomorrow for a meeting. I'll call Nora next, or is she there?"

Nora grabbed the phone from Hawk, "I'm here, Lieutenant. I asked Hawk to stay over tonight. I didn't want to be alone."

"Good idea. Did you hear what I told Hawk about coming in later?"

"Yes, thank you. I think we can use the short break."

After sleeping in until 10 o'clock, Hawk woke up from a restless night. The episode with O'Leary aggravated his nightmares. In blurry dreams, he visualized men pointing smoking guns at him. The embankment of that ditch that he purposely drove the police vehicle into to escape being killed, all came back to him with vengeance. And a new nightmare—his throat clamped down so tight that all oxygen was cut off, his dead body dumped by a crane into a junk vehicle shortly before being crushed in a scrap yard.

Soaked in sweat, he awoke to the pleasant aroma of sizzling bacon and hazelnut flavored coffee wafting into his room. It took him a few seconds to realize that he was in Nora's guest room. His breathing was still shallow and rapid, and his throat hurt and burned. The thought of Nora putting around in the kitchen relaxed him.

Looking in the mirror, Hawk was taken aback by the ugly black bruises, reminders of O'Leary's fingers digging into his throat. He shivered at the thought of how close once again he came to death. After a quick shower, he dressed and joined Nora, who was humming a song he did not recognize. She looked fresh and exceptionally pretty this morning. Her welcoming smile warmed him inside and out. "Hello, sweetie," she said. "I hope you don't mind me calling you that. After all, you are sweet and my hero. Of course, I'd never call you that while at work." She suddenly appeared horrified by the bruises. "Oh, you poor dear, your throat! Does it hurt badly?"

"A little." Hawk smiled and, with a raspy voice, said. "To answer your other question, I don't mind at all. It feels good hearing those words. And you are definitely my hero. If it hadn't been for you knocking O'Leary off of me, forcing him to release his solid grip on my throat, I wouldn't be here talking to you. There is no one like you." He came up to her and gave her a kiss on the cheek.

Nora laughed. "I guess we belong to a mutual admiration society. Do you know that song? My father sang it a lot. He said he heard Teresa Brewer sing it *On the Hit Parade* when he was a kid, whatever that was?"

"No, I can't say I do."

"Look it up on Spotify." Hawk found it and played it. The happy song of the 1950s brought broad smiles to their faces. "I'm a little giddy this morning. It feels so good to know that O'Leary is in jail. I feel like the weight of the world was lifted off us. We're alive!" She looked at Clint. "And I'm so happy that we're together this morning."

Hawk's severe commitment issues flared up. *Uh, oh! Does she want me to agree to that? That might lead to a conversation about living together. Although, I might just like it. But what if I don't? How would I get out of it and still work in the same unit with her?*

"Whatcha thinking about, so deep in thought?" Nora asked.

Fast on his feet, Hawk answered, "I'm thinking shop unfortunately. One of those Hollister siblings or one of the spouses is a true murderer, or maybe all of them are in cahoots. We have our work cut out in this case."

"Yikes. I was hoping that you'd be concentrating on something more pleasant." Her super-smiley face suddenly fell with a half-smile remaining.

Hawk saw the transformation and knew that she would rather discuss their present of being together for breakfast. And he wanted the same thing but just could not bring himself to commit to it. He liked being with her and looked forward to seeing her every day. She was perfect for him, but strangely, Marcie Turner's face kept popping up in his thoughts. Earlier, Marcie asked him to quit being a cop and join her in California. And while O'Leary was out there making threats, it did not seem to be a bad idea. But he also knew that he would not want to give up his job. He loved it. And he knew that even though he was fascinated with Marcie, he was not sure he really loved her.

He realized that he would have to decide between the two women that really seemed to want him sooner than later. He did not want to string Nora along. He knew he needed to settle down, marry and have children before he got too old to chase them around the house and crawl all over the floor playing with them. He caught how her old partner, Detective Seth Morgan, eyed her and flirted with her in that interrogation room. Hawk suspected that he would make a move on her, as would many other men. With Nora wanting to get married and have a family, she may give up on him and start dating others. *Damn! I need to decide what I want.*

"Nora, when are you going to Pueblo? I think I'd like to ride along. The last time I was there was a trip to the Mental Institute about five years ago."

"Oh, you checked in, did you?" Nora teased.

"Nooo! I delivered a patient pursuant to a court order."

Nora's mouth widened into a broad smile. "Great. How about next weekend?" After he agreed, Nora asked, "What do you want to do until 2 o'clock? It's a shame to waste the morning just lying around, and if you're up to it, it'll be good to get some rays. It's a beautiful day out there."

"Let's go to the zoo. I've never been to the one in Denver. But before we do, I need to stop by my house and change clothes."

At 1:45 o'clock, the two detectives walked into the station. By that time, everyone heard of the detectives' exploits. "High-fives" were given as they made it up to the second floor.

Orlinski said, "Remind me not to spend any time with you guys." He laughed. "But hey, I'm glad you're alive. You couldn't have just shot the bastard rather than trying to fight him?"

Hawk said, "Yeah, I probably should've done it if I'd known how unbelievably strong he was. Nora saved the day again."

"And he mine," Nora said. "So, what's the meeting about?"

Orlinski laughed, "Probably mostly about you guys. I'm sure, though, that the captain wants an update on the Hollister case now that James and Kay Hollister were murdered as well."

Nancy Salazar and Harry Ling walked into the unit, appearing exhausted after investigating the shootings of James and Kay Hollister. Other than a casual greeting and inquiring how Nora and Clint felt, they did not say much and proceeded to their desks. Following them a minute later was the tall and lanky figure of Mortimer. He wore a light-gray suit that looked only slightly out of date, a big change from his other vintage suits. Unfortunately, his new outfit was a size too large, hanging loosely on him, giving him an appearance of a scarecrow. His shoes were the black pointed-toe pair that seemed to be his favorite. His shirt was bright green with a rose-colored bowtie and matching suspenders. As always, he looked awkward, but for some reason, more so today.

Um oh, Nora thought, *MacGregor will not like his clothing again. The poor guy tries so hard. Maybe I should take him shopping. But then probably Josephine would kill me. Maybe I ought to give her a call and tell her what MacGregor wants.*

Mortimer immediately approached Hawk and Ricci. "I heard about your capture of an international fugitive. I should've been there. We're partners, you know. On the other hand, after I told Josephine about it, she said that I was lucky that I wasn't there. Maybe she's right."

Mortimer's eyes followed Nancy and Harry to their desks, then told Hawk and Nora, "I don't think they really want me working with them. They're nice, all right, but I don't feel as comfortable with them as I'm with you. They seem to clam up when I'm around, and when I ask them about an area of Denver, they don't seem to know any history of it like you folks do."

Hawk asked, "So what do you think of the James and Kay Hollister shootings? Were they the targets, or was it a random drive-by?"

"Oh, I believe that they were specifically targeted. Someone that was an excellent marksman. It wouldn't be easy to shoot so accurately from a rolling car. I know that it wasn't a drive-by as Nancy and Harry think."

Nora asked, "Oh, why do you think that?"

"The shot was too accurate. But there is a witness that thinks it was a drive-by. So maybe that's what it was."

"Really? Did they see the shooter or describe the vehicle?"

"That's all I know because Nancy talked to him while Harry was with the M.E. and I went inside to talk to the bartender."

Hawk asked, "Didn't you ask Nancy?"

"Yeah. I tried. But she was too busy talking on the phone."

Hawk and Nora returned to their desks. Harry and Nancy came up to them. "Tell us about your latest adventure," Harry asked.

Nora hesitated, "If that's what you call it, I guess it was quite an adventure that I'd never want to live through again. Ever!"

Nancy said, "We're so sorry. Will you get some counseling?"

"We'll see," Hawk said.

"I'm sure they'll make you," Harry said. "I had to go through it after I shot a suspect and had to get an okay from the shrink before I could come back to active duty. Anyway, we want to hear every detail about it. Can the four of us get together for lunch? Lunch is on us."

Before Nora could answer, Mortimer came up. "Is there something that I need to know?"

Harry answered, his voice irritated, "No, Mort, we're just asking them what happened?"

"I told you before, Harry, don't call me Mort." His voice raised. "I hate that name. Besides, I want to hear what happened myself."

Both Hawk and Ricci noticed the antagonism between the two of them. Nora said, "I'm sure all of you will hear all about it from the brass soon enough." She nodded toward the hallway. "And there they are. Right on cue."

But it was only Lieutenant Perez who stepped out of the hallway. He looked their way and motioned with his finger for Hawk and Ricci to follow him.

"Before the meeting, Captain wants to see both of you in her office. Good luck."

Mortimer began following the two detectives when Perez stopped him. "Holliday, the Captain only wants to see Hawk and Ricci."

Captain MacGregor met them at her office door and pointed to the chairs. After the detectives and Perez sat down, she gazed at them for a minute before speaking. "What I can't figure out is why it's always the two of you?"

Hawk asked, "What do you mean?"

"You know exactly what I mean. You seem to have danger follow you around like a dark cloud." She looked hard at them, her face grim, her jowls hanging. "I suppose I should be pleased to have two top notch detectives in my unit. But I don't know what to do with you. Should I break you up?"

Nora said, "No, ma'am. I don't think that will work. We cover and protect each other. We are very careful and do everything by the book. We make an excellent team, and if you keep us together, we'll even get better over time."

"By the book, huh? I haven't received your reports yet because Lieutenant Perez wanted to give you a break and give you some time off. But I read his report and the officers' reports and I'm concerned how you handled O'Leary's capture."

"Oh?" Hawk sounded concerned.

"Yes, oh, Detective!" MacGregor slammed both fists on her desk. "From what you told Perez, O'Leary came in from the kitchen with a gun in his hand. He saw you and was about to shoot you, but you, in your poor judgment, decided not to use your weapon. Instead decided on a wrestling match with him. Why, in the hell, didn't you pull the trigger when you had the chance? From what I understand, you had the element of surprise on your side."

Nora started to explain when MacGregor lifted her hand to silence her.

Hawk considered the question, "If I had known how strong the man is, I certainly would've taken another course. He looked small to me at first glance, shorter by more than a head. His weight, according to Interpol records, showed him at 160 pounds. I honestly thought I could tackle and take him down easily.

"Shooting him in Nora's living room would leave such a mess, ruin her carpet, maybe holes in the walls, and she'd have to live in the house where a man died, reminding her of the terrible incident. Then there is all the paperwork to follow, being placed on administrative leave, investigated by Internal Affairs and taking a chance that someone else would see it differently and come to the conclusion of unjustified shooting." Hawk stopped. His heart was racing. MacGregor continued to study him, her face still grim, her eyes squinted. "I thought of these consequences and tried to formulate a plan that would capture him alive. After all, he might have valuable information as to who hired him and maybe info that the FBI or Interpol may want. With Nora's help, it worked. Not as smoothly as I had hoped, but it worked."

MacGregor sat silently in thought, her full lips puffed out. She looked at Nora Ricci, then at Clint Hawk. "All right. I think you should've just shot him in self-defense when he was there to kill you and Ricci. But now that you explain your reasoning. I can see your point. Next time, and I hope they'll not be a next time, don't think of the consequences but protect your lives. Just pull the damn trigger." She gave them a half-smile for the first time. "Now get out there and join the other detectives. I want an update on the Hollister cases."

CHAPTER 33

MacGregor sat down on Orlinski's side chair as always while Perez stood a few steps to the side. She did not look happy. Her pale lips turned down. She gave an appraising glance at each detective before she spoke. Then her gaze returned to Orlinski. "Detective, you've been working on the financials of the Hollister children. Are you done with that?"

"Yes, Captain, I feel I've done all that I can."

"So, tell us, who's the murderer?" Out of nowhere, MacGregor's frown turned into a mischievous smile. "Or should I ask Josephine?" She laughed and looked at Mortimer.

Everyone else laughed, but Mortimer didn't get the joke. Startled, he sat up and said, "Oh, you must have said something humorous. But if you want to know Josephine's opinion—"

"No, Detective Holliday. I was only kidding."

"Oh, I see. But if you want my opinion, we need to concentrate more on the butler and the maid. I got bad vibes from them."

MacGregor took a closer look at Mortimer and his hanging suit. She shook her head and rolled her eyes, mumbling, "Gads! I got to do something about his clothes." Then she turned her attention once again to Orlinski, "Based on their finances, who's the murderer?"

"As far as I'm concerned, they all could be. All have financial difficulties."

"Who is in the worst shape?"

Orlinski looked over his notes. "I'd say probably it's George and Rhonda Hollister. He seems the most overextended and really needs some immediate cash."

MacGregor gazed at Hawk and Ricci. "Did you interview them yet?"

Nora said, "Not yet. We have made an appointment to see them at 4 o'clock this afternoon."

MacGregor then turned her attention to Harry Ling and Nancy Salazar. "What about the shooting of James and his wife, Kay, I believe?"

Harry answered, "We don't think it was random. They were targeted. We have a couple of witnesses but nothing to indicate who might've done it. Possibly an iffy description of the shooter's car. One witness said it was dark gray. Another that it was black. One thought that it was similar to her car, a Nissan Altima. Another bystander seemed to have confirmed that. So, if we can believe them, then I guess we need to look for a dark Nissan, but there're a ton of them out there. There weren't many people out on the street. If there's no convention goin' on, that part of downtown, close to the convention center, is dead at night. All the action is in LODO. We'll go back and search for cameras and hit the homeless in the area. Maybe they saw something."

Nancy added, "The shots were clean. James was shot right in the forehead, while Kay's was square in the heart. The guy was a great shot and knew what he was doing."

Mortimer said, "I was there with them, per Lieutenant Perez's directive. I looked at the expressions on the victims' faces, and I'm sure that they recognized the shooter and walked up closer to the vehicle." Harry and Nancy exchanged glances. Nancy rolled her eyes and blew out a quick breath.

Perez said, "Really? How did you come up with that?"

"The more I think about it, I believe that the shooter shot the victims after he stopped his car on the street as the Hollisters walked out of the bar. He either called them over or they saw who it was and came up closer to him. The bodies were found by the curb, where he shot them. I don't believe that it was possible for someone to shoot with such precision from a moving vehicle."

Harry said, his voice argumentative, "Maybe they were just going to cross the street."

Mortimer argued back, "For what purpose?"

"That's probably where their car was, somewhere on that side."

"No. After I saw them positioned by the curb while you and Nancy were busy, I went inside the bar and asked the bartender if he had seen anything or whether he knew what car the Hollisters drove. He didn't see anything, only heard two shots. But he told me that James always drives his older model red Mercedes when he comes downtown. I looked for it and found it parked a block away on the same side of the street. There was no reason for the victims to cross the street."

MacGregor addressed Nancy and Harry. "How does Mortimer's reasoning help us here?"

Harry said, "Doesn't make much of a difference. We already determined that they were targeted. We still need to find out who did it."

Perez said, "It does help us, Ling. If Holliday is right, we need to concentrate on who James and Kay knew."

Mortimer said, "To me, it's obvious that it would be one of the family members since James was to inherit the bulk of his father's estate."

MacGregor stood up. "All right then. Let's do this again after all the suspects are questioned." She turned and went back to her office, as did Perez to his.

Nancy came up to Nora. "So, when can we have that lunch? I'm dying to know the details of what happened last night."

"Nancy, if it's all the same to you, I need a few days before I can talk about it. It's just too raw, and I don't want to think about it. All I can tell you is that we went through hell."

CHAPTER 34

GEORGE AND RHONDA'S house, located in the upscale suburb of Cherry Hills Village, was at least a twenty-minute drive from the station. As Hawk and Nora walked out of the station to arrive on time, Mortimer was at their heels per orders of Lieutenant Perez. Prior to their departure, the Lieutenant slipped Hawk the keys to an older Chevrolet Tahoe, formerly used by detectives in District 5. "It's now for your use." He smirked, "I wonder how long it will remain in one piece."

"I like this vehicle," Mortimer said as he slid into the back seat. "It's got more room than the Explorer. We don't see too many of these in the Tampa police department."

Hawk said, "These are pretty popular in the metro area."

As Hawk drove, Mortimer watched the surroundings with great interest. "I'm glad we're traveling for a distance, and I get a chance to see more of the metro area. I keep asking Josephine to go for a ride and show me around, but she just says it's too much bother and doesn't want to use up gas. Anyway, it's better without her since I get to learn a little about the history of the area when I'm with you. I doubt that Josephine is interested in history."

Nora said, "Mortimer, I'd be happy to tell you what I know about an area of Denver, but I'm no real historian. You can look all this up on Google. I was thinking, if you want to discover more of the region, why don't you just get into your car and drive around?"

"Oh, no! I don't think Josephine likes it when I leave her alone on my days off."

Hawk laughed, "What would she do, beat you on the head with a broomstick?" Nora chuckled.

"Oh, I don't think she'd do that. She'll just act all grumpy and throw snake eyes at me when I'd return from a trip like that."

Nora said, "And you certainly don't want that, Mortimer."

"Oh no. Her grumpiness sometimes lasts all evening, making me feel guilty."

Hawk said, "I'm sorry about that. I'll tell you what, though. Instead of taking the fastest route to Cherry Hills Village using I-25, I'll take you on a more scenic route so that we can show you more of the area. I think we'll still make it there on time."

Mortimer seemed as excited as a kid that was told he could have ice cream. Hawk chose to turn on Cherry Creek Drive from Washington Street, then make a right onto University Boulevard, and then follow that street all the way south to Cherry Hills Village.

As they passed Arizona Street, Mortimer said, "That's the street I turn on to get to Josephine's house. She lives a few blocks down to the west on High Street. It's a nice area, but a little too quiet for me."

Nora asked, smiling, "You like it wild, do you, Mortimer?"

"Oh, no. Not wild, but I'd like to see more people out and about. I hardly see anyone in the neighborhood. And the ones I do see, they seem to want to be left alone. I feel like I don't belong there." He paused, seemingly deep in thought. "So, Nora or Clint, what can you tell me about where we're heading?"

Hawk glanced over at Nora and smiled, "Go for it since it still bothers me to talk."

"Well, let me see." She thought a moment. "That area that is now called Cherry Hills Village is at the southern boundary of Denver. In the old days, it was simply called Country Homes. Mostly wide-open fields with some mansions of the wealthy and famous Denver people. Back in the late 1930s and early 40s, as more houses were built, the residents of the area, wanting to keep it semi-rural, came up with zoning restrictions requiring approval for new construction. They fought to keep stores and other commercial activity out, and to this day, there are none. Today it's incorporated as a city and it's a lovely place, one I wish I could afford." Nora paused again. "What about you, Clint, are you acquainted with the place?"

"Oh, I've been through it a time or two. I had a girlfriend that lived in Greenwood Village, and I drove past the place."

"Oh yeah. What happened? You broke up?"

Hawk thought for a moment. "Yeah. It was a while ago. She was looking for a steady relationship and I wasn't ready then."

"Oh, are you now?"

"I'll have to think about it."

"Anyone I know?" Nora giggled.

Hawk ignored her question. "Well, we're almost there. We just crossed Hampden Avenue, and now we're in Cherry Hills Village. Notice the red street signs."

Nora was disappointed that Hawk didn't answer her question, even though she asked in jest. She decided to drop the subject and said, "Clint, do you know why those signs are that color?"

"To stand out from the others, I suppose."

"Well, maybe, but supposedly the color was picked to match the shoes that the city clerk wore on the day they were deciding what to do about street signs. I mean, the town started out on a shoestring operation, haha. No pun intended. The police department was in the patrol car, the city clerk operated out of her home, and the city council met on someone's back porch."

Mortimer said. "That's exactly why I like traveling with you. I would never have known such details on my own. It makes it interesting to know those facts as we drive through." Hawk and Nora glanced at each other and laughed, not at Mortimer, but at his excited mood, the first they had seen from him since they met him."

"Oh, did I say something funny again?"

"No, Mortimer," Hawk said, "We're just happy that you're enjoying yourself."

"Oh. Yes, I guess I am. Thank you."

Nora's cell rang, showing Nancy Salazar as the caller. "Hello, Nora, I understand that you and Clint are on the way to interview George and Rhonda Hollister."

"Yes, we're almost there."

"I got some good news from Chet at the crime lab. Evidently, the investigators found a crumbled paper cup in the back of a trash can that sat next to the toilet. I don't know if you know this, but when Harry went out to the country club to get some info on George and Rhonda Hollister, he spotted them drinking a beer at a table. Being experienced, he waited for them to finish, then snatched the empties, placed them in a bag, and brought them over to CSI for fingerprint and DNA analysis. Asked for a rush on it. He had a hunch that an analysis might be handy. Well, my friend, he hit the jackpot. Guess what?"

"Nancy, what? Don't keep us in suspense. You're on speaker with Clint and Mortimer."

"Hi, guys! Chet was able to match George's and Rhonda's prints and DNA from the beer bottles to the throwaway cup found in the trash can."

Hawk smiled as Nora gave him a "high-five."

Mortimer asked, "Oh, did I miss something important? My mind was focused on a big bird just circling around. Wondering if he found something to eat." Thinking that it was unusual for him not to have listened to the call, Nora relayed Nancy's conversation.

Hawk turned onto Quincy, past the new City Hall, Police, and Fire Station combination, then drove east. Not too far from the Kent Denver private school, he made a left turn onto a side street. "We're almost here. It's one of these huge houses."

Mortimer began to sneeze. Then took out a handkerchief and blew his nose. "I wonder what these people will be like. Remember, we've been told that George Hollister has a horrible temper. Make sure he doesn't have a gun on him."

Hawk said, "I bet that with us, he'll be on his best behavior. But here's what we should do, let's try to separate them and talk to each individually."

Nora said, "That may be more difficult than you think."

"Let's try. I'll take George, and you take Rhonda."

Mortimer said, "I'll be with Nora if that's all right."

CHAPTER 35

THE SOUTHERN-STYLE house with its inviting wrap-around veranda was big, sitting on at least an acre of land. As Hawk turned into the circular driveway, it reminded him of old plantation houses that he had seen in Mississippi. Before he was able to shift the Tahoe into "park," both George and Rhonda Hollister stepped out of the house and waited for the detectives to exit the vehicle. George was tall and stout looking, slightly overweight, wearing casual brown slacks and a light-green golf shirt. Rhonda was much shorter and had a trim figure with long platinum-blonde hair. She wore black Bermuda shorts and a white T-shirt with the word "Paris" stenciled over the Eiffel Tower. While still in the car, Nora said, "That's strange. I bet they don't want us inside their house."

The Hollisters invited the detectives onto the porch and pointed to the six colorful Adirondack chairs that lined the wall of the pale-yellow wood-shingled house, indicating where they wanted them to sit.

Since Hawk's plan was to separate George from Rhonda, he had to figure out how. After introductions, an idea struck him. Hawk said to George, "Mr. Hollister, when we drove up, I noticed a horse in your corral. I love horses. Grew up with them in Texas. Could we walk over there and take a closer look? It's been a while since I've been around a horse."

George blew out a breath, his round cheeks expanding like those of a trumpet player. "That's a strange request from a detective. But hey! If that's what you want, I see no harm in it."

They walked around the side of the house on lush green Kentucky bluegrass, then connected to a well-maintained gravel path that led from the back of the house to a barn and corral. The palomino gelding with its long white tail and matching white mane ran up to the edge of the corral, lifted his head, and nodded in a welcoming gesture. "That's such a beautiful animal," Hawk said.

"A real golden beauty. He's a quarter horse, isn't he?" Hawk rubbed the horse's nose and the side of the neck.

"Hell, if I know. Not my horse. It's too much damn bother."

"Oh? Whose horse is it?"

"It's my daughter's. After she begged me to buy one for months, I finally relented. But she has to take care of him. I want nothing to do with this beast. I hate horses and that damn animal knows it."

"I'm sorry to hear that."

"Look, Detective, you didn't come out here to pet that horse. What's the purpose of your visit?"

George took a step back to the house, but Hawk didn't move from the corral, horse snuggling up to him. "Let's stay here a moment. I'd like to be with this fine animal for a few more minutes if that's all right with you?"

"We'd be much more comfortable on the porch."

"I'm sure, but it's just that the place, the barn, and the horse bring back memories of when I was a kid visiting my grandparent's place near Tyler, Texas. By the way, I wish to apologize for my bad manners. I meant to express my condolences for the huge loss of your father and now your younger brother." Hawk carefully watched George's reaction.

He had no visible reaction. "That's the way life is. You're here one day, and the next, you're gone. My father was old. He lived a good life, and in the long run, his death was maybe a blessing since he had cancer and would've probably suffered. Probably already affected his brain."

"How long had he been sick?"

"Actually, I don't really know. I only found out about it a few days ago."

"Mr. Hollister, as I stated on the phone when we arranged to meet at your home, I do have a few questions about your father's murder. Since you were at his house the night he was murdered, you, along with your other siblings, are persons of interest. As such,

I am recording our conversation, and even though you are not under arrest, you should know that you have the right to an attorney…" Hawk continued advising him of his Miranda rights.

"Look, Detective, I have nothing to hide. I did nothing wrong, and I don't need a lawyer."

Hawk got his permission to continue with the questions and asked, "You mentioned that your father dying might be a blessing to him since he had cancer. Why's that?"

"Look, Detective Hawk, if you're fishin' around trying to see if my father and I, or my brother, for that matter, were close, then let me just come right out and tell you. No. No. No. We were never close, at least since I was a teenager. He didn't understand me and wanted me to follow in his footsteps, but I had no interest, especially working with him where he'd continue to control my every move. Rhonda and I decided that we didn't need him, and we both felt more at ease when we didn't talk or see him. Much less stress." Hollister came closer to the corral and as he did so, the horse backed off. Hawk noticed the horse's fear or perhaps dislike of the man.

"But you took his money from the trust. I assume you needed him for that?"

George's cheeks on his round, puggy face puffed out. He rubbed his thumb over his sagging chin. "Listen, man, of course. I took his money just like everyone else. Why wouldn't I? I didn't ask for it, but since it's offered, why not?"

"Your financials are such that you needed the five thousand you were paid from the trust. It helped give you the lifestyle that you now enjoy. You also needed to inherit from the father that you despised to get out of the financial crunch that you got yourself into. And now that he took it away, that pissed you off. I suppose you would've been mad enough to kill."

Hollister's breathing became heavy; his voice raised as he placed his hands on his hips. "You had no right to check my financial situation without a warrant. Are you accusing me of murdering my father?"

"Well, you certainly had a strong motive."

"Sure, we relied on the money. I admit that not receiving the trust payment or inheriting a substantial sum will hurt us. But I didn't kill my father. I couldn't do such a thing. It's not in me. I bet some people told you that I have a bad temper. But the truth is I'm like a barking dog that doesn't bite." The veins on Hollister's temples popped out, blood surging through them. His face was red, his hands curled into tight fists, and his breathing turned from heavy to shallow and rapid.

"Mr. Hollister, now that your father is deceased, who inherits his estate?"

Hollister, still fuming mad, said, "Just to point out what kind of a bastard my old man was, he said that he'd wait a week before changing the trust and the will. He didn't. He just brought us to his house to torture us by telling us we're cut off."

"How do you know that he didn't wait the week?"

Hollister hesitated. "I believe I heard it from one of the siblings."

"Oh, which one?"

"I can't remember. Maybe it was James before he was shot down."

"So, you knew that James was to inherit under the will?"

Hollister looked away from Hawk; his hands trembled. "Yeah, I think James told me."

"It wasn't James. You knew about the new will, and you knew the contents because you stole a copy of it from the lawyer's office, didn't you?" Hawk looked George straight in the eyes. George looked away. At that moment, Hawk took a good look at George's sneakers. He remembered admiring the exact pair at a Dillard's store a few months ago, with brown leather and white soles. *I'll have to ask Chet if they would match the muddy imprint on the back door of the law office.*

George's red face seemed about to burst. In a loud voice, he yelled, "Hell no! I didn't even know that someone stole a copy of the will. That's a bunch of crap, accusing me of something that I had no knowledge of."

"But you saw the copy of the will, didn't you? Come on, George, you can't keep a thing like that secret. One of the siblings will verify our information sooner than later, and the cat will be out of the bag." Hawk didn't have any particular information, but he played a hunch.

George took a long time to answer. "Okay, Detective, I'll tell you the absolute truth. Someone left a copy in a manila envelope on our porch by the door. I have no idea who left it. I called all my siblings except for James and his wife for a meeting. None of them knew how it was that I was provided a copy, and everyone acted surprised that someone had left it for me. We had no idea how anyone got ahold of it. That's the absolute truth."

"Then, at that point, everyone in the room knew that James was to inherit the bulk of the estate?"

"Yes. We were all extremely pissed."

"Would you be so kind as to provide that copy you received along with the envelope? It'll go a long way in showing your cooperation with this investigation."

George thought hard about it. "If it'll help and get you off my back, I'll give it to you."

"Thank you."

"And the next day, after everyone found out that James was to inherit, he was murdered. Very convenient and rewarding to the rest of you, isn't it? Did you have anything to do with James' and Kay's slayings?"

"Of course not. I have an old double-barrel shotgun that I used years ago trying to hit clay pigeons. I don't particularly like the gun and haven't shot it for at least ten years. I understand that James and Kay were killed by someone that was a marksman with a pistol, and I have no freakin' idea who would've done it. I can't believe that my brother or my sisters could've done anything like that. It was probably some freak, random shooting."

Hawk thought of something with that statement. "Mr. Hollister, how did you know that your brother and sister-in-law were shot by a marksman?"

"Well, an officer from your department called us and advised us that my brother was shot. After I asked how and when it happened, I believe he mentioned that he died from a clean shot to the forehead and most likely did not suffer. I just assume that whoever shot him was a marksman."

"But you were able to take someone's life away not by a gun but by a more devious method when you switched the medications in your father's bedroom, knowing full well that he was allergic to aspirin."

"Damn you, Hawk. I did not kill my father." Hollister's breathing once again was deep and rapid, his fisted hands raised. Hawk didn't move but glared at the suspect watching his chest heave in and out as he breathed. After Hollister cooled off a bit, he said. "I admit that I knew he was allergic, yes, but I wasn't in his bathroom the night he died."

"Well, now, Mr. Hollister, I know you're lying. We have a couple of witnesses that saw you and Rhonda coming out of the bathroom." George's eyes widened. "And more importantly, we found the small paper cup that you and your wife used when you were in the bathroom. I can only assume that both of you had such headaches from the devastating news your father gave you that you each took an aspirin and washed it down with water using the cup." George's mouth flew open. "And, as it appears that you had aspirin available, it was easy enough for you to switch the medications."

George didn't look Hawk in the eye. Instead, he looked toward the house. Taking in some deep, regular breaths, he said, "You're guessing here, and you have it all wrong. You're making up a story that you'll never be able to prove, hoping I'll slip up and confess to something. But I don't have to slip up because I didn't do it."

"We have your and your wife's prints on the paper cup, and we have a DNA match to the both of you. You both used the same cup to wash down the aspirin. And since you're lying about that, what else are you lying about, George?"

George looked frantic. "All right, all right. I admit that Rhonda and I were in the bathroom. I just didn't think it looked good, considering the situation. But we were not the only ones. As far as I know, everyone, even James and Kay, were upstairs looking the old place over since it probably was the last time we'd see the house we grew up in. You're right. Both Rhonda and I had some real bad headaches, like the one I have now. We saw the dispenser with the paper cups, and Rhonda gave each one of us a pain pill. I'm not sure it was an aspirin. It might've been Celebrex, which she usually uses. She says it's gentler on our stomachs. I also admit that I saw the pill dispenser that my father used, but neither I nor Rhonda messed with it. Shit, I wouldn't even have known that would be a way to kill a person."

Suddenly, George began walking back to the house in a huff. Over his shoulder, he yelled out. "We're through here." He suddenly stopped and turned, "You don't have any proof of anything illegal that I had done. If you had, you would've arrested me. So, get off my property."

"Mr. Hollister, please wait a minute," Hawk yelled back. "Before we leave, can you give us the copy of the will and the envelope it came in as you agreed to do?"

"All right, I'll bring it out, and I swear that I didn't take it. But leave immediately after that."

CHAPTER 36

WHILE HAWK had George cornered by the corral, Nora Ricci accepted Rhonda's invitation to sit down on one of the comfortable porch chairs. Mortimer Holliday remained standing. Rhonda asked him to sit down once more, but he refused. Nora saw that he made Mrs. Hollister extremely nervous by hovering over her and asked him to sit down. Finally, he relented but continued to glare at the woman.

"Mrs. Hollister, thank you so much for agreeing to see us. Please accept our condolences over the deaths of your father-in-law and brother-in-law. I'm so sorry that they were victims of homicide."

Rhonda nodded gravely, "Yes, it is so sad. A real tragedy to hit our family."

"As such, we're bound to investigate their deaths, and we're interviewing all the family members for more information."

"Oh heavens, dear. I really don't have much to say other than what, I'm sure, you already heard from everyone. And, we certainly didn't have anything to do with the deaths of William or James. Our consciences are clear."

"That may be true, but I need to get your side of what happened. We know that you all were invited to a very contentious dinner at William Hollister's house recently."

"Oh yes, it was very unpleasant. Everyone was mad and argumentative. I know that George and I received horrible headaches from the event. I'm sure everyone there did as well. Except, of course, James and Kay. They seemed fine with the turn of events."

"What do you mean?"

"They knew that they'd inherit everything and, as far as I'm concerned, were smug about it."

"Did you know that they'd inherit everything?"

"No, not until later."

"Oh. The contents of the will hadn't been disclosed by the lawyer yet, so how do you know what's in the will?"

Rhonda's seemingly etched, forced, pleasant smile faded for the first time since they arrived. She straightened up from a semi-slouching, relaxed position, her eyes as big as saucers. "Oh, my, I misled you. I really don't know what's in the will. We just assumed that it would go to James since William mentioned that one of the children will inherit most of it." She glanced at Mortimer, whose eyes seemed to penetrate deep into her soul.

"Did you know that a copy of the current will was stolen from Mr. Windsor's office?"

"No. I didn't know that. Who would've done a thing like that? Surely, you don't think George or I had anything to do with it?"

"Regardless of who stole it, did you see the copy of the will or hear someone tell you what's in the document?"

It took a long time for Rhonda to answer. She avoided Mortimer's stare and concentrated on her feet. Without looking up, she said, "I don't think so. You'll have to ask George that."

Nora said, "Whoever stole that copy had to be one of the children or their spouses. Any idea who would've done that if it wasn't you?"

"I have no idea. All I know is that it wasn't me or George."

"How do you know that it wasn't your husband?"

Rhonda, gazing toward the Detective's vehicle, finally answered after a long pause. "Because George wouldn't have done a thing like that. I know him like the back of my hand after thirty years of marriage, and he's no criminal."

Mortimer cleared his throat, then sneezed. "Ma'am, please don't insult us with such blatant lies."

Rhonda fidgeted in her chair, "What in the hell are you talking about? I'm not a liar."

Mortimer continued, "Yes, you are. I know when people lie to me. Both you and your husband saw that copy, and probably so did all the other siblings. Just come out and tell the truth because if you lie about this, we'll definitely focus on you and your husband in these murders."

Rhonda looked to Nora for help but didn't get any. Instead, Nora asked, "Mrs. Hollister, had you gone into William's bathroom the night that he died?"

The woman took a brief glance at Mortimer, her breathing quick and shallow. Trembling slightly, she answered Nora in a slow, low voice, "I don't remember. It was very hectic that evening."

"Well, let me refresh your memory. We have fingerprint and DNA evidence that both you and your husband were in that bathroom. That's where you most likely switched a cancer pill with one of your pain pills. I assume it was an aspirin or something that would trigger a severe allergic reaction in William."

"Now, I believe you are lying to me. How would you possibly know that? There wouldn't be any fingerprints or DNA evidence, as you called it, since we didn't touch anything."

"Mrs. Hollister, you touched the faucet to pour water into a small paper cup so that both of you could take the aspirin. A paper cup that was found behind the trash can in the bathroom had your fingerprints and your saliva on it."

Mortimer said, "Yes, and that's when you and George noticed that your pill looked so much like the cancer pill that William takes nightly from a weekly pill dispenser. You knew that he was allergic to aspirin, and so you switched the pills."

Rhonda stood up, turned and ran into the house, screaming, "That's not true. That's not true. We did not switch the pills." They heard her lock the front door.

Nora and Mortimer looked at each other. "What do you think, Mortimer?"

"I wouldn't rule them out as suspects. As a matter of fact, I think they did it."

They walked down the three steps and around the house to see if Hawk was done. She saw the two men appeared to be in an animated conversation. George flayed his arms about as though he was directing a Boeing 747 into the gate. "Let's not bother them," Nora said to Mortimer. "We'll go wait by the car."

A few minutes later, they saw George stride toward the front of the house while Hawk followed a few steps behind. Since the door was locked, George banged on it until Rhonda opened it. Nora caught her tear-stained puffy face and suddenly felt bad. If they were not responsible for the death of William, then they put her through needless drama. But the evidence surely pointed to them.

Hawk came back and remained by the door. Nora didn't understand why until she saw George return and shove a manilla envelope into Hawk's chest.

CHAPTER 37

NORA EYED the manilla envelope held by Hawk. "What's in the envelope?"

"It's supposed to be the stolen copy of the will that George said was delivered to him by an unknown person, if you believe that. At least he gave it to us without a fight. Perhaps there may be a print or a drop of saliva on the papers."

Nora said, "Wow, that's interesting. And he just agreed to give it to you, just like that?"

"It is surprising, but after a few questions, he admitted that he had it. Wouldn't it be something if we found a print? Unless there are none other than George's, then that kinda' points the finger at him again."

"Clint, what do you think? Did George and Rhonda murder their old man?" Nora asked as she began walking toward the driver's door. "I'd like to drive, if you don't mind."

"Sure, go for it." He handed the key to Nora, then slid into the passenger seat. Mortimer had already squeezed himself into the back.

After Nora pulled out of Hollister's driveway, she again asked Hawk, "What do you think? Are they the culprits?"

"So far, the best evidence we have certainly points to them. George finally admitted to me that they were in the bathroom. And that they pulled out an aspirin or a Celebrex for their headaches. He admitted that he saw the pill dispenser. Admitted that he had a copy of the will and that he knew that James would inherit."

Mortimer said, "Isn't that enough to arrest them?"

Hawk said, "I suppose we have probable cause to do so. And who knows, with some brow beating, they'd confess to switching the pills and maybe even to shooting James and Kay, but…"

"But what?" Nora asked.

"I'd like to talk to Cynthia and Sam first and possibly again to Benson and Consuela before hauling George and his wife in. They're not going anywhere."

Nora smirked, "And don't forget your girlfriend, Tina Dionisio. Remember she wants to talk to you alone? Just you and her, with some hot information about William's murder." Nora chortled.

"Nora cut that out. She is not my girlfriend. It has always been strictly professional."

Mortimer said, "Oh, I didn't know you had another girlfriend, Clint."

Hawk raised his voice, "I don't. Nora is just kidding."

"Oh, I see. I guess I missed something."

Nora said teasingly, "Yeah, but she wants to be your girlfriend," Nora laughed again, infectiously. Even though Hawk's anger began to simmer, it did not last long. He cooled and laughed companionly along with Nora, leaving Mortimer to wonder what was so funny.

After the detectives left, George plopped down on the family room couch. His insides shook as he thought about what he said, what he admitted to. He thought that he would be much more in control, but somehow Hawk was able to get information and admissions out of him. He knew he was always bad at lying, and Hawk caught him in lies. *I should've been straightforward with him. Now he will continue to focus on Rhonda and me. Oh God! What have I done?*

Rhonda brought them each their favorite drink, a stiff martini with two olives, no ice. She gave one to him and, after sitting down next to George, began sipping her own. George downed his in one gulp. Raising his head, he looked right at her and drew a pained breath. "Rhonda, I screwed up royally. That Hawk caught me in lies. I don't feel good about it. I expect the cops to pick me up in the next few days and maybe you as well."

Rhonda listened to George's lament. Nervously, her fingers tapped on her knee while her heart pounded against her chest. "I didn't admit to anything, as far as I know. But I'm surprised by how much they know. If only I didn't suggest that we take that Celebrex for our headaches, but you were whining like a baby about how much your head hurt. Why didn't you put that small cup into your pocket, George? I can't believe that you threw it in the trash and even missed the trashcan. Now they know that I lied as well. I told you that we should get a lawyer, but no, you're so frickin' stubborn and so frickin' cheap."

"Rhonda shut up. I don't need you making me feel worse than I already do. You told me to get Marlene Livingston, the hotshot lawyer from the club. But even though she must keep it confidential, how would I be able to go back there just knowing that she knows our business? I couldn't look her in the eye."

"That's bull crap, George. You could've gotten someone else."

"Oh, shut up. Bring me another drink. Scotch this time."

"You had enough. We got to think through this. I think we need to get an attorney now more than ever."

"Rhonda, we just can't afford it."

At that moment, George's cell rang. "That's all we need now. It's Cynthia."

"What does she want?" Rhonda asked. "She never calls. Well, answer it, George."

"Hello, Cynthia. What's up?"

"George, you sound terrible. Anyway, stupid Sam made an appointment with the Denver detectives to meet tomorrow at our house all the way out here in Vail. Just want to know if they had interviewed you yet?"

"Yes, as a matter of fact, they just left."

"What kind of questions did they ask?"

"Oh, just the standard questions like how my relationship with the old man and whether we had any idea who could've killed him or James." George was not about to tell her any more than that, especially not about the copy of the will. He did not want her to be overly prepared while he was blindsided.

"You mean that's all? Come on, George, they asked you more than that, I'm sure?" George decided to push her buttons, his favorite pastime when they were growing up.

"Actually, Cindy, I told them that I thought it was you that killed Dad."

"What?! You sonofabitch! You didn't really say that did you? I don't believe it."

George laughed. "Gotcha."

"You bastard," Cynthia yelled into the phone. "You almost gave me a heart attack. You're cruel, as always. That's why I never call you or want to see that ugly mug of yours." She clicked off.

George's smile faded quickly as he thought of his own predicament with the police. Rhonda listened to the conversation on the speaker and shook her head. "I don't know how you can joke at a time like this. We may be going to jail. You should've been more careful. I still can't believe you threw that cup away like that."

"Look, get off my back. You already nagged me about that cup. I made a mistake, okay? They still have to prove that we switched those damn medications. Just because we used the cup for our own aspirins doesn't prove anything. You were smart to walk away from any more questions. I wish I had. I need another drink. Shut up and go get me one!"

"Get it yourself, you jerk." She gave him a long nasty sneer. "Yeah, drink up, you idiot. They won't give you any booze in jail."

CHAPTER 38

AFTER THE three detectives made it back to the station, they wrote reports on the George and Rhonda interviews. Since Hawk interviewed George and Nora and Mortimer talked to Rhonda, they met afterward and exchanged their statements.

Sitting around Nora's desk discussing the case, Mortimer announced that it was later than he thought and he needed to get home for dinner. "Josephine is waiting for me with some cauliflower casserole, and she was specific that if I come late, it won't taste as good if it's reheated. Actually, truth be known, and I'll never tell her, but her casserole is not that tasty even if it comes right out of the oven." Hawk and Nora smiled but remained silent. Mortimer continued, "We're still going to Vail tomorrow morning?"

Hawk said, "Yes, we are. It'll take us a couple of hours to get there. We should leave around 7 o'clock."

"Oh, I thought the appointment was for ten."

"It is, but with all the tourists, sometimes it takes a little longer than two hours, and I want to make sure we get there on time. If we arrive too early, we could always look around a little, perhaps grab a cup of coffee."

"Oh, I'll have to explain that to Josephine. She has a set time for breakfast, and she'll probably not be willing to break her routine."

Nora snickered, "I'll tell you what, Mortimer. If she doesn't make breakfast for you, we'll stop at a drive-through and get all of us a breakfast sandwich and coffee."

Hawk said, "Can't you make your own breakfast, Mortimer? What's the deal?"

"Oh, Josephine said that the kitchen is her province and that she'll be in charge of all the cooking. I don't want to upset her by moving pots and pans around."

"Okay, Mortimer," Hawk said. "We'll meet here at seven tomorrow morning, and we'll grab some breakfast."

After Mortimer left, Hawk took Nora's hand and gently squeezed it. "What about a nice dinner somewhere tonight?"

"Clint, I'm pretty beat. The incident with O'Leary took a lot out of me and I need to crash. My couch, and a Netflix romantic movie, is what I need. I think you should go and relax. You were as wound up as me, almost choked to death."

"I guess you're right. I could use some downtime." Nora nodded, powered off her computer, stood, and grabbed her black leather handbag. Hawk stood as well. "Let me walk you to your car."

They walked silently across the parking lot. At Nora's vehicle, Nora turned toward Hawk, pulled him toward her, and kissed him hard on his mouth. With a mischievous smile on her blushing face, she slid into her car. From the open window, she called out, "That'll give you something to think about," and laughing, she drove away. Hawk had a wide grin as he saw her stick her arm out of the window and wave goodbye.

Hawk had a pleasant night for a change. He had no devastating nightmares of guns pointed at him or people trying to kill him and slept well with passionate thoughts of Nora going through his mind.

The next morning, the three detectives took off for Vail in the police Tahoe. A minute after they left, Mortimer asked, "When can we stop for breakfast? I imagine that we need a full stomach to travel in the mountains."

Hawk said, "I know a place along the way where we have a choice of eateries, Mortimer. We'll stop there, and you can buy your breakfast."

"Oh, I buy? Let me see how much money I have." He looked in his wallet. I guess I can't buy too much. All I have is five dollars on me."

Nora said, "Don't you have a credit card?"

"Oh, I do, but Josephine and I agreed that we'll only use the card for emergencies."

Hawk glanced at Nora and shook his head. "I'll tell you what, I'll charge the meals on my card then hope that Perez would approve the expenditures and reimburse me But let's keep the cost down."

Mortimer nodded and thanked Hawk.

Hawk made his way onto the Sixth Avenue freeway and, after twenty minutes, turned right at the Indiana exit to Chick-Fill-A. Hawk and Ricci each ordered an egg, bacon, cheese biscuit, and a cup of coffee. Mortimer ordered two breakfast sausage muffins and a side order of waffle fries. Instead of coffee, he chose a milkshake. "Josephine would really be mad at this order, so don't tell her."

Nora said, "Don't worry. Our lips are sealed. Besides, we never met her or talked to her…how can you eat all that anyway?"

"Oh, I find that after one of Josephine's meals, I'm usually still hungry. I guess I need to make up for it."

Feeling sorry for the poor guy, Hawk couldn't help wondering why he was hanging around that woman. *Are they truly in love?* He asked Mortimer, "Do you have a picture of her with you?"

"Oh, no. She doesn't like being photographed. When we first met on the cruise, I took a couple of pictures of her, but she asked to see my digital camera and, without my permission, deleted them."

Nora and Hawk exchanged glances, looking concerned.

Nora asked, "You sure she inherited all those millions that she told you about?"

Appearing puzzled with the question, Mortimer sneezed, then coughed three times in a quick sequence. "I don't understand why you asked, Nora. She told me a rich uncle had died and left his whole estate to her. She doesn't want to talk about it much, and I don't know any more than that. I believe her. I certainly must trust her if we're to be married. After all, I told her the truth about my aunt."

Hawk asked, "Your aunt, what about her?"

"As I told Josephine on our cruise, I have a rich grandaunt who's worth millions. Her husband died a few years ago and now she's all alone as she never had any children. So, my brother, Seymour, and I are the only heirs." Mortimer fell deep in thought. "I guess one of these days, I'll wind up a millionaire as well. Unfortunately, probably sooner than later, because Seymour told me that Aunt Marian is not doing well at all."

Nora said, "Oh, that's too bad. How old is she?"

"She just turned eighty-nine. I'm sad about it. She's a great lady who took care of us after our parents died in an auto accident outside of Miami. The negligent driver was one of those crazy Miami drivers that think they're on a racetrack on I-95. I really need to go visit her, but I haven't accumulated any vacation time yet. Josephine says that she'll go with me and is encouraging me to go. Told me to just take a leave of absence. She wants desperately to meet my aunt."

Hawk said, "Mortimer, what would you do with all the money?"

"Oh, I haven't thought about it much. Josephine told me that she'll invest it for me, so I'll leave it up to her to decide that, I suppose. She's really good with money."

Hawk said, "Sounds like it. Never spends it."

"Yes, she's very practical." Nora arched her eyebrows.

After they finished eating, Hawk made his way back onto the Sixth Avenue freeway and shortly afterward exited onto I-70 West. Once on that interstate, they entered the foothills of the Rocky Mountains and soon the tall mountains themselves. Mortimer's neck twisted from side to side taking in the majestic scenery. However, the curvaceous, up-and-down road made him car sick. His nausea became worse after about an hour, and he asked Hawk to quickly find a restroom.

Luckily, the exit for Georgetown, an old mining town, was a mile away. Hawk sped up and got off at the exit, turned left into the town, and made his way onto a gas station/store combination near the interchange. The Tahoe barely came to a stop before Mortimer rushed out of the vehicle and ran into the store. That was the fastest Clint or Nora had seen him move.

The other two detectives remained in the vehicle. "Poor guy," Nora said. "That'll certainly ruin this trip for him. He was really looking forward to it. What do you think about him inheriting all that money?"

"Appears that Josephine is sure interested in it."

Nora said, "If she has all that money, why would she want more, considering she doesn't do anything with it?"

"Supposedly, she has all that money. For all we know, she may be a scam artist. I mean, look at Mortimer. I feel sorry for him."

"Yeah," Nora said, "Now, I'm a little suspicious of her myself."

"Anyway, I'm sure Mortimer will figure it out someday, hopefully, sooner than later. He's a detective, after all. But just in case, I think we need to have a long talk with him."

"But you're forgetting; love is blind."

"I wonder how much they're in love. I think he's lonely and wants companionship. But she should wise up and start feeding him if she wants to keep him." He looked at Nora and quickly changed the subject. "So, were you able to relax last night?"

"I suppose so. Except I had a call from my parents, then my brother, bugging me about taking that job as a manager, then my former partner, Seth Morgan, called, then—"

Hawk turned sharply toward her, interrupting, "What did Morgan want?"

"Oh, he's been asking me out to dinner and wondered if I could do it this weekend."

A green-eyed monster suddenly rose his head inside Hawk. "I thought we'd be going to Pueblo this weekend. Besides, did you tell him that your boyfriend wouldn't like that?"

Nora's eyes flew open as she twisted her neck towards him. She chuckled. "Oh, and who would that be?"

"Me, of course."

"I didn't know that. Does that mean that I'm your girlfriend, then?" She giggled.

"Well, I guess so. What do you say?"

She unbuckled her seatbelt and threw herself at him, kissing him passionately. After she came up for air, she asked, "Does that answer your question?"

Hawk laughed in amusement. "I'm not sure. You'll have to tell me again." Both laughed heartily.

A few minutes later, Mortimer came back, his face paler than usual, which was hard for Clint and Nora to believe possible. He carried a bottle and a little bag. "I bought some Dramamine tablets. I had to use my credit card since it was an emergency. I wonder what Josephine will say. Do you think that Lieutenant Perez will reimburse me for them since we're on official business?"

Nora said, "You can always try it, Mortimer."

They continued on I-70, up and down and from curve to curve until finally, they made it to Vail pass. Vail was on the other side of the summit to the west. In the extra hour that it took from Georgetown, Mortimer's pill seemed to help with the motion sickness, but now he was complaining that he couldn't breathe very well. "There's not enough oxygen up here. I'm feeling lightheaded, and I think my heart is bouncing around. How high is this mountain anyway?"

Hawk said, "From what I remember, it's almost eleven-thousand feet, maybe three or four hundred feet less. But hang in there; we're almost there. Vail's elevation is just a little over eight thousand."

Mortimer continued breathing shallowly. Nora and Hawk were concerned. Hawk sped up to get to a lower altitude, and as he did, Mortimer's breathing seemed to stabilize.

"I'm sorry that I'm such a nuisance. Coming from Florida, we're not used to all the curves and high altitudes. This is the first time I have seen anything like this. I feel that I'm entirely in another world somewhere. Even though I've had a problem or two, I wouldn't miss it for anything. Josephine must've been here and seen these imposing mountains, but she certainly hadn't taken me here."

Nora said, "You need to get into your car and just drive around here. A quiet place, away from everyone on a mountain top is an experience like no other. It almost cleanses your soul."

"Oh, I'd like to do it, but even if Josephine lets me do something like that, my old car wouldn't make it to the top."

Hawk interrupted, "There's the town of Vail ahead of us."

"Yes, Mortimer, "Nora said, "If we have time afterward, we should have our lunch there. It's like being in a German or Austrian ski town."

"That'll be great, but I don't know if I'll be able to eat anything."

Nora punched in the address she had previously programmed and touched the Google Maps app. "We're about fifteen minutes away from the Maxwell house."

Mortimer began to sneeze, one after another, then followed the sneezes with a cough. *He's nervous about the interviews;* Nora knew him better now.

CHAPTER 39

THEY DROVE past Vail a few miles, and then at an exit ramp, they turned right into a narrow valley bordered by mountains. Once there, they followed a winding road up a mountain until they came to a wrought iron gate held up by two white stucco pillars. A white plastic fence ran along the front of the property. Hawk got out of the vehicle to open the gate, but it was locked. A heavy-duty keypad was attached to the post. Looking around, he caught a camera hanging off a tall pole. *They must know we're here,* he thought.

He was right. Suddenly, the locking mechanism clicked, and the gate swung open. They drove up a steep, narrow gravel path up a hill, and once they reached the top, a wide two-story log house with a five-car garage loomed ahead about a quarter mile away.

"Boy, this place is really secluded," Nora said. "I don't think I'd like to live so isolated from others."

Hawk said, "Hard to borrow a cup of sugar when you need it."

Mortimer cleared his throat twice, then sneezed, then coughed. "Are we going to try to separate them?"

"I think it's a good idea," Nora said. "Any ideas how you're going to do it this time, Clint? I don't see any horses around," she jested.

"I'll come up with something."

Mortimer said, "Who will take on Cynthia? She's the volatile one of the two."

"Nora said, "I'll do it. She may be more comfortable with another woman asking questions."

"Good," Mortimer mumbled. "I'll be with Clint."

The driveway led them to the front door. Threatening steel-clad clouds gathered, and a crisp mountain breeze immediately lowered the temperature—a refreshing change from the summer heat of Denver. Mortimer complained that if he had known how cold it will be, he would've brought a heavier jacket.

Since the Maxwells' knew they were there, the detectives expected them to wait by the door. Instead, Nora rang the doorbell. There was no answer. She rang it again, hearing chimes inside. After waiting another long minute, Hawk grabbed his phone to call. As he did so, Cynthia angrily flung the door open. The stout woman was dressed in faded blue jeans and a brown khaki shirt and had bare feet. Her auburn-dyed short hair was neatly styled, obviously by a professional stylist. Her slim husband, an inch shorter than his wife, stood behind her, dressed in casual blue pants, a black T-shirt, brown sandals, and white socks.

Contrary to Cynthia, Sam gave the detectives a smile. Cynthia said, "Well, I see you made it here. But you've wasted a trip. Are you still on this stupid kick that my dear, precious father was murdered somehow? And if he was, do you really believe one of his kids could've done it?"

Nora said, "We are here because that's what the evidence shows."

"Sam and I don't believe it for a moment. You're just making this all up to put a feather in your bonnet. Making up a murder just so you'd look good to your superiors. You'll look like real idiots when it is proven that my father died a natural death."

Hawk asked, "Oh, what do you know that we don't know?"

"I just know that no one in our family would've killed our father. So maybe you should leave us alone. If you really think someone did, then who is it that's in charge of his medication? Huh, bright boy?"

Hawk asked, "Who?"

"Geez, you're really dumb. Did you forget that it was Benson or Consuela, or whatever her name is? They took turns handing out my father's meds. You should be going after them, not us."

Nora asked, "May we come in?"

Cynthia didn't answer right away. She continued to stand in the doorway, glaring intently at Nora. Finally, she snarled, "Hell, you want to waste everyone's time, then come in. I'll give you just a few minutes, then get out."

Mortimer said, "Listen, lady, we're here as a favor to you. I got carsick driving out here."

"What do you mean as a favor to me?"

"We should've had you come to the station instead, like it's usually done. So, we'll take as much time as we need, or you'll be coming into Denver with us or escorted by officers."

Nora and Clint glanced at each other. Nora's eyes went wide. *He's at it again with his aggressive behavior toward witnesses. This is an interview, not an interrogation. I hope he didn't ruin my approach to this.* Cynthia blew out a hard breath and sucked in some air. She didn't say a word, but her face turned red.

Once in the house, Cynthia pointed them to a massive distressed-oak dining table standing in the center of the formal dining room, an elkhorn chandelier hung above. Through the floor-to-ceiling windows on two of the four walls in the spacious room, a magnificent view of the wooded mountains instantly caught their eyes.

Before they sat down, Hawk addressed Sam. "Mr. Maxwell, I noticed a five-car garage attached to the house. Are you a collector of vintage vehicles by chance?"

Smiling broadly, Sam said, "I sure am. I got two in there that are my pride and joy. Would you like to see them since you look like a man that would admire them?"

"Oh, that'll be a thrill. Lead the way."

Mortimer followed Hawk and Maxwell as he led them down a hall and through a gourmet kitchen. The room was impressive, with two islands and a long wrap-around granite countertop. Above and below the counter were custom-built crème-colored cabinets with a shiny copper hood over the gas cooktop. Hawk noticed that the walls were bare in the kitchen, as were the other walls in the house. Except for one small portrait of a young man in the study, there were no decorations, posters, paintings, or pictures of the family.

The house was beautiful but lacked charm and coziness, giving it a cold, austere feeling.

They strode through the mudroom and then through a nine-foot-tall door leading into the spacious garage. When they passed through the mud room, Hawk noted several pairs of shoes lined up on the floor next to a bench. He spotted a pair of men's blue New Balance sneakers, the white soles stained by mud. He thought, *according to Chet Watkins, the design of the soles used by the burglar that broke in at Windsor's office were, most likely, those of New Balance. Interesting. Might be just a coincidence, though, but probably not.*

Just as the men entered the garage, Mortimer grabbed Hawk's arm and said, "Sorry, Clint, but I'm not doing well. My nausea has returned, and I'm so sleepy that I can't seem to keep my eyes open. Or think. I think the high altitude is getting to me. I need to go and sit in the car for a while, if you don't mind."

Overhearing, Sam said, "Here, let me open the garage door for you. This high altitude plays tricks on you if you're not used to it."

Hawk observed Mortimer drag himself out of the garage. *I bet he swallowed too much Dramamine. That'll make you sleep.*

Hawk then focused on the vintage vehicles. "Oh my gosh! A yellow 1949 Buick Roadmaster convertible. It's one of my most favorite classics. And oh geez, a 1959 Cadillac Fleetwood. I can tell by those bullet shaped taillights. These cars are worth a fortune. How did you ever find them? And in such great shape. You must've fixed them up to look this good."

"Hell, no. I was told when I bought them at car shows that everything on them was original. I had them checked out and that's what my mechanic also said. But, boy, you sure know your cars."

"Oh, you bet. I'm a sucker for vintage cars." Hawk noticed a smaller car in the end of the massive garage covered with a tight-fitting tarp. "And what's under that cover? Surely, it isn't another one of your treasures, is it?"

Sam laughed. "No, not at all. We're storing it for our son now that he's on active duty with the Army."

Hawk took a closer look at the covered vehicle and saw that a portion of the back fender and tire was left exposed. He noted the gray color. He also was able to deduce the make of the car by the wheel cover logo. He turned his attention back to the classic autos and walked around them, observing the interiors. Addressing Sam, he said, "Now that we have all this electronic gadgetry on the new cars, it's a pleasure for me to see the old dashboards. Simple, yet very functional." Sam nodded. Pointing to the cars, Hawk continued, "Anyway, Mr. Maxwell, I can keep drooling over these, but we need to get down to business."

Sam said, "Okay. Let's go back in and join the ladies."

"Actually, I think it'll be much more pleasant if you could show me around your beautiful place here while we talk. To me, it'll feel like a wonderful hike in the backcountry somewhere. I love the mountains."

Sam laughed, but Hawk knew that his laugh was more out of nervousness than merriment. "Sure. I'm glad to show off my little property here."

They walked out of the garage. Hawk glanced at the Tahoe and noticed Mortimer's head bobbing up and down as though he was fighting sleep. The two men walked around the house to the back. Sam said, "I'm surprised you came all the way out here. Surely, you don't think that I'm a suspect, do you?"

"No, not at all, but since you were at that dinner with your father-in-law, you are considered a person of interest, and I'll be recording our conversation so that there are no misunderstandings. Can we talk frankly?"

Sam hesitated for a minute before answering. "I guess. I have nothing to hide. Sure, why not?"

"Now, if you feel uncomfortable with any of my questions, you certainly have the right to remain quiet and call your attorney."

"I told you I have nothing to hide. So go ahead and ask what you need to. I understand you're doing your job."

Hawk continued, "Fine then. I hate to say anything bad about a man's wife, but Cynthia sure seems to have a temper, doesn't she?"

Sam chuckled. "She can be that way at times. Her father's death has really upset her, and she's more uptight than usual. I must admit, it's been rough for me lately."

"She was pretty mad when William Hollister said that he was cutting everyone off, I hear."

"Well, yeah. What do you think? We all were. Except, of course, James and Kay. They knew they'd inherit all of it, except for what Benson and Consuela were to get."

"Oh, how did you know that James and Kay would inherit everything?"

Sam was about to answer, then he suddenly hesitated. Hawk could see the marbles rolling around in his brain, trying to come up with a good answer. Finally, he said, "You know, I can't quite remember where I heard that. It might've come from lawyer Windsor or possibly from George."

"You're referring to your brother-in-law, George Hollister?"

"Yes, him. He seems to be right on top of everything when it comes to that."

"Oh, do you think that he might've even switched the meds to kill your father-in-law?"

Sam hesitated again. He raised his head and seemed to stare at a pine tree. "I hate to think that he or even Rhonda would do a thing like that. But he was pretty upset that his father was cutting him off. He was really relying on the trust payments and inheriting a bunch of money. I think he may have some severe financial problems."

"But as far as we've garnered, you and Cynthia are in the same boat. You also need that money."

Sam took in a deep breath; his hands quivered. He once again turned away, and while seemingly staring at a boulder, he said, "Yeah. It would appear that way. But we have an option to get out of it. With the way this real estate is selling around here. With all the folks from Denver, California, Texas, New York, and Chicago clambering for mountain property, I think we'd be able to sell the place for a profit if we needed to. Sure, we hoped to get that extra five thousand a month from the trust and eventually inherit. Then pay off this huge loan we have, but sometimes that's the way it goes." He paused, looked down at his sandals, then at Hawk. "George and Rhonda seemed to take it harder than the rest."

"I understand that Cynthia threatened her father at the dinner."

Sam turned away again. "I really don't remember that…everyone was yelling and screaming."

"But you wouldn't put it past her to threaten her father?"

"Well, in the heat of the moment, she might've, but she gets mad, blows off some steam, and then as quick as she gets riled up, cools off."

"From what I heard from everyone so far, everyone seemed to visit William Hollister's bathroom. Although, I'm not sure why it was so important to gawk at the bathroom. So, my question is, when you and Mrs. Maxwell went into the bathroom to look around, had your wife cooled off by then?"

Sam looked at Hawk, his eyes wide. Hawk noticed a slight tremor in his upper lip. "Cynthia wanted to go into every room upstairs so that she could remember the house she grew up in; as it seems like you said, everyone else did too. So, I'm pretty sure we did as well."

"Was anyone else in there? It's a big room and you could hold a meeting there." Hawk chuckled.

"I believe so. I think I saw Darren and his bimbo girlfriend. Wait! I just remembered. I saw the wench pull something out of her handbag while in the bathroom. They looked serious about what they were doing."

"Oh, what do you think she took out of her bag?"

"To me, it looked like a flat tin or a container of aspirin or something like that. You definitely need to check that out, Detective."

"I certainly will, Sam."

"You know, Darren's an alcoholic, the black sheep of the family, and he'd be the type to convince his girlfriend to switch an aspirin product for a med that William took. And I really don't know that woman, but I wouldn't put it past her to do something like that to help Darren inherit his share. Then she'll twist him around her little finger, get the money and dump him. She just looks like the type that would do it."

"Did you see what she did with those pills, if they were, indeed, medications of some sort?"

"Nah, they saw me look in and she quickly turned away while Darren gave me a dirty look. We walked out and then waited for them to leave, I believe, before we went in and looked around."

"Did you notice the pill box full of meds?"

"Not really. I probably should've taken a good look to see if Darren and that woman did switch something around."

"Of course, having William Hollister dead would help Cynthia inherit her share."

After pausing, Sam said, "Well, yeah. But we would never want to get our share that way."

Hawk and Maxwell kept walking slowly, and about two hundred yards from the house, the detective noticed a makeshift shooting range with a tall, ninety-degree embankment carved out of the hill to prevent slugs from sailing over the property. In front of the embankment were bits and pieces of broken glass and shot-up cans. He spotted a few spent shells of various calibers, mostly 22's, along with empty shotgun shells. Hawk said, "Looks like you do a little target shooting."

"Yeah, it's kind of a hobby for Cynthia and me."

"It's good to have a hobby. You must be pretty good."

“I’m all right, I guess. It’s Cynthia that can shoot the cap off a beer bottle.”

Hawk decided not to ask any more questions and pretended not to show any interest in the range. Though, he made a note to himself of what he should do once he’s in his vehicle.

It seemed that Sam wasn’t concerned whether Hawk saw the shooting range or not. The smallish man seemed excited to show off to Hawk his latest purchase. They kept walking another fifty yards or so to a large log shed, the logs matching the color of those on the house. As they entered, Sam said, “This is my latest toy, Detective. It’s an M-5 John Deere utility tractor. I got a snowplow for winter and a weed cutter for summer to go with it. I’m having a ball just driving this thing around the property. I’m even thinkin’ that I should plant something, but not too many crops grow around here. Do you want to take it for a spin?”

Before Hawk could decline, they heard Cynthia yell out in her booming voice, “Sam! Sam! Where in the hell are you? Get in here!”

CHAPTER 40

INSIDE, NORA was face to face with Cynthia, sitting across the table from each other. Nora scooted up to the table while Cynthia sat further back, her hands crossed over her wide chest, and her face portrayed a frightful frown. Cynthia glared at Nora with her dull gray narrow eyes as if she'd strangle her any second, making Nora feel uncomfortable. She had a job to do and had to get through the interview with the hostile woman.

In an unsuccessful attempt to warm the frigid air between them, Nora said, "I just love your home, Mrs. Maxwell," glancing around. There were no paintings, pictures, or knickknacks except for a single portrait of a young soldier hanging on a wall across the hall in an adjacent room used as a home office. Nora asked, "Is that fine-looking man there in the photo your son?"

"Yes. Listen, Detective. I know what you're doing. You're trying to make this pleasant, but every second that you're here, taking me away from my work, makes this a miserable meeting. This is no social visit. Now get on with what stupid questions you have."

"Of course. What are you working on?"

"It's none of your damn business, that's what."

Nora cleared her throat, but before she was able to ask the first question, Cynthia sprang up and leaned over the detective, her hands splayed on the table, her round face thrust forward. Not knowing what to expect from the woman, Nora sat back and slid her chair away further away from the table. The rage in the woman's expression and her usually dull eyes shooting arrows caused Nora to shudder, wondering if she should prepare herself for a possible assault. *I've taken down some really nasty criminals, and I could certainly take down this fat bitch. Come on, woman, give me a chance.*

"Let me save time here," Cynthia bellowed, "I know what you're going to ask. So here it is. Yes, I was furious at my father. He had no right to cut us off. Yes, I might've said something in anger to him that I didn't mean." Spittle flew out of her mouth as she leaned closer to Nora. Nora slid her chair back a little further, embarrassed at her own retreat. "Yes, we were all mad at him, except for James and Kay, who had this crappy grin on their faces. Yes, we went upstairs with everyone else. Sam and I went into my old room, and I took a few knickknacks and threw them in the box. There was a lot of complaining from all of us, especially Darren. He was drunk as always, spouting that he'd figure something out and stop this foolishness on Dad's part. He called him a senile old man whose time was up." Cynthia gasped for deep breaths, her chest heaved, and veins pounded in her temples.

"Now I told you all I know, now you can leave." Nora's dark blue eyes stared back into Cynthia's as she sat silently. *You're not going to get rid of me that easy, woman.*

Nora said, "Mrs. Maxwell, would you please sit down? We'll certainly leave soon. Thank you for the information. It did save some time. But I can't get over what a beautiful house you have, and the setting around it is breathtaking. It would be exceedingly difficult for you, I'm sure, to lose it."

"Lose it? What in the hell are you talking about? Who's going to lose it?"

"It is our understanding that, ah, you were counting on the monthly trust payments to keep yourselves afloat. And I believe you expected a large inheritance from your father to pay off the mortgage."

"Are you for real, missy? You come into my house and insult me like that?"

Her heart raced as Nora said, "No, I certainly don't want to insult you. I'm just stating the facts that have come to light as we investigate your father's murder."

Cynthia flared up, "There are two things wrong with your statement. First, there was no murder. My father died from old age. He was senile and didn't know what he was doing in the last few months of his life, evidenced by his being unduly influenced by James and his conniving wife. That's why his will is invalid." Cynthia's face turned red. "But it doesn't really matter now that James is dead. We'll still inherit our share. So, you're full of shit, lady."

"How do you know that since James died, you'll inherit? I don't think the will has been read yet, has it?"

Cynthia was about to blurt something when she suddenly caught herself. "That's just what we heard, that's all. I guess we'll find out next week when that old lawyer finally gets around to it."

"Could it be that you saw a copy of the will at George's house the other day?"

"How do you know about that? That sonofabitch brother of mine could never keep his damn trap shut."

"Ah, isn't it such a coincidence that once you found out how the will reads, suddenly James and Kay are violently killed?"

"Coincidences happen. Shit happens. But it doesn't mean that we had anything to do with it."

"But it sure was lucky for you, wasn't it?"

Nora noted Cynthia's trembling hands. "Sure, it was lucky. There is some justice in this world, after all...but we had nothing to do with James's death."

"Any idea who might've done it?"

"I don't have the foggiest. If I had to bet, I'd say it was a gang drive-by. You should be out there right now looking for the gang rather than harassing Sam and me like this."

That's funny; who's harassing whom? "How did George get the copy of the will?"

"Ask him. I think he lied to us when he said that someone left it on his doorstep."

"But you already knew what was in the will before you went to George's house, didn't you?"

"No, we did not!"

"We know that someone broke into Attorney Windsor's office, and the only thing that they took out was a copy of the will. And we saw and heard you at his office sounding really upset that the lawyer didn't provide you a copy."

"Sure, I was. And so what? I didn't break into his office."

"And didn't you threaten poor Mr. Windsor that you'll get a copy one way or another?"

Cynthia paused, and blew out a hard breath. "Is that what that old fool of a lawyer told you?"

"That's in the report that the Golden Police detective emailed us last night."

Cynthia's tone softened, "Maybe I might've said something like that. But then, I have a habit of mouthing off without thinking. Most of the time, I really don't mean what I say."

Nora said, "But sometimes you do." Cynthia remained silent. "And you followed through with your threats and killed your father and your brother."

"You're full of it. Of course, I wouldn't do anything like that. Get out! Get out now! I had enough of you—"

Before Cynthia finished her sentence, Nora interrupted, "All right, I'll leave, but before I go, could you please answer whether you and Sam went into your father's bathroom that evening?"

Cynthia was shaking. She seemed to be unable to breathe, and Nora thought she might be having a heart attack. She finally took some deep breaths and seemed to calm down. Looking out the window, she said, her voice calmer, "You just can't take a hint, can you? Okay, I'll answer this question, then please leave me alone. "I don't remember if I did or not. Probably not, because it just so happened that quite a few of my siblings and spouses were in my father's bedroom when I peeked in. I had such a horrible headache, and I wanted to get out of that friggin house."

"Oh, I'm sorry. Did you take anything to relieve your pain?"

"I had to. Luckily, I had a painkiller in my purse. Always carry an aspirin or Advil because I'm susceptible to headaches. As a matter of fact, I have a hell of a big one right now because of your friggin accusations."

"So you took an aspirin that evening?"

"I told you. I had to." Cynthia's anger rose again. She glared at Nora, then quickly turned and complained, "Where in the hell is that husband of mine? What are they doing in the garage for so long?" She stood and walked out of the room. Nora heard her heavy steps down the hall. Then she heard a door open, and Cynthia holler out for Sam. When she returned, her hands were fisted and trembled. "Listen, woman. We're done here. Now get off my property and take your damn partners with you!"

Nora said, "Yes, of course. We'll leave, but we may have to continue this interview, possibly an interrogation, at the police station in Denver."

"Screw you. Get out! Get out!"

With her insides trembling, Nora switched off the recording, snatched her purse and her small notebook, and walked out of the door being held open by Cynthia. Her face was the color of a boiled lobster. Nora didn't see anyone in the Tahoe, so she walked around the house looking for Hawk and Mortimer. She saw Hawk and Sam by a shed a short distance away and slowly strolled toward them, wondering where Mortimer was.

Nora didn't feel good about the interview. She tried hard not to allow the vile woman to intimidate her, but Cynthia got to her. No matter how tough and professional she attempted to be, she felt that Cynthia was able to ruin her timing and prevented her from following through with questions. *I could've handled it much better. I wonder how Clint would've handled her.*

Taking deep breaths to calm down, Nora slowed her pace as she walked toward Hawk. She purposely focused on the nature around her. She heard birds chirping away, some engaging in song and saw a chipmunk scurry on some rocks a few feet away. The cool mountain summer breeze felt refreshing on her flushed face. In the distance, an amazing peak with a few strands of snow above the timberline made her wish that she was there on top of the world, escaping the ugliness that she experiences every day. As she approached the men, she heard Cynthia scream again, "Sam! Sam! Where in the hell are you? Get in here!"

She heard Sam say, "Oh, oh. That's the second time she's yelled at me to come in. I'm in the doghouse again, maybe the dungeon, this time by the sound of it. The queen calls." Sam barely said goodbye to them as he hastily high-tailed it back to the house.

"How'd it go?" Hawk asked Nora as they stood side by side, watching Cynthia wait for Sam at the patio door, her expression mean and stern.

Nora chuckled as they started back to their vehicle. "I'm ready for a diversion from this detective business, at least for a day. I could sure use that short trip to Pueblo. You need to get away as well. By the way, where's Mortimer?"

CHAPTER 41

FROM A distance, the Tahoe looked empty. Hawk and Nora eyeballed the surrounding landscape hoping to see Mortimer wandering about, perhaps taking in the tranquil nature. Suddenly, the calm was interrupted by the shrill voice of Cynthia from inside the house as she berated poor Sam. Obviously, she didn't appreciate him leaving her alone with the overbearing detective.

Gazing at each other with amusement on their faces, Nora asked Hawk where Mortimer was.

"I'm not sure. I thought he went to the Tahoe."

"No. I walked by and didn't see him there. Where could he be? Surely, he didn't go into the house. Cynthia would've kicked him out faster than my uncle's mule when that nasty animal was upset. Besides, I think that Mortimer is a little afraid of her."

Hawk remembered seeing Mortimer's head bobbing up and down, fighting sleep. "You worry too much. I bet he's in the vehicle taking a snooze. I don't know how much of that Dramamine he took, but I bet it was too much."

They approached the SUV and after looking in the back seat, they saw Mortimer crunched up in a fetal position. Hawk chuckled. "See, I told you so." Once they opened the doors to the vehicle, they smelled the unpleasant air of someone giving off gas. Nora fanned herself with her hand and both she and Hawk left the doors open for a minute to air out the vehicle. They laughed silently, looking at each other. Suddenly, they heard a loud snore, then a whistle, followed by another, then another. Neither Hawk nor Nora could hold in their laughter. Mortimer wasn't awakened by the laughter as he proceeded with his snoring, only changing the pattern from a cannon to machine gun fire.

Still laughing, Hawk and Nora slid into the vehicle. Hawk drove down the steep hill to the street and stopped. He looked at Nora. "I'm going to call Perez about a warrant."

“A warrant? What did you discover that would give us probable cause?”

Hawk told Nora what he saw parked in the garage and the shooting range while walking with Sam. Nora’s eyebrows rose almost to her hairline. *How does he do it? He’s so darn lucky. Here, I struggle with that bitch while possible evidence just seems to fall into his hands.* “I think you may have enough, especially with the strong motive for taking James out. Sure, let’s go for a warrant, although a judge may disagree.”

Hawk grabbed his phone and punched in the number. “Lieutenant, we’re still in Vail, and we believe that we have something here. How soon can you get a warrant to search the Maxwell property?”

“Really? What’cha got?”

Hawk told him about the Nissan that matched the possible description of the shooter’s car that a witness had described to Detectives Salazar and Ling. Hawk further reported on the shooting range with shell casings of various calibers strewn about and the earthen embankment that most likely had slugs embedded in it. He also informed Perez about the New Balance sneakers stained with mud that might match the imprints they found on the ground and the back door of the law office.

“It’s a long shot, but if we search for slugs in the embankment and the casings on the ground, we might get lucky and find one that’ll match the ones used on James and Kay Hollister. If we surprise them now, we might even find the weapon used in the slayings. Lieutenant, I think that they’ll spill the beans if we pressure them a bit in interrogation. Not sure, though, about Cynthia, but I believe that Sam would sing like a bird.”

Perez asked, “If I can get the warrant, and that’s a big if, how do you propose that I get it to you? It’ll take at least three hours for the warrant and the time to send it over with a couple of officers.

Nora said, “The local sheriff would surely cooperate, maybe even send a couple of deputies to help us search the place. We should go over and ask for his help, and you can fax the warrant to his office.”

Hawk said, “That’s a great idea. That way, we won’t be stepping on his turf. I’ll call Chet Watkins to see if he made any progress on the sneaker footprints. If he did, it’d help us compare with the ones I saw in the Hollister’s mudroom.”

“All right, then,” Perez said. “Let me know what the sheriff says. By the way, what’s that awful noise I’ve been hearing in the background? Sounds like a battle.”

Hawk and Nora let out a boisterous laugh. Nora said, “That’s our friend, Mortimer, sleeping off Dramamine. He got pretty car sick on the way here and must’ve taken too many pills.”

“Oh, God! There’s always something with Holliday.”

After Hawk clicked off, he called CSI Watkins. Chet said, “Yeah, I haven’t had time to send you a report on those shoes, but I did some research, and I was right. The sole is from an older model New Balance. It’s fairly old and worn. I can tell you that whoever wore them favored the inside of the foot. In other words, more of the sole is worn on the inside than the outside. If you look at the shoe, you could tell that the shoe leans to the inside. There also seems to be a small pebble or something like that embedded deep in one of the grooves.”

Nora asked, “Any way you could finish up the report and email it to me? We’re waiting for a warrant to search and if we could have something in writing, it’ll be easier to match the shoes or collect them for evaluation.”

“Nora, I’m totally swamped here. But just because it’s you, I’ll bust my ass and get you something in an hour. Just add that to all you owe me.”

Nora laughed. “Thanks, Chet. You’re the greatest. And the best.”

Hawk shifted into “drive,” and as the vehicle began to move, he suggested that they head for the Sheriff’s office. He looked at the back seat. "Do you think we should wake up the sleeping beauty and fill him in on what's going on?"

"Sure." Nora turned toward the back seat and gently shook Mortimer's shoulder as she said, "Mortimer, wake up. Wake up, Mortimer!"

The man yawned, then looked around, not knowing where he was for an instant. Then realizing that Nora was gazing at him, he sprung up. "Oh, oh. I'm sorry. I must've fallen asleep. Are you finished with the Hollisters'? Are we going back now?"

Hawk said, "No. We're on our way to the Eagle County Sheriff's Office." Mortimer looked perplexed, so Hawk filled him in on what he observed and the request for a warrant."

"Oh. That sounds good. Maybe we can have lunch soon. For some reason, I'm really hungry. It is on the expense account, right?"

Nora said, "Maybe we should get a quick bite to eat before we see the sheriff."

"I'd rather contact the office first to make sure that they watch their fax machine for a warrant," Hawk said. "I hate to be eating when it comes in, and they don't know what to do with it. Some idiot may even throw it away. Might also see if the sheriff is in to tell him what we're up to. Okay?"

"Good idea. I'll google it to see where the office is." She looked it up and frowned. "The sheriff's office is in Eagle, thirty miles away."

Hawk suggested, "See if there's a substation in Vail."

Nora's eyes fell back to her phone. A couple of seconds later, she said, "Yup. There's one. Good. It's on Eagle Road. I'll have *Maps* direct us."

"So, can we eat first?" Mortimer insisted.

"I don't think you should be eating much," Nora said. "We still have to drive back through curvy mountain passes."

"I think I'll be all right. If necessary, I'll just pop in another pill." He paused. "But if you think you need to go to the sheriff's office first, I can wait."

CHAPTER 42

THE SHERIFF just happened to be at the substation. He was a tall, slim, and handsome man in his late forties with a full head of neatly combed salt and pepper hair. His freshly pressed uniform fit him like a glove. The four stars on his collar and the badge on his chest shone brightly under the fluorescent lights as he gave them a toothy smile. He introduced himself as Albert Paxton, his white teeth sparkling in contrast to his dark olive complexion.

After presenting him with their credentials, the three Denver detectives explained the purpose of their visit and asked for his assistance since they assumed that it was the sheriff and not the local Vail police that had the jurisdiction out in the county.

Paxton was pleased to oblige them, indicating that the Hollister property was indeed outside the limits of Vail. He indicated to the detectives that his office would watch for the warrant and call them when it came in. Paxton also assigned two deputies to accompany the detectives to the property and help with the search. Hawk noticed that while he spoke to them, his eyes seemed to wander constantly to Nora. Clint did not blame him. She was certainly pleasing to look at, but he did not like what he thought were her overly friendly smiles at the Sheriff.

"Well, if that's all you need from me," Paxton said, "I need to go to the substation in Edwards right now. Here is my card. Call me if there's anything else I can do." He gave the card to Nora. Focusing on her as he repeated, "Anything at all. I'll be available." In return, Nora thanked him and handed him her card. Hawk sucked in a deep breath. He saw the flirt for what he was and suddenly didn't like the guy—more than pleased when Paxton left.

"He certainly seemed friendly," Nora said as the three detectives walked out of the building.

"A little too friendly with you, Nora. And you relished his attention."

"Whoa, there, partner. Are you jealous or something?" She laughed, slapping Hawk on his arm.

Hawk did not respond. "Let's go eat. Mortimer, are you ready?"

Mortimer seemed to be in a daze. His eyes seemed to be focused on the mountain to the west. Then he suddenly came to but seemed to lose sight of where he was at the moment. "Mortimer," Hawk repeated. "Are you ready to eat?"

Mortimer shook his head rapidly back and forth as though he needed to clear his brain. "Did you say something, Clint?"

"Yes. Let's go get some lunch."

"That would be good. Sorry that I didn't hear you, but I've been admiring that mountain with the ski runs and thought how nice it would've been if I had been a different person. Wouldn't it be something to escape to the mountains and ski all day long in winter and climb every mountain during the summer? But then, I'm not that person. Even in Florida, with all the water around it, I dunked myself into the ocean only a few times in my life. I didn't like the feeling of not seeing what was under and around me or what could bite me, or I'd step on a barb of a stingray or get stung by a jellyfish." Clint and Nora exchanged glances in bafflement. Nora felt sorry for Mortimer. It was apparent that he had personal issues all his life.

Hawk said, "We all can't be the same. We all can't be skiers or surfers, can we?" Mortimer nodded in silence, his face looking more sad than usual.

They settled on the Little Diner for lunch. Nora chose the place because she called it a "cute café with an inviting red door." Mortimer carefully studied the breakfast and lunch menu and asked Hawk how much he was allowed to spend. Hawk told him to pick any one item. When the pleasant young waitress walked over, they ordered drinks and asked if they could order the meal right away. Nora took a ham, tomato, and cheese crepe, Hawk took the

Pannekoeken or the German pancake, while Mortimer ordered a bacon cheeseburger and asked for extra bacon.

When the food came, they were stunned by Hawk's large pancake, at least two inches high. "That looks so good," Mortimer said. "I need to tell Josephine about it. Maybe she can look up how to make one. Of course, it'll have to be a vegan one."

Nora laughed, holding her fork in the air with a chunk of crepe on it. "I don't think it'll taste quite the same if you have no eggs in it."

Hawk offered the other two detectives a piece of his pancake. Mortimer quickly took him up on his offer, and Nora tasted a small piece of it. They agreed that it was delicious. As they were halfway into their meals, Nora's phone rang. It was Sheriff Paxton. "Hello, Detective. May I call you Nora?"

"Yes, certainly. What's up?"

"Just heard from the office in Vail. Looks like you got your warrant. My men are ready to proceed."

"Give us another fifteen minutes, and we'll be at the substation."

"Too bad that I won't be able to assist you. But remember, if there's anything I can do, please call me. Perhaps sometime when I'm in Denver, we could have coffee together."

"That sounds fine. Thanks for your help, Sheriff."

"Oh, call me Al."

Nora had a smile on her face because she knew that Clint was boiling inside. *Good. He'll appreciate me more.*

"Why did you agree to have coffee with the lecher?"

"Clint, it was just a friendly thing to do, especially since we want no trouble out of him in his jurisdiction."

"Oh. Did I miss something? Is something wrong?"

Both Clint and Nora answered almost in unison, "No, nothing is wrong."

Hawk continued, "Nora seems to have an admirer here in Vail."

Mortimer surprised them by saying, "Oh. I bet she has several all over." Hawk arched his eyebrows as he glanced at Nora. *She does look great. I really don't blame the Sheriff.*

Nora seemed to read his thoughts. Smiling sweetly, she mouthed a kiss in his direction. They both laughed.

"Oh. Was there a joke I missed?" Mortimer asked, perplexed.

"No, Mortimer," Hawk said. "Nora just made a funny face, that's all."

The deputies assigned to help them search the Hollister property were as opposite as they could be. Jack Trimble was in his forties with a huge beer belly. His uniform was too tight and generally looked sloppy, but Nora thought that he tried to compensate for his soft appearance by appearing hardnosed with a scowl on his face. The other deputy was Todd Garcia, a thin, short man with a friendly smile. Exuding a high level of energy, he seemed excited to accompany the Denver detectives. Hawk asked that they bring their metal detector, and once the deputies left the building and got into their Ford Interceptor, Hawk followed them to the Hollister house.

"The Hollisters are in for a big surprise," Hawk told Nora and Mortimer.

"Oh. Do you think they'll give us trouble?" Mortimer asked. He began to sneeze, followed by a couple of coughs.

CHAPTER 43

THE GATE was locked. Hawk pressed the button, and a few minutes later, Cynthia's voice came over the intercom, "What in the hell do you want now? Get off our property. I'm not opening the gate, so skedaddle and take all those people with you."

Hawk said, "Mrs. Hollister, you must open the gate if you want to keep it in one piece. We have a warrant to search your property."

"The hell you do. Now get out. You're on our property, and if you try to get past that gate, you'll be shot." Upon hearing that, Mortimer quietly slid back.

Hawk said, "That's not smart of you at all. There are five of us with official warrants, and two are Eagle County deputy sheriffs. You do not want them to arrest you for trying to shoot police officers."

They heard Cynthia shout at Sam to get his assault rifle. "And bring me mine."

Nora said, "Mrs. Hollister, please be reasonable. The next group of people here will be a SWAT team. Do you really want that? Please open the gate and let us in so we can do our job. I know that losing your father and your brother is very stressful for you, but we must clear you of any suspicion of their murders. Once we look at a few things and find nothing, then we'll be out of your hair."

After a minute of silence, Cynthia mouthed, "Hell, I guess you can't fight the freakin' government. All right. I'll open the gate but do your thing fast and be out of our lives." The intercom was still on when they heard Cynthia tell Sam to put the gun down. "The bitch is right. They'll have SWAT destroying our house."

The gate swung open, and the two vehicles began their steep climb up to the house.

Cynthia and Sam Hollister stood with arms crossed over their chests at the front door. They tried to look tough, but their hands trembled. Cynthia asked, anger washing over her ruddy face, "Show me that damn warrant." After Hawk handed them a copy, she and Sam studied it. "I don't know if it's legal or not. We need to call our attorney. What are you looking for anyway?"

Hawk said, "You're welcome to call your attorney, but we'll proceed anyway. We'll let you know if we find what we're looking for. In the meantime, please stay in your dining room until we finish. It shouldn't take long. To save time, tell us where you keep your weapons. I see two AR-15s on the table, which we need to remove for the time being for our protection and yours. But where do you keep the rest?" As he waited for an answer, Todd Garcia took the weapons off the table and took them to his vehicle.

Reluctantly, Sam said, "I have a gun safe in the basement."

"What's the combination to the lock?"

He gave them the numbers. Hawk asked, "Where else? Any in your bedroom?"

Cynthia and Sam exchanged looks. Cynthia said, "Of course. I got a Colt 1911 pistol, a 45 caliber, in my nightstand drawer. I'll get it for you...I don't want you trampling around in our room. Stay out of there."

Nora said, "Sorry, Cynthia. That won't work. We'll have to check it out. Do you have any other weapons in that room?"

"No."

Mortimer said, "You also have a 9mm in that room, don't you?"

Cynthia's face turned red, her hands still shaking, "No, no, no. I told you that I didn't have any more guns in our bedroom."

"Your body language is giving you away," Mortimer quickly responded. "You're lying to us, and that's the room we should search first."

Cynthia rose quickly, forcing Mortimer to take two steps back. "Are you calling me a liar?"

"Yes, ma'am, I am, indeed. I know when people lie to me. So where in that room do you keep any other weapons?"

"I told you that I don't have any more weapons in the room, you moron. Stay out of our bedroom. I'm warning you."

Hawk said to Cynthia, "Please sit down, Mrs. Hollister. We'll try to be careful with your belongings, but we must do our search." Cynthia sat down in a huff. Her lips were squeezed together, breathing hard like a bull ready to charge.

He addressed Mortimer, "Stay with the Hollisters and entertain them while we search the house."

Mortimer looked petrified. He asked if he could talk to Hawk in private. After they stepped outside for a minute, Mortimer said, "Ah, I don't know how to entertain. I can't sing or tell jokes. Besides, she is very volatile. Perhaps one of the deputies could do that."

Hawk suppressed a laugh. "No, Mortimer, that's just a figure of speech. Just sit down with them and make sure they don't leave the room. And remember anything that they say to each other."

Mortimer went back into the room. Sam appeared as though he was ready to cry while Cynthia threw daggers with her eyes. Feeling extremely uncomfortable with the situation, Mortimer said, "I'm going to sit here with you, and I'd appreciate it if you do not address me unless, of course, you want to confess."

"Confess? To what? You know, you're as crazy as a loon."

"I've been told that, but it no longer bothers me." After that, the Hollisters sat silently while Mortimer turned his chair slightly to the side so that he didn't have to be subjected to their hateful stares.

Nora and Hawk agreed that she and Todd would search the house while Clint and Jack would search the garage, the shed, and the shooting range. Nora and Todd made their way to the upstairs bedrooms. They found the master and began their search. On each nightstand, they found a weapon in the drawer. On what appeared to be Sam's side of the bed, the weapon was a Colt 45 revolver, while on Cynthia's side, it was a Smith and Wesson M+P 9 Shield EZ. "Hey, it's a 9mm. Let's bag this one, Todd."

Todd asked, "Do you think this 9mm could be the murder weapon?"

"Possibly. It would be a lucky break if it were." Nora then began to search the huge closet. "This closet is bigger than half of my house," Nora mumbled. "But it doesn't seem large enough for them. All the rods are bulging with clothes." She wasn't sure if Todd heard her or not since he was searching the dresser in the bedroom. Nora took out several tops and laid them on the bed. She slid the remaining clothes aside from rod to rod. She knew from experience with her parents that they hid valuables behind the clothing. Her father even made a secret compartment in the wall.

With the flashlight on her phone, she shone the light onto the wall. At first glance, she didn't see anything unusual. Then when the light fell onto the baseboard, she noticed some plaster powder at the very edge where the thick carpet met the baseboard. From that spot, she carefully examined the wall, running her fingers up and down, feeling the texture. Upon looking closer, she noticed that a rectangular piece of the drywall was thinly and neatly sawed about chest high from the floor. She grabbed the nail file out of her purse, came back into the closet and nudged it into the almost unnoticeable narrow crack. With the file, she pried the cutout piece of sheetrock out and, with amazement, looked into the opening. *Oh my God! I can't believe this! What luck!*

Hidden in the cache was a pistol. Excitedly, she called for Todd to come and look. After taking a photo of the inside of the closet, then of the opening in the wall, Nora removed the weapon that was propped up vertically against a stud. Lying next to the gun was a small cloth bag. Inside were gold coins. As both she and Todd gazed at the gun and the gold in amazement, Todd blew out a whistle. "Wow. This is the most exciting thing that happened to me today, maybe the whole month," he almost sang the words.

"Let's have another evidence bag," Nora said as her nitrile-gloved hand extracted a Sig Sauer 9mm from the cache. "I bet you a dozen donuts that this is the murder weapon. Why else would they be so careful hiding it? But then, if it is the murder weapon, why did they even bring it into the house and not dispose of it somewhere?"

"People do strange things," Todd Garcia said. "What about this sack of gold?"

"We'll leave the gold where we found it. Let's go down and confront the Hollisters now. Well, maybe I should tell Hawk about the find first."

CHAPTER 44

MORTIMER RUBBED his eyes with his left hand, sensing that Cynthia's evil eyes were still drilling into him. Still turned away from the table, he didn't want to have any kind of unpleasant confrontation now that he was alone with them. *Why am I this way? Josephine tells me all the time I need to be more aggressive, more assertive in my work. She's right. I'm a third wheel to Clint and Nora. I'm not needed. I don't produce anything. I just exist. I wasn't that way in Tampa. I was my own man. I was respected for the difficult crimes I solved. Here, I'm afraid to step on anyone's toes. I take a backseat to everyone. Well, dog-gone-it, I need to do something constructive for a change if they keep me in the Denver Police Department.*

He turned toward the couple across from him. With his typical grim face and piercing gray eyes, he stared back at them. They immediately lowered their heads. He studied them for the first time that day. *They're scared. They're nervous as hell. They feel an impending doom that will befall them, so they act out—angry, irritable, and argumentative. They're feeling on edge. I can see their rapid breathing, their chests heaving. They're sweating, and their hands tremble. Now is the time to force them to confess.*

Cynthia and Sam were startled when Mortimer spoke up after many minutes of silence. "You people are guilty as sin. And you know it. You're tired of the guilt. From fear and lack of sleep, the devastating nightmares ever since you killed your father and your brother and his wife."

Cynthia was about to open her mouth, the veins on her temple about to pop, when Mortimer raised his voice, "Keep quiet! Listen to me. I don't want a word out of you unless I ask! I am recording our conversation."

Cynthia closed her mouth. Sam sunk lower in the chair. His face was as white as snow on the tall peaks visible out of their huge windows.

"Now I know what will ease the fire that is destroying you on the inside. The fire that will consume you unless you put it out. The only way would be to set yourself free of the burn within you is to come clean and tell me what you did. You must lift the burden that is devouring you. I can see your pain in your faces, in your bodies."

At that moment, Hawk and the deputy entered the house, and as if planned, Nora and Todd met them as they came downstairs. All four wound up in the family and heard Mortimer's voice. Nora and Clint had never heard Mortimer speak like that. Hawk lifted his arm to stop them from going any further. Standing there quietly, they listened.

"You're full of shit with your hokey accusations," Cynthia shouted back. She laughed mockingly. "We feel no guilt since we did nothing wrong. We certainly didn't kill our father." Her voice dropped off a bit when she added, "And we had nothing to do with James's and Kay's murders either."

Mortimer continued, "We know you did, and so do you. That's why you've been sitting across from me, breathing so hard that I can hear your hearts pounding in your chests. Why are you trembling, Sam? It's fear knowing what consequences you face." Sam dropped his head, his fingers tied into knots, squeezed together.

"Now, I'm going to do you the favor of making you feel better by admitting to me exactly what you did. You can't lie to me. I know when people lie. That's why I'm so successful. Before you admit your wrongs and lift the burden off your conscience, I need to advise you of your right to remain silent because anything you say could be used against you. In your case, the silence would defeat the purpose of making it easier on yourselves both health-wise and maybe getting a break from the DA. You also have the right to an attorney, and if you can't afford one, the court will appoint one for you. Do you understand those rights?"

Cynthia gave out a hysterical laugh. "Do you think we're idiots? That we'll be taken in by the bullshit that you've thrown around? You have nothing on us. You can't prove a damn thing. So why don't you shut up, and all of you get out of our house."

Mortimer asked, "Then you waive your right to an attorney, and I can proceed with my questions?'

Cynthia laughed again, but her voice trembled as she said, "I do want an attorney, and I'm not answering any question. You think that we are idiots, don't you?" Her eyes blazed with venom.

"Actually, ma'am, to answer your question. Most criminals are idiots; otherwise, they wouldn't be in the position you're in with the prospect of spending the rest of your lives in a penitentiary. You should understand that most times, people who cooperate and come clean get a better deal from the DA and the judge. So, it would behoove you to tell me now before they find more evidence against you."

"They won't find a damn thing, you ugly smartass."

Sam said, his head bowed low, "I'm sorry, Cynthia. But I don't want a lawyer. I'm going to tell them."

Cynthia shot out of her chair, stood over Sam, and whacked her husband across the head. Sam cried out, "That's it! I can't take your abuse any longer." Sam slid his chair to the side and, with a desperate look, said, "The Detective is right. I can't carry the guilt and shame any longer. I must get it off my chest."

"Shut up, you idiot! Cynthia was about to belt Sam again when Mortimer's tall, lanky body stood up, and his chest expanded as he fiercely growled at the raging woman to sit back down. She did in a huff, her red face seemingly on the verge of exploding. He looked back at Sam and said, "Go on, please."

Sam hesitated. Mortimer sat silently, his stern face and piercing eyes fixed on Sam.

"Don't you say anything," Cynthia hollered. "I'm warning you!"

With his head still down and drooping off his neck, he avoided Cynthia's shooting eyes. Addressing his wife, he said with bravado, "You're the one that made me break into the lawyer's office and steal the will. Told you it was a horrible idea. Then later, you insisted on taking a drive into downtown Denver. I begged you to leave James alone, but you had to talk to him." He glanced at Cynthia. "How can you convince anyone of anything if you immediately start calling him a thief? Why would he listen to you when you threatened him and Kay and yelled out that they'll be mighty sorry? Why would they want to share their inheritance with all of us? We never gave them the time of day. I know you carry a gun in your purse, and who knows what you'll do."

Sam turned his attention back to Mortimer. "That's why, Detective, I gunned the engine on my son's car and took off before anything bad happened. And just as I did that, we heard gunshots. Without stopping or looking back, we took off so that no one could blame the shots on us. That's the gospel truth, Detective."

"Are you happy now, you moron? You're crazy. Why are you making up a tall tale? We never broke into the lawyer's office, nor were we at the scene of James' death."

"No, Cynthia. For once, I'm going to stand up to you and say it like it is. The guilt is killing me from the inside, just as the Detective said. I've never broken into anyone's property, and I need to clear my conscience."

She screeched at Mortimer, "You can't believe a word he says. He has a problem with reality. He's delusional. You have no evidence at all to substantiate what my crazy husband made up. He lives in a fantasy world easily influenced as he was influenced by your stupid and pathetic words."

Hawk and Nora stood still as statues, mesmerized by Mortimer's questions and the responses he elicited, especially from

Sam. Hawk whispered to Nora, now is the time to show them the evidence."

They left the deputies in the family room and boldly strode into the dining room. Cynthia's eyes bulged out at seeing what they carried in transparent plastic bags. One of the bags contained Sam's old New Balance sneakers. Hawk said, "Mortimer, this will help with your interrogation. Detective Ricci found a 9mm pistol on the nightstand and another in a hidden compartment behind the clothes in the closet. We believe that one of them is probably the murder weapon. And deputy Trimble and I recovered several 9mm slugs from the embankment of the shooting range. I bet that some of the slugs will match the striations of the ones used in the murders."

She rose quickly from behind the table, "You people are as insane as my freakin' husband. That hidden gun belongs to our son, and he asked us to keep it safe and out of sight while he's deployed. I can't believe you found it. We never killed anyone, and you'll find out after you test those weapons. Now take the damn weapons and get out," her fingers balled into a fist as though ready to punch someone in the gut.

"Sit down!" Mortimer ordered Cynthia. She opened her mouth, took a deep breath and slowly complied. Sam sat silently, his eyes closed, his right hand squeezing his forehead. The three detectives let Cynthia and Sam sit for a few moments before Hawk asked Mortimer to do the honors and arrest them for breaking and entering the Windsor offices for now.

"Wait," Nora said. "We have no jurisdiction over the break-in. That's Golden's turf. Let me call that detective and see what she wants to do?"

"Damn, I got wrapped up in the moment and forgot. Yeah, do it."

Nora went outside and made the call. After fifteen minutes, she came back in, "They'd like the sheriff to hold them until a couple of officers drive up and pick them up."

Deputy Garcia was happy to comply and quickly handcuffed the couple. Mortimer said, "We'll see what these weapons and slugs turn up. You may be charged with murder yet."

"No way," said Sam. "We didn't kill anyone."

As they were being escorted to the deputies' vehicle, Cynthia looked absolutely miserable. Her head and shoulders slumped, and tears streamed down her cheeks. She glanced at Nora and said in a trembling voice, "We had nothing to do with James, Kay or Dad's death. You won't have any proof of that because we didn't do it."

"We'll see, Mrs. Hollister," Nora answered. She suddenly felt a tinge of pity for the belligerent woman. As they sat in the back of one of the sheriff's vehicles, Nora informed the Hollisters that they'd secure the property and set the alarm. She also asked if there was someone that could take care of the place. They uncuffed Sam long enough for him to call their daughter. While he made the call, Nora kindly thanked the deputies for their help and for securing the Hollisters until such time that the Golden officers arrived.

CHAPTER 45

THE THREE detectives followed the Vail Sheriff's cruiser down the steep hill and out the gate. Ten minutes later, Nora and Hawk sighed with relief as they finally entered I-70 and were on the way back to the station.

Viewing the backseat passenger in the rearview mirror, Hawk said, "Mortimer, I'm proud of you. Good job with those people. Whatever made you decide to interrogate them?"

"Oh, I got tired of just sitting and trying to avoid Cynthia's nasty looks. I decided that enough is enough, that I'm a detective after all, and I need to get more involved with the cases we work on together. At least that's what Josephine says I should do. So, I stared hard at the couple and began the usual speech that I'd successfully used many times in Tampa. I saw people who were not typical criminals but might've been desperate enough to commit criminal acts. I played on their guilt and how hard it was on their health. This time I got lucky. But only because Sam was the weak link. Actually, I feel sorry for him. His wife rules with an iron fist, and he does everything she wants…." Mortimer paused, falling deep in thought. "I suppose I know how that feels."

"What do you mean by that?" Nora asked.

"Oh. Nothing, I guess. I was just thinking that Josephine is also a little bossy. Anyway, I don't want to talk about it. I will tell her about what we did and about the beautiful rock formations and the scented pines that I saw today. The air was spectacular, maybe even a little intoxicating, whatever that meant, because I'd never been drunk in my life. The mountain air certainly made me sleepy. That and the pills knocked me out, and for that, I apologize." He paused again. "Uh, oh. I forgot about the sharp curves in the road. Hmm, hopefully, I won't get car sick again. But I still have some of those pills left if I need them. But boy, did they ever knock me out."

Nora laughed, "You were sure out for a while."

"I guess that's funny."

"Mortimer, I have never heard you laugh," Nora said. "Do you ever? Surely you and Josephine sit around and laugh at movies or shows?"

"No. Josephine and I don't find anything to laugh about. I remember laughing when I was a teenager. But somehow, I just don't do it. I had a pretty rough time as a teenager. Always bullied. Now, I really don't find anything to laugh about."

"That's sad," Hawk said. "Laughter is good for your health."

"Oh. I'll tell Josephine that. Although, I think she laughs, but not when I'm around."

Nora and Clint exchanged glances. Hawk shrugged.

Nora asked, "What do you gentlemen think about Cynthia and Sam denying that they killed anyone? Do you think they're telling the truth?" She didn't let them answer but continued talking. "Hopefully, the pistols and the slugs we found will prove that they were the killers, at least as far as James and Kay. We really don't have any definitive evidence that they caused William's death. Actually, unless they admit that they did it, we really have no clue as to who did it. They are the most logical choice since Sam already confessed to burglary. And I bet it was at the direction of Cynthia. Why stop with one crime?"

Hawk said, "All the heirs have a strong motive to get rid of William and then, once the contents of the will were known, to eliminate James. Any one of them could've switched the meds or pulled the trigger. But you must be a great shot to put a bullet in the head of James and another in Kay's heart. As far as I can see, only Cynthia, maybe Sam, fits the bill."

Mortimer groaned, "I think I'm getting sick again. I better take a couple of these Dramamines." He popped them into his wide mouth and washed them down with a gulp of water. Wiping his thin lips with his sleeve, he continued, "I don't think that Cynthia or Sam killed the father. Most likely killed James and Kay, though. My money is on George for William's death."

Hawk asked, "Why?"

"I don't trust him as far as I can throw him. Didn't you say, Clint, that his wife had such a headache that she had to take an aspirin? And George admitted that she took it right in the bathroom with the father's pills right there out in the open. We found their fingerprints on the small paper cup. She had the aspirin out, and it was easy to switch the meds…whoa, Clint, pull over. I got a problem."

Hawk quickly pulled over to the narrow shoulder, and Mortimer barely had time to force the door open and retch. Nora crinkled her nose and turned her face away from the pungent smell as the door remained open for a couple of minutes. When Mortimer sat back and threw his head back against the headrest, Nora offered him another bottle of water. With labored breathing, he gulped it down.

A few miles down the road, Hawk and Nora heard him snoring. "Poor guy," Nora said. "Okay, Clint, what do you think? Did Cynthia and Sam switch the meds?"

"That's a tough one, Nora. I don't even have a hunch as to who did it. Everything leads to Cynthia and Sam at the moment. Maybe, Sam will admit to it. I don't think Cynthia would ever. I hope that our friend in the back advised them of their Miranda rights before eliciting a good confession out of Sam."

"He told me he did," Nora said. "He said it's all recorded."

"Hopefully, he knew how. I recorded part of the interrogation as soon as we sat down in the family room. At least we'll have that part as a backup. Mortimer has to transcript the confession and sends it over to Laura so that she can charge them with breaking and entering. After that, we need to get the couple back to our station for further interrogation. I'll talk to her about it."

"Oh, Laura, is it now? I BET you'd like to talk to her. That red-haired Golden detective certainly had her eyes on you, and you loved the attention."

"Come on, Nora. This is ridiculous. I see her only as a fellow detective." Nora playfully stuck her tongue out at him.

They were startled by Hawk's phone as it played *Bad to the Bone*. Hawk handed it to Nora as he maneuvered the Tahoe around a hairpin curve. Nora said, "It's a Denver number, but it doesn't show the name."

"Put it on speaker."

"Hello, is this Detective Hawk?" The pleasant voice sounded familiar to both Clint and Nora.

"Yes. What can I do for you?"

In a soft, pleasant tone, the woman said, "Detective, you should remember the sound of my voice by now. This is Tina Dionisio." Nora tensed up. She hated the woman.

"Hello, Tina. I haven't been able to call you back yet about the Hollister case. Do you still think that you could help us with it?"

"Well, if you come over to my condo tonight, I have, indeed, something important to tell you. Something that will solve the case for you."

"Okay. My partner and I will be there. Just name the time."

"Your partner. No. I specifically told you before that you must come alone."

"In that case, I won't come to your condo, but we could meet for coffee."

"How about dinner then? I know this great Italian restaurant in the Highlands area that you'll love."

Nora's mouth scrunched up; her breathing became hard.

"What's that snoring I hear in the background?" Tina asked, chuckling. "That isn't your partner sleeping on the job, is it?" Nora was ready to explode.

"Oh no, not at all. It's someone else. Listen, Tina, we need to keep this professional. If you really have something for me, I'll meet you for a cup of coffee at Starbucks on the Sixteenth Street Mall at six. It's walking distance from your Condo. Will you be there?"

She hesitated. "All right. If that's how you want to play. But I'm not going to give up on you, and we'll have that romantic dinner together sooner than later."

Nora felt that her veins were about to burst. She wanted to throw the phone out of the window. It took all the restraint she could muster to keep silent and not yell at that woman. *I can't believe what I'm hearing. She's trying to steal Clint from me, that bitch! She's doing it on purpose because she knows that I hate her and knows that I'm listening. And Clint is loving every minute of it, I'm sure.*

Hawk said, "Tina, I'm flattered, but you should realize that I am in a relationship that I'm very happy with." Still breathing hard, Nora's frown now turned into a toothy smile as she gazed at Clint.

Tina said, "Oh, that's all right. I thought that you and that Italian detective were pretty chummy with each other. I'm patient and will wait for you to come around. I can size up a man quickly, and I know you're not the marrying type. You'll be looking for someone new soon enough." Nora's smile disappeared; her heart resumed to pound.

Hawk replied, "Tina, we're really off the tracks here. Do you or do you not know something that can help us in the William Hollister murder? For example, did you actually see someone that switched the medications? I don't want to waste my time." Nora could see that Clint was getting angry with the woman, which pleased her.

Tina heard the irritation in his voice and realized that she needed to take another approach. "Look, Detective, of course, you understand that I'm teasing you? I really do know something, but I don't want to go to your station. If you like, you can bring your girlfriend with you. But, please, do not bring that tall, weird man that calls himself a detective. I can't stand to look at him. I thought that he was rude and insensitive, and I didn't want to face him again. If he comes, I won't tell you a thing."

Hawk said, "Fine. Detective Ricci and I will see you at Starbucks at six."

Hawk gazed at wide-eyed Nora, her face serious. "I don't like that woman. Maybe, I shouldn't go with you because one more pass or flirt at you, and I don't know if I'd be able to keep my temper."

Hawk laughed. "Nora, you're just too jealous. You heard her. She was playing games with me and actually with you, that's all. Don't you know that I'm not rich enough for her? She goes after money."

"I'm not sure about that at all, Clint. She's trying to reel you in. A game? Maybe. She might want to win you over, make you fall deeply in love with her, then drop you like a hot potato, just for the fun of it."

Hawk laughed. "I'm not that naive. I survived worse." He laughed again and enjoyed the attention from Nora.

Nora didn't laugh. "Oh, you think so, do you? All men are naïve most of the time. All she has to do is strut her sexy body, and you'll be hot to trot. So, watch out for her." Nora looked back at the snoring Mortimer. "I'm glad he's sound asleep. She wasn't too complimentary to him, was she?"

A minute later, both Nora and Clint received a text from Captain MacGregor. "Finn O'Leary escaped while being transported. Head straight to the station. Now!"

CHAPTER 46

REVENGE CONSUMED Finn O'Leary. He craved the satisfaction of killing Clint Hawk and Nora Ricci. The thought that they were only doing their jobs and had nothing personal against him never crossed his mind. His obsession was to escape and make sure that he eliminated those two detectives.

While he sat in a Denver cell, O'Leary had plenty of time to think and agonize over how he, a clever man, let his guard down to such an extent that two insignificant, piddly detectives from Colorado managed to outsmart, outmaneuver, and take him down. How did they manage to be one step ahead of him? Afterall, he outwitted the best at Interpol, Europol, Scotland Yard, NYPD, Boston police, and even the FBI. What happened to his talent and savvy to get away without a trace, with everyone clueless as to who he was? He was smart enough to arrive in this country illegally with the ability to lose himself in the general population. *How in the hell did the bastards, Hawk and Ricci, find out who I am? And that I was after them? It doesn't matter. I'll break out, and they won't be around much longer.*

He could not get over his mistakes, dwelling on them. *How could I have been so dumb? But the stupidest one is that rookie detective for not shooting me when he had a chance. What a fool he is! He thought he could wrestle me into submission, but I easily overpowered the bastard. I almost put his lights out if it hadn't been that freakin', fierce Ricci woman with her powerful kicks. Boy, I'd like to kick her around for a while after I have my way with her.* O'Leary laughed out loud, yet no one heard or paid attention to him alone in his noisy jail cell. Over and over, he pondered and focused on the mistakes he made. He regretted playing mind games. His biggest mistake was that he did not shoot them the many times that he had a clear, unobstructed shot. He could have been long gone, out of the state and on his way to Brazil. *But that's okay. No more cat-and-mouse games this time. Soon, I'll be out. It'll be fast with a quick shot to the head.*

From the moment O'Leary was arrested by Nora and transported from her house to the Denver City Jail, his mind laboriously worked on how to get out. Prepared for any opportunity to escape, O'Leary saw a chance during booking. His sharp, perceptive coal-black eyes spotted a large paperclip on the floor, mostly hidden from view by the lip of a cabinet. After his mugshot was taken, he pretended to trip over his own feet and fell conveniently close to the paperclip. He quickly snatched the object and slid it into his mouth. After the guards thoroughly searched him, he slipped the paperclip into a rubber-soled shoe issued to him, along with socks, orange pants and an orange shirt.

A day later, O'Leary's demand to his public defender attorney to schedule a special bail hearing paid off. With a smirk on his arrogant face, he climbed into the jail van for transport to the Judicial Center. This was his first opportunity to break out. He sized up both armed Denver sheriff's deputies as one shoved him into the Chevrolet van. A metal cage surrounded the interior passenger compartment of the van. The two deputies, one overweight and unenergetic, the other small, wiry, and slight of build, sat in the front, whereas he sat next to the sliding door. The deputies felt safe with O'Leary in the back cage. After all, his hands were cuffed on his front-facing wrists, shackles on his ankles.

As soon as the van left the garage, O'Leary went to work. With both hands cuffed, he leaned down and retrieved from his sock two stiff, straightened strands of wire which he had formed from the paperclip. Although it took at least a minute to maneuver his cuffed hands and work the lock, he was able to free himself from the cuffs. Once his hands were free, he inserted the wires into the shackles lock. The lock was more complicated, and it took O'Leary three minutes to finally free his feet.

Believing that he'd soon arrive at the Judicial Center's garage to be led up to the courtroom, he feigned violent seizures with rhythmic muscle contractions, jerking movements of arms and legs purposely striking hard the metal cage to create discord. For greater dramatic effect, making his condition seem more frightening and in severe distress, he rolled back his eyes, showing the whites, tried to foam his saliva and blow it out the corner of his mouth. He made as much noise with the jerking of his legs and arms on the metal cage as possible and held his breath for as long as he could.

Wide-eyed, the deputies weren't about to take the blame for not rendering immediate aid, even though it was just a few blocks to the courthouse. The last thing they needed was to have the inquiry and possible liability for them and the City to have a death on their hands and in their records. The driver, the thin deputy, pulled off to the curb on Broadway, next to the Denver Art Museum. As he dialed 911, the other deputy slid off the passenger seat and strode the few steps to open the locked door and render aid. As he opened the door, O'Leary cocked his powerful legs back and, with a smashing kick to the chest of the big man, knocked the deputy to the ground.

Without hesitation, swift as a leopard, O'Leary leaped on the supine deputy and went for his weapon. The deputy was not able to resist. He was knocked out by slamming the back of his head hard on the cement. Meanwhile, the thin deputy took cover behind the van, the radio in his left-hand pleading for backup. His drawn gun was in his right hand. Seeing that the deputy would soon have a clear shot at him as he cornered the rear of the van, O'Leary swiftly aimed and squeezed the trigger shooting the man in his right arm with the other deputy's gun. The deputy dropped both the radio and weapon as he yelped with pain. He took cover behind the van, applying pressure on his wounded arm in a feeble attempt to stop the flow of blood.

"Step away from the van," O'Leary barked. "I want to see you running away before I finish you off." The deputy did not argue and took off. O'Leary jumped in the driver's seat and sped down Broadway, disregarding red lights. A few blocks later, being first in line, he stopped at a red light. Still wearing the orange prison garb, he leaped out of the van and dashed up to a car in the adjoining lane. Pointing a gun at the petrified driver, he ordered him out. The frightened middle-aged man flew out. O'Leary pushed him aside and slid into the Toyota Highlander, continuing down Broadway before turning left on Evans Avenue. Noticing a navigation system, he switched it on and found the "Home" icon.

It took him twenty minutes of a drive to reach an upscale neighborhood called Lowry. Following navigation prompts, he located the victim's two-story stucco and brick house quickly by watching which garage door opened after pressing the programmed opener on the rearview mirror. Pleased that it took him a good distance from the scene of his escape, he figured that he'd have a few moments in the house to find what he needed, assuming, of course, that no one was home for him to deal with. As far as the man he carjacked, he knew he would be tied up with a police statement and didn't worry about him returning to his house any time soon. But the police were another matter. If they are on the ball, they could track the stolen vehicle by GPS. Nevertheless, it would take some time, he hoped.

With no other car in the garage, he parked the Toyota, closed the wide door, and made his way to the door leading into the house. Luckily, it was unlocked. As he entered, the alarm warning beeped and continued to beep, but the alarm had not yet gone off. He had to hurry. He needed clothes, and he remembered that the man he carjacked was about his build. As he ran up the stairs to the bedroom, the alarm went off. It shook him for a second, but he knew it would be at least a minute or two before the alarm company called and several more minutes before the police arrived. He also knew that the owner of the house would be notified as well. He really had to hurry.

He found the master bedroom, saw some loose dollars on the dresser, grabbed them, then sprinted to the closet and quickly pulled out a pair of black pants and snatched a checkered button-down shirt. He threw off his jail-issued shoes and slipped his feet into the man's black Nike sneakers. *They're a little big, but they'd do.*

Taking three steps at a time, O'Leary galloped down the stairs and out of the house into the garage. Once the door fully opened, he squealed out in the Highlander and took off. After a short distance, he turned north onto Quebec Street. He knew he had to ditch the car fast because the cops must already be tracking the vehicle because of the GPS.

Ahead on the left, he spotted a busy Safeway grocery store. He swung into the parking lot and looked for an older vehicle, one that did not have GPS. He could not have asked for a better one for what he had in mind when he spotted a faded-gray older model GMC Sierra pickup with a crew cab parked a distance from the entrance. He hoped it was owned by an employee that wouldn't discover that it had been stolen for a few hours. Leaving the Highlander several spaces away, O'Leary sprinted over to the GMC and quickly picked the lock. Sliding in, his head low, he hot-wired the vehicle and took off in less than a minute, heading for the District Six police station.

O'Leary intended to seek out a spot in the parking lot across from the station on Washington Street and wait for Hawk and Ricci to walk either into or out of the building. From that vantage point, he could easily gun them down with the Glock 9mm that he snatched from the deputy. It was a good weapon used by the FBI, and he used a similar one with precision knowing exactly how high to adjust for the drop of the bullet at a certain distance.

As he approached the station from the east on Colfax Avenue, he watched officers on foot searching parked cars and at least a half-dozen patrol vehicles scanning the area around the station. *Damn! They figured it out! They are already on the look-out for me here. Shit! I got to get out of here.* As he proceeded west, O'Leary encountered a slow-moving police vehicle heading in his direction on Colfax. *If they already know the description of the vehicle, I'm toast.* As they were about to pass each other, he held his breath and held the pistol in his right hand, ready to use it if necessary. But something seemed to catch the officer's attention on his side of the street, and didn't even look O'Leary's way.

A little flustered, O'Leary formulated a new plan. Initially, he thought it was best to get out of Colorado as soon as possible, but now he decided that it would be better to lay low for a week or two. During that time, he would catch Hawk and Ricci off guard when they least expected it. *Besides, it may be hard to get out of the Denver area now anyway,* he rationalized. On Pennsylvania Street, he turned left, and then a block later, on Fourteenth Street, he headed east. Now was the time to hide in Aurora in that rundown, cheap motel he had booked for a month using a fake ID and paying in cash a day before he was arrested. He learned that a good gangster hides fake IDs, passports, and quick cash in several places where he may want to run to or lay low for a time. That's exactly what he did. He hid the fake documents and five one-hundred-dollar bills in a narrow space underneath and in the back of the noisy heating and cooling unit in the room. *But first, I'll need to ditch this truck and get other wheels before it's too late.*

CHAPTER 47

"OH, GOD! Not again," Nora moaned. "Not sure if my body can handle any more distress." She clasped her hands, bowed her head, and said a short prayer. With a shaky voice, she asked, "Clint, what are we going to do?"

Hawk sighed and blew out a deep breath as he rubbed his forehead. "We must stay calm and focused. We'll get O'Leary. The way I see it, with all law enforcement looking for him, he's got to get out of the area in a hurry. He may even lose interest in us at this point. He has more to worry about than gunning for us. But having said that, we need to be on alert." Hawk tried to soothe the grim situation, but deep down, he had a sinking feeling that they would meet up with O'Leary. *He has a mission—that of revenge.* He stretched his hand out and stroked Nora's hair, then gently massaged her neck. She turned toward him, forcing a weak grin. He hated to see her so stressed. He missed her beaming, captivating smile but realized that she would not be at peace until O'Leary was caught or eliminated.

Suddenly Mortimer snorted and sat up like a jack in a box in a fit of sneezes. "Oh, sorry, I must've dozed off. I see we're still in the mountains. How close are we to the station? I sure could use a rest stop."

Hawk said, "We're not too far. We passed Floyd Hill and headed toward Genesee. How are you feeling?"

"Oh. I guess I'm good."

"It'll be probably another thirty minutes with traffic. Can you wait?"

"Oh. No, I don't think so."

Geez, it's like traveling with my sister's kid. "Okay, I'll stop when I'm able."

Nora turned to face Mortimer. "You were sleeping and hadn't heard of the jail break. Finn O'Leary escaped, and I fear that he'll be after Clint and me again."

"Oh, that's not good. Not good at all. If he's serious, the best chance to get you," he hesitated, "and actually, me as well, since we're together, is to wait for us near the station. That would be foolish, though, because of all the cops around." He paused for a minute. "So, never mind."

Nora said, "Actually, he would be crazy enough to do something like that, thinking that no one would expect to see him there." She turned toward Hawk and noticed his clenched jaw. "Look, Clint, I don't think he'll try my house because surely he would realize that would be carefully guarded."

Hawk said, "He's crazy enough to try anything."

"Don't forget to stop for me," Mortimer said.

"I won't. There's a Home Depot not too far ahead, right off Colfax and Highway 6. I'll stop there."

"Thank you. I didn't know Colfax goes all the way out here, so far from downtown."

With an uncharacteristically gruff voice, Nora said, "Colfax Avenue is the longest commercial street in the United States. It's over twenty-six miles long."

"More interesting facts for me to tell Josephine. By the way, Nora, you never told me about the history of Vail."

"Mortimer! Are you serious? Do you think I can think of anything else other than that creep, O'Leary?"

"Oh. I suppose you're right? We need to concentrate on catching him, shouldn't we?" Mortimer had a sneezing fit again.

As they waited for him to return from the restroom, Hawk squeezed Nora's hand. It felt cold even though the temperature outside was in the high eighties under a bright, sizzling sun. "Nora, we'll be all right."

"I'm sure of that. But having this feeling that someone is lurking to kill us again—" She shuddered. "What makes you so calm, anyway? I know you're tense and probably shaking on the inside, yet appear stoic."

"I'm trying to be. You're right. My heart feels like it's in my stomach, but we have to stay sharp and focused. So, let's take some deep breaths and relax a bit. Come on. Count with me: one, two, three, four." Nora complied. "There, don't you feel better now?"

Nora managed to chuckle nervously. "Oh, you're so good. I feel like a new woman, ha, ha."

"Well, don't change too much. I like the old Nora." Hawk laughed to lessen the stress.

After Mortimer returned, Hawk continued the trip on Highway 6, at which point it turned into a freeway. They sat silently almost all the way into downtown Denver. The silence was interrupted by a phone call from Lieutenant Perez. Hawk answered, placing the call on speaker. "Okay, we think we know what vehicle Finn O'Leary may be in. It's a 2003 gray GMC Sierra four-door, short bed and has a dented right front panel. It was taken from a parking lot close to where O'Leary was last picked up by the GPS in the carjacked vehicle. Of course, by now, he might've stolen another."

"That's very helpful, thanks," Hawk said.

Nora added, "Lieutenant, we've been discussing that he should be in a big hurry to get out of the area. If he wants to do us in, he'll need to know where to find us. The logical place would be the station."

"I thought of that. I had just now issued a BOLO for the truck. Shortly, several cruisers and officers on foot will patrol the area around the station."

Hawk said, "Maybe we should stop such obvious patrols. Let him set up to take a shot at us. He'll be easier to find if he doesn't suspect anything. We just have to be more cautious, which we'll be."

"Nope. No way. That's too risky."

Nora said, "I'd rather know where he is rather than he knows where we are later and then bushwhack us."

"Sorry, Ricci. I've discussed this with MacGregor, and she agreed to the patrol activity around the station. She said you'll be going to a safe house until he's caught."

Hawk said, "We may never catch him. He'll always be a threat to us. We must go on with our lives."

"Hawk, you discuss this with MacGregor, but her mind is pretty well made up."

Hawk banged on the steering wheel. "Damn! Go to a safe house?! O'Leary has a sixth sense. He'll know where to find us and then escape without a trace. From what I've been able to read about him in the FBI files, he's as slick as oil."

"Maybe the Captain is right," Mortimer said. "You and Nora should take precautions. It's for your own good. At least try it for a couple of days and see what happens."

Hawk and Nora exchanged glances. Hawk shook his head and mouthed "no" to her. Nora shrugged. "I really don't know what to do. I agree with you, Clint, that being locked away in a safe house while O'Leary is out and we're doing nothing about it is not for us, that's for sure. Who knows how long we'd be holed up…I'll go with you to talk to MacGregor and see if we can talk her out of it."

The three detectives sat silently again for a few minutes until Mortimer cleared his throat, "I can hardly wait to tell Josephine all of this and what a day we had. Don't forget we probably solved the Hollister cases. That's a big deal. Too bad we have this psychopath to deal with. Kind of takes the luster of solving a big case away." He remained silent for a moment. "By the way, can you drop me off a couple of blocks from the station? I think I'd like a short walk since we had been cooped up in the car."

Chicken. Hawk thought. *But I don't blame him. If he rides into the station with us, he realizes that he could also be a target if O'Leary is lurking out there.* "Sure, Mortimer, anything you say."

Nora looked at Hawk and rolled her eyes, her face in a frown.

From Sixth Street, Hawk turned left onto Clarkson Street, a one-way roadway with two narrow lanes heading north to the east entrance of the station's parking lot. As he approached Fourteenth Street—just three blocks from the station—he slowed to let Mortimer out. As he did so, he noticed a gray GMC Sierra stopped at a red light on Fourteenth. His heart started to pound as he spotted a large dent in the front passenger panel over the tire. He squinted his eyes to try to get a better look at the driver.

Mortimer prepared to exit the vehicle, his hand on the door handle. Instead, Hawk gunned the engine shouting, "That's the truck! O'Leary!"

CHAPTER 48

HAWK SLAMMED on the brakes hard, his Sig 380 drawn. Nora understood her partner's maneuver and drew her gun. Mortimer, who had his seatbelt unfastened already, was thrown into the back of Nora's seat. Before he could react, a bullet whizzed through the driver's window, barely missing Hawk and Nora. Then another flew above Mortimer. "Get down," Hawk screamed. Nora quickly took cover in the footwell. But Mortimer flew out of the car and bent low behind the hood of the Tahoe, and began shooting at O'Leary, giving both Nora and Hawk a chance to flee the Tahoe and join Mortimer.

O'Leary took another shot. He knew he had to conserve his bullets, and his shots had to count. He was out of the GMC, took another shot at the three detectives and began a swift run down Fourteenth Street away from them. Hawk and Nora took chase, Hawk shouting over his shoulder for Mortimer to call for backup. O'Leary ducked into an alley, and they followed, their bodies drenched in sweat. They spotted O'Leary as he ducked behind a metal four-ton dumpster. Hawk and Ricci took cover in a narrow alcove of a doorway as a couple of bullets shattered the bricks lining the building. Chips from the bricks pierced Hawk's gun hand, causing it to bleed. They returned fire.

"Cover me!" Hawk shrieked to Nora, his breath labored. "Keep him down!"

Nora fired one shot after another in O'Leary's direction as Hawk scampered toward the container, but O'Leary began shooting back. Hawk took cover at another doorway and motioned for Nora to cease her fire. O'Leary poked his head just slightly over the dumpster and shot at Nora. Hawk fired a shot. It came close but sailed over O'Leary's head, causing the criminal to stoop further down.

At that moment, a police cruiser pulled into the alley behind O'Leary. It was Corporal David Hopkins, Hawk's jealous competitor at the academy. Hopkins carefully exited his vehicle, his gun drawn, pointing at the criminal and taking cover behind the open car door. Hawk kept edging his way toward O'Leary, ready to either pounce on top of the dumpster and take him that way or come around the container. Hopkins roared out, "Throw out your weapon, O'Leary. It's over."

O'Leary froze for a few seconds, thinking. He knew he could shoot the cop down, but he sensed that Hawk was nearly on top of him. As he hesitated, Hawk sprinted and sprang onto the dumpster, his weapon a few inches from O'Leary's head. "Throw down that damn weapon," Hopkins roared.

"Give it up," Hawk bellowed. "Throw your gun out in the open, you sonofabitch."

O'Leary knew that he had no choice. *It's no use. I need to save myself and fight another day. Let them take me. I'll get out one way or another, as I always do.* He laughed mockingly as he tossed the gun into the middle of the alley. He stood up, looking proud, his chest out and his arms outstretched.

Ricci stood next to Hawk. O'Leary had a defiant smirk on his face. He looked at them, threatening, "This ain't over. I'll be back as soon as I escape again. I told you that there's no jail that can hold me." Again, he laughed, this time a blood-chilling laugh that shook Nora to the core.

"You bastard, you're going to be locked up and spend the rest of your worthless and soulless life in solitary confinement." Nora felt better for the outburst.

O'Leary sneered. "Don't count on it, lassie. I'll be back. You'll never know when I'll do you in." At that moment, Hawk came up to him and forcefully twisted him around and shoved him hard into the steel container as he unceremoniously jerked his arms back and cuffed him."

O'Leary laughed again. "It will be a great pleasure to torture you before I do you in. You could loosen up the cuffs a bit, though, mate. They're cutting off my circulation."

"Good! Corporal Hopkins, read him his rights and take him in."

Hopkins smiled. "It's a pleasure, sir."

While Hawk and Ricci were in pursuit of O'Leary, Mortimer called for backup and began to run toward the alley. However, he tripped on an uneven piece of sidewalk and fell, his gun flying out of his hand. He scraped his hands and knees, even ripped one of his pantlegs. He lay on the ground for a minute before a passenger in a stopped vehicle jumped out and helped him up. Mortimer thanked him, grabbed his gun, and hobbled toward the alley. He made it in time to see O'Leary standing with his hands high in the air. Breathing hard and in pain from the scrapes and banged-up knees, Mortimer rejoiced, *yeah, they got him.*

He then walked up to Hawk and Ricci. Hawk said, "Mortimer, it's all over. He's been caught. You can relax now."

They both noticed his limp and a torn pantleg. Nora asked, "What happened to you? Are you alright?"

He didn't answer at first until Nora asked him again. "Oh. Yes. I'm fine. Just tripped and fell. These stupid shoes that Josephine found for me are just too big. I don't care what she'll say, I'm going to throw them away…but I've been thinking as I walked over here about what I should do with my life. I often wondered if I was cut out for this violence. I've never been shot at while in Tampa."

"Well, hang in there, sport," Hawk said. "It isn't always this way."

"I know. I'll have to tell Josephine about this day and see what she thinks."

After the three detectives were back in the Tahoe, its windows shattered and bullet holes in the body from O'Leary's bullets, Nora asked," Clint, we're not going to meet with Tina Dionisio after all of this, are we?"

"I think we should do as planned. I know we're shaken up, but the Hollister case goes on."

Mortimer looked startled. "Oh, we're not through with the day yet? But I called Josephine and said that I'll be home shortly."

Hawk said, "You certainly need to be with Josephine right now. Nora and I can handle it."

"Oh. Good. I really feel that I need to stretch out on my bed for a few minutes. I would do it on the couch and maybe watch some PBS, but Josephine doesn't like me lying on it for some reason."

Nora finally laughed and kept laughing as Hawk joined in.

"Oh, did I say something funny again?"

Nora said, "Not really, Mortimer. I apologize, but it seems to me that you have more rules and regulations in your home than the zoning department."

"Oh. I never thought of that."

CHAPTER 49

THE POLICE station was abuzz with O'Leary's capture as Hawk and Ricci dragged themselves upstairs to the Homicide Unit. Mortimer Holliday went home after announcing that he was tired and his knees and hands hurt from the fall. The two detectives still had a couple of hours before their meeting with Tina Dionisio. Now they wanted to do nothing more than sit back in their chairs and let their minds and bodies calm down from yet another traumatic experience. They knew that they really should call it a day. Nora again suggested that Clint cancel the appointment with Tina. But Hawk was adamant that it should be followed through in case she really knew something that would help them in the Hollister murders. "Stubborn, aren't you," Nora said.

Their hope that they would not be bothered by anyone at the office after the last incident was nothing but a pipe dream. Stan Orlinski strode up to them and wanted to know all the details of O'Leary's capture. While they were describing it, Detectives Salazar and Ling came into the Unit and rushed over to hear about it. All three listened avidly as Nora portrayed the horrible scene in much detail, particularly how Hawk spotted the vehicle O'Leary was in and how brave he was for rushing toward the shooter while under fire. They stood wide-eyed and listened. Nancy shook her head back and forth, quietly mumbling, "I can't believe that. That's incredible. Holy cow!"

Hawk said, "Oh, Nora. You're exaggerating my role in his capture. It was Corporal Hopkins that pulled up at the right moment. If it hadn't been for him distracting O'Leary, I don't know how it would've ended. And don't forget to tell them that you're the one that kept him pinned down. That way, I was able to closer, keep him in a crouching position and allow Hopkins to find him wide open and vulnerable. And then don't forget Mortimer's role."

"Oh, what did he do?" Harry Ling asked.

"Mortimer was the first to jump out of the Tahoe as we were dodging O'Leary's bullets. It was Mortimer who began firing back at O'Leary, pinning him down and giving us enough time to exit our vehicle and shoot back and chase him into the alley."

Orlinski said, "Good for Mortimer. You all did well. I've been here twenty-five years and have never been shot at. You sure seem to attract gunfire. Let's hope it's the last time. By the way, I'd like to invite all of you and your spouses or dates, whatever, including Mortimer and his famous Josephine, to a BBQ this Saturday. Let's celebrate another one of your escapes from death. I'll have my date—" He stopped and looked at Hawk. "Yes, Clint, I'm now dating Monica Pachek. And just in case you're wondering, it's going great. Anyway, we'll cook up some Polish kielbasa along with a barrel of sour kraut, pierogi and other goodies. And, of course, plenty of beer."

Nancy readily agreed, as did Harry Ling. Hawk looked at Nora, and with a sour face and even tone, he said, "I think that we're going to make a trip to Pueblo this weekend, right?"

Nora saw how unexcited Hawk appeared about making a trip to Pueblo. *He really doesn't want to go and meet my parents. I'm sure he thinks that's just too much of a commitment for him. I wonder if he's really serious about me or if I'm just convenient to be with at the moment. Just like Tina said, he's not the marrying type.* She could not help but sigh when she said, "Actually, Clint, if you don't mind, let's make it to Pueblo another time. The BBQ sounds like fun." She really wanted to meet Josephine and hoped that she and Mortimer would agree to come.

No one had seen Orlinski so excited about anything. He swiftly rubbed his hands together, smiling widely. Nancy said, "Boy, Stan, I can't believe what a woman in your life did for you. I wish my husband had such enthusiasm." They all laughed.

"Okay then. I'll invite MacGregor and Perez, also. You don't mind, do you?"

Everyone shook their heads in the negative, and the party was on.

At that moment, Captain MacGregor called Hawk and Ricci into her office. "Um, oh," Nancy joked. "You're in trouble now." They all laughed except for Hawk and Ricci.

Lieutenant Perez sat on the brown vinyl couch as they walked in. MacGregor was behind her desk. With sarcasm, she said, "I see that you managed to stay alive, at least for another day. Sit down."

Hawk laughed, thinking that she was making a joke of it. He was wrong. "Detective Hawk, it's no laughing matter. You both chased a known killer into an alley without getting backup first. It ended well, and thank God that you are both safe, but you could've very easily been ambushed. I don't want to lose my two best detectives over hotshot decisions."

Hawk said, "Captain, we were extremely careful. We just didn't rush into the alley without first determining where O'Leary went. We saw him hide behind a dumpster. We checked out spots in the alley where we could take cover, and we did."

Nora added, "Besides, if we waited for backup, he would've disappeared. If that happened, we'd remain a target leaving us exposed to his whims as to when and where to pick us off. My nerves can't take it for much longer, having that hang over my head. We had to do what we did."

Perez spoke for the first time. "Captain, I agree with them. They had to go after him and catch him. And I admire our detectives for being alert enough to notice him in traffic, of all things."

MacGregor stared at each one of them for a minute. "I don't like it, but I can't argue with the results." She suddenly had a half-smile on her chiseled face and a change in tone. "Okay, I did my duty as your Captain and gave you the spiel that I believe I had to do. Personally, I want to congratulate you for spotting him and arresting him. Next time get backup before going into a situation that could very well have been a trap. By the way, where's Detective Holliday?"

Not wanting to get Mortimer in trouble, Hawk and Nora both hesitated before speaking. Finally, Nora said, "Captain, in following us to the alley, he tripped and fell, scraping his knees and the palms of his hands. He even tore a pantleg that he was really upset about. He thought that Josephine would be extremely angry about that. Mumbled something to the effect that now she'll have to go searching for another used suit. Anyway, he was hurting, and the mountain trip really wore him out. I watched as he barely dragged himself to his car. He said that he really needed to go home. Besides, he was very brave when he was the first to risk his life getting out of the police vehicle under O'Leary's barrage of bullets coming at us. Mortimer pinned the creep down so we could get out and begin to pursue him."

MacGregor shook her head, her jaw tight. "All right. You two should also go home now. You look like an 18-wheeler ran over you."

Hawk said, "We will, but first, we have an appointment with a witness in the Hollister cases. I think it's important to keep it. As they say, 'Strike while the iron is hot.'"

"All right, if you can manage, do that, and then take the morning off. Sleep in late. The Lieutenant updated me about the arrests you made today. Keep up the good work. Do you think that Sam and Cynthia murdered the old man?"

Hawk said, "It sure looks like it, but I don't have the gut feeling. Of course, they deny it. As for the murders of James and Kay, we'll know more once their 9mm weapons are tested."

"All right. Keep me posted."

At their desks, Nora fell into deep thought. She thought of Clint's meeting with Tina. *I really don't need to be there. Clint might even get more information out of her if I'm not. She doesn't like me, and I don't like her, and she knows it. With me there, she might just clam up tight. Besides, if I'm going to have a trusting relationship with Clint, I need to give him space.*

She turned her head toward Hawk, who was leaning back in his chair, his eyes shut. "Clint, I said that I'll go with you to interview Tina, but I think it's best that you go alone. Besides, I'm really dragging. I don't know why, and maybe I didn't eat the right food or what, but this fear of O'Leary, especially since he almost killed us in my house, just crippled me mentally. When I'm overstressed, I get very tired physically. If you don't mind, I think I'll follow MacGregor's advice and go home. You don't mind, do you? I need to recharge myself."

"Nora, you do look pale. I'll cancel the meeting for tonight with Dionisio. She'll wait until tomorrow."

"No, no. Clint. Keep the appointment. Once I lay down and calm myself, I'll be good as new and will be able to fight the battle again. You look so worried. Please don't. I just need some time to myself. Oh, and don't let that woman wrap you around her little finger." Nora attempted a laugh, but it came out weak. "I shouldn't worry. I know you'll be professional."

"Of course I will. At least let me drive you home."

"No. I'll be all right. I just need to stretch out for a while." She studied Hawk. "Frankly, I don't know how you do it. Why aren't you all stressed out to the point where you can't function?"

"It was an awful feeling, having a psychopath lurking out there, that's for sure. It seems that with his arrest, I'm all pumped up. However, later this evening, I'll conk out. Hopefully, without all the nightmares, I can't seem to escape."

"I'm so sorry that you're still plagued by those nightmares. Today's incident certainly doesn't help."

Nora rose and checked to see if anyone was watching. Unfortunately, Orlinski was eyeing them, and she couldn't get away with planting a kiss on Clint before she left. A friendly "good-bye" was all Clint got.

Glancing at his silver-colored Tag Heuer watch, Hawk noted that he had over an hour before meeting Tina at 6 o'clock. He needed to work on reports that were stacking up from all the recent activity. He could not get into doing them. He tried to present a tough exterior as though O'Leary did not worry or bother him. Just another day in the office. But his nerves were a mess. He kept it all in. But now he felt limp, his mind drained.

Meeting Tina seemed such a chore. Hopefully, with a strong cup of coffee and a rush of caffeine, he would be able to carry on a decent interview with her. After that, he could stretch out on the couch and watch some mindless TV show before succumbing to sleep.

Time dragged on as he sat back in his chair, going through the motions of looking over his notes. Strangely, Marcie popped into his mind. He pictured the usually radiant blonde as she pleaded for him to quit the police force. She couldn't stand that in the future. She'd worry and wait for him to come home every night. Her words— "We could move to California together, and you could set up a private practice in psychology"—appeared in his thoughts. *"Why can't I get Marcie out of my mind? I wonder what she's up to."*

He slapped himself slightly on the cheek and shook his head. *Why can't I get over her? She just isn't right for me. Besides, I love what I do.* He peeked at his watch again and decided that it was time to go, now curious about what Tina had to say.

CHAPTER 50

FINDING A parking spot in downtown Denver is always a challenge. If Hawk had the official police vehicle, he could have left it in a loading zone; however, the Tahoe assigned to him was damaged with O'Leary's bullet holes. Perez told him that he did not even know if he would be able to get another vehicle. Everyone that had been assigned to him had been either destroyed or damaged. "Your track record sucks," were his exact words.

Driving his personal Jeep Cherokee, Hawk finally found a spot a block away. Luckily, Perez gave him a placard that read, "Police Department: Official business." He stuck it on the dashboard and walked away without paying the meter.

He arrived at Starbucks five minutes before six. Tina was not there yet, so he found a corner table and sat down. He imagined that he would have to buy her a coffee anyway, so he'd wait and get him at the same time. Five minutes passed, then ten minutes. Irritated, he decided to give her another minute, and then he would leave.

Just as he was about to walk out, his eyes fell wide as he saw the "Barbie doll," as Nora described her, saunter in. She looked like a million dollars. He noticed all the men in the store twist their necks in her direction. Hawk did not know the brand of the tight-fitting blue sleeveless dress with a white polka-dot pattern, but he knew that it must be expensive. It certainly looked expensive. He stood as her hips swayed toward him. After asking her to sit, he noticed a large emerald pendant hanging from a thick gold chain. In addition, three gold bracelets adorned her slender wrist and an elegant Chanel gold watch on the other. A large emerald ring, also set in yellow gold, matched her pendant. Setting her leather Prada handbag down, she displayed perfect teeth as she gave him a beaming smile.

"What would you like, Tina?" Hawk asked. "I haven't ordered my coffee yet."

"Oh, I'm not picky," she said in a crème-smooth voice. "I'll take whatever you're having."

Hawk came back with two cups of black coffee. "Would you like some cream in that?"

"No, black is fine. Thank you. So where is your girlfriend? Couldn't take the competition, I see." She laughed in merriment.

Hawk smiled, saying, "No, we had a gruelingly long day today. She needed a break."

"Oh, poor baby. Listen, Clint. May I call you Clint?"

"I'd prefer detective."

"Okay, but if we're going to have dinner together, I can't keep calling you detective, can I?"

"We're not having dinner together. I'm here because you have something important to tell me about the Hollister case. Or are you misleading me?"

"Oh, no, not at all. As I said over the phone, I'll solve the case for you. But, Clint, honey, it's silly for us to sit here when it's dinner time. I'm famished, and I'm sure you haven't eaten yet, either. Let's just walk down Sixteenth Street Mall. I know a charming place where we can talk in peace."

"Tina, that would be inappropriate. You may be a witness to something you're about to tell me. If you're ever called to testify in the trial, a defense attorney will make a big deal out of us having dinner together. He'll allege that there is a collusion. Any relationship other than strictly professional could undermine the case."

"So? Let them think that…it sounds good to me. I mean a relationship. Don't you think?" She laughed again.

"Okay, stop with the jokes."

"I'm not joking. I think we should have dinner tonight and see where it goes from there."

Hawk chuckled. "It won't go anywhere. I already have a girlfriend. Besides, what do you want with me? I'm obviously out of your league."

Tina laughed, "It really doesn't matter, but you are in my league. I've checked you out, Clint. You're wasting your time as a cop. You come from a very prominent Texas pioneering family with high-flying friends."

Hawk's smile evaporated as he leaned back in his chair. He crossed his arms over his chest. "What?" His voice grew louder. "What are you doing, checking up on me and my family? Is that why you're interested in me? Just because you think my family may have money?"

"Clint, Clint. Darling, listen to me."

"Tina, please don't call me honey or darling. I'm not your boyfriend. I'm here only on official business. So cut that out!" His voice rose again. Some of the people turned their heads toward them once again.

"Don't be angry. I'm only trying to help. You have a golden opportunity to make millions as an investment banker or financial planner. You're smart, good looking and with your family connections and the people I'd introduce you to, the sky's the limit. I'll help you get started. We could even be partners in a company of our own. Just yesterday, I picked up a whale of a good client. The guy's worth millions. My management fees and commissions would set me up for life. You can have the same opportunity."

Hawk laughed and leaned toward her, his wrists on his knees.

"I'm serious. This is not supposed to be funny."

Hawk said, lowering his voice, "Tina, please back off. My parents' business is theirs. I'm not part of it. I'm doing what makes me feel good about myself. I'm helping people with their life-and-death situations, and I know I'm making a difference. To me, that's worth a hell of a lot more than money. My salary is enough for me to live comfortably. So don't worry about me. Besides, aren't you seeing Darren Hollister?"

"Oh, him. I like him. That is when he's sober. But he's got a real problem. I can't stand drunks. Don't think I'll be seeing much of him anymore. Besides, he's got a drinking buddy by the name of

Spike or something like that. I can't stand him. To me, he's dangerous. Gives me the creeps. I don't know where Darren met him, probably in some dive because the guy looks like he crawled out of a cave somewhere. Mean looking, dude. His eerie dull blue eyes look soulless. I bet he'd kill his mother if you paid him to do it. Other than getting stinkin' drunk together, I don't see why Darren is even with him. I'm sure I know why he's with Darren. I'm sure Darren pays for all the drinking."

Tina stretched out her arm and gently touched Hawk's shoulder. "Getting back to financial planning, you have me wrong. I threw that out as a suggestion, that's all. Of course, I'd love to get to know you better, and from what you just told me, I admire you even more. I just wish that you'd take me more seriously as someone that could make you happy. I'm tired of losers or lechers. I need someone solid as a rock. So, whenever you get tired of that Ricci woman, call me." She winked as she chuckled.

Hawk smiled. "Okay, Tina." Hawk was about to tell her, "Don't hold your breath," but held off, thinking that might really piss her off. He needed to know what she had on the Hollister case. *Or does she have anything? Or did she want to see me only to recruit me? I have to get her back on track.* "I'm flattered, but I'm here as a detective, and you said you can solve my case for me. Shall we get down to business? I'll turn on the recorder, okay?"

Tina's demeanor changed. Her smile faded, her face portraying disappointment, "All right, Detective Hawk, I didn't come forward sooner since I thought you'd be around to question me anyway. At the Hollister dinner, after the old man had his nasty say to his kids, we all stomped upstairs. Everyone was fricking. George said that he was so upset that he could've strangled his father right there and then. Imagine that. Cynthia said something to the effect that she'd help him. It was unnerving to watch all the madness and fury going on. Only James and his wife seemed to enjoy it and had obnoxious smirks on their faces. I'm surprised that they weren't killed there on the spot."

Tina took a swig of coffee, as did Hawk. "Go on, Tina. What else happened?"

"The siblings and their spouses first went into the rooms that they grew up in. I followed Darren into his. He was a little tipsy but managed to throw some of his childhood memorabilia into a small U-Haul box that I guess was provided by Hollister's butler. He's a creepy guy if you ask me. I wouldn't trust him." She paused and took another sip of coffee. Again, Hawk did the same.

"Then, I guess all of them left their boxes on the beds and began going from room to room looking at everybody else's. I saw Rhonda grab a few odds and ends out of each room and, I suppose, take them back to her box. Then, it seemed everyone took a turn going into the old man's master bedroom and, I guess, into the bathroom. Darren and I, with Ashley tagging along, stopped to view William's fancy bedroom and bathroom. I remember discussing with Darren and Ashley the pill organizer that looked just like my grandmother's." As Tina looked intently into Hawk's eyes, she reminded him of a dog he had in Tyler. Lucky's sad, pleading eyes usually got him what he wanted—usually that extra scrap of food.

"Ashley left the bathroom a minute before us, and we headed back to Darren's room, where he collapsed on his bed and told me he had to rest for a second. I sat down in a chair and waited for him to wake up, but he was sound asleep. So, I thought I'd go back to that master bathroom, get a few more ideas for my remodeling job, and freshen up a bit. You know, comb my hair, put on some lipstick, that kind of stuff." When Tina talked about lipstick, she protruded her lips, trying to bring his attention to her seductive cherry lips.

Hawk noticed and was embarrassed at himself for gazing at them maybe a little too long.

"As I entered the hallway, I was stopped by Cynthia, who was very pleased, in no uncertain terms, to inform me that I had no business being in their house. She said that soon, the house would be hers and riffraff like me would not be allowed. You can imagine how that upset me."

"Yes, I imagine that would," Hawk said.

"Yes, for sure. Anyway, I watched Cynthia walk towards the father's room, so I went back to Darren, hoping that he was awake. But before I did, I saw the housekeeper come up the stairs and make her way toward William's wing of the house.

"After a few more minutes, I got tired of waiting for Darren, so I walked out into the hallway again and lingered there, watching the siblings in animated discussions at the top stair landing. After some finger-pointing, mostly by George, some of them began to leave.

"At that time, I slipped past the few people still talking and made my way to the bathroom. I loved that master bathroom. Couldn't seem to get enough of the way it was designed and decorated, all in marble and unusual 3-D wallpaper. Just as I was at the door, I saw a reflection in the mirror of the person shaking out a white pill from a bottle, which I now assume must've been aspirin, dropping it into the pill container. I didn't think anything of it at the time, and I just walked in. As I did, I noticed her quickly scoop what looked like another white pill into her palm. I definitely surprised her because she looked totally shocked at me coming in like that. Again, at the time, I didn't quite understand what she was up to. I thought it strange but didn't think anything of it even after I heard that meds had been switched, causing the old man's death."

"All right, Tina. Don't keep me in suspense. Who was it?"

Taking a last sip of her coffee, she looked at Hawk and told him who she saw.

CHAPTER 51

ON HER way home, Nora ran into unusually heavy rush hour traffic, but she was in no particular hurry. She felt drained as she sat back in the seat, her mind traumatized. It was as if the car was driving itself home.

With low energy, she made her way into the house from the garage and plunked down on the sofa. Closing her eyes, she threw her arm over her face and tried to unwind, perhaps even catch a nap. However, her mind was so hyper with thoughts of O'Leary and how it all ended that she was not able to calm down. She thought of the way she acted and was ashamed of herself for acting so nervous, so unprofessional. *How embarrassing. What does Clint think of me now? I know that he was frightened as hell, but he didn't show it.*

She could not understand what washed over her. She has had several dangerous incidents where she was precariously close to death. In those, she was strong, courageous, and able to fight her way out. *I'm a tough girl. So, what's wrong with me this time? Maybe it's not knowing where and how the evil came from. The first time that psycho came after us, we expected him. We thought it would be at my house. This time it was different. He was out there somewhere, capable of picking us off at his pleasure before we guessed when he'd strike. This time it could've happened any moment today or a week or two from now without us having a chance to defend ourselves. Was that it? The unknown that made a difference.*

Nora sat up, stretched her neck, and went for her phone. She needed to be pampered. She needed love and affection. She wished Clint were there to hold her, but he was not. Only her parents would invariably make her feel better. Whenever she felt that she needed support and, ultimately, a build-up of confidence, that is who she called. She needed to hear their always exuberant and praising words, the same ones she had heard since she was a little girl. They made her feel that there would be no more worries or fears.

Both were on the phone, genuinely excited to hear from her. Although they heard from her yesterday and the day before, it was as though they had not heard from her in months. She would not dare tell them about O'Leary, not about the first time or now. Or taking down hired killers with her kicks, or facing death by a mastermind of corrupt cops or the many altercations as a patrol officer. They knew that her chosen career was extremely dangerous, and they tried repeatedly to dissuade her from it. However, if they heard of the grave incidents where she came to a breath from dying, and not only once, but Nora would also never, ever hear the end of it. They will beat her down until she resigns. She did not put it past her father driving down with a U-Haul and physically moving her back to Pueblo. She laughed for the first time since O'Leary escaped thinking of her father and her brother carrying stuff out of her house. There would be no discussion. Of course, she would never agree to anything like that, and they knew it.

The conversation was longer than usual. She wanted to hear everything about every member of the extended family and whatever gossip about friends that her mother was glad to share. Finally, her mother asked, "So, what's up with your knight in shining armor? When are we going to meet him? You've been promising to bring him down here, and if you don't, papa and I will go up there and take you both out to dinner."

"No, mom. We'll make it. We have this complicated case we're working on, and we're both very busy. I'll let you know. It'll be soon, I hope."

She felt better after a talk with her parents. She clicked on the TV and began mindlessly watching the tail end of a news program. Her mind was not on the show, but Clint's meeting with Tina sure was. She did not believe that Tina had anything concrete to offer. *It was a ruse to see Clint again, try to inveigle him with her charms and body. That's all it is. I should've gone with him. They're most likely having dinner together and having a great time. She would've talked him into it. It might be easy because he may not be that serious about me. He warned me that he has a problem with commitment.*

She felt so insecure about her relationship with Hawk. She was not even sure if there was a relationship. He never expressed that he loved her. He said that she was his girlfriend, but she was not sure that he really meant it. *I just don't feel it. I should've forced myself to go. What a fool I am. Women seem to gravitate to him, and he likes the attention. So how can a guy like that settle down and be with one woman for the rest of his life? I guess it depends on how much in love he is, and so far, he hasn't shown it.*

After those thoughts poured out of her tired brain, Nora became sad. The sharp ringtone of her phone startled her.

"Hello, Nora, this is Chet, Chet Watkins from the Crime Lab. I know it's getting late, but I wanted to get this information to you as soon as possible."

"Yes, hi, Chet. What's the info?"

"You know the pill organizer from the Hollister house?"

"Yes, what about it?"

"We planned on working on the box; however, because another case had an emergency priority, we had to set it aside 'til later. Then we had this new intern that showed up, and I didn't know what to do with her, so I asked her to check the box over carefully to see if she could find any evidence that would be useful. You know, it was just something for her to do."

"Okay. I imagine you have something for us then."

"Well, this college student is pretty sharp, all right. With fresh and young eyes and using a powerful magnifying glass, she spotted a tiny black hair tucked upright in the corner of the pill compartments that was labeled for the day that Hollister died. It's from an eyebrow. We ran a DNA on it, and we found no match in the database, but it appears that there is familial DNA with William Hollister."

"So, the hair belongs to one of his children, then?" Nora asked.

"That's what I think. One of the daughters, most likely."

"Oh. You sure?"

"Yup. There's heavy makeup on the hair."

"What color is it? I mean the makeup."

"It's dark, almost black, I'd say. Okay, Nora, got to run. Inform Hawk of this, would you?"

Chet punched off, and Nora came to life. Excited, she paced the room, saying to herself, "I know who killed him! I know who did it!"

She grabbed the phone to call Hawk, but as she did, the phone chimed. Clint was calling her. "Hi, Nora. Have you eaten yet?"

"No, why?"

"I'll be right over with a pizza and some beer."

"You didn't you have dinner with that vixen, Tina?"

"Of course not. I resisted her charms and her invitations to eat out, and now I'm starving. Oh, by the way, when I'll come by, I'll tell you who switched the meds."

"Oh, I already know who it is."

"What do you mean you know?"

Nora laughed. "I'll spring the surprise on you when you come."

CHAPTER 52

THE NEXT morning, Hawk and Ricci met with Lieutenant Perez to discuss who, they were sure, caused the death of William Hollister. Hawk described to him who Tina Dionisio saw switch medications. Nora came to the same conclusion after Chet Watkins told her that the eyebrow hair was from a woman related to William. She remembered one of William's daughters having heavily made-up eyebrows.

"Good work," Perez said. "What about the other murders? You think she done it?"

Hawk answered, "We have no idea at this point. I kinda doubt it, though. We still think that Cynthia and Sam Hollister are our primary suspects in that case. They admitted they were there and certainly had the opportunity."

"Do we have a report on the ballistics yet?" Nora asked. "I think it'll be crucial to know the exact trajectory of the bullets and an idea from what range they were shot. We know that Sam's car was right in front of James and Kay."

"No, I hadn't seen it yet. What are you thinking, Nora?"

"Well, if the slugs came from a distance further away or at an angle away from where Sam stopped his car, perhaps Cynthia or Sam didn't do it."

"I'll call the crime lab and see where they're at with that," Perez said. "Also, I'll contact the ADA and get an arrest warrant. It shouldn't take too long based on what Dionisio saw and your recollection of the heavy-lined eyebrows. When you arrest her, make sure you find something that would have her DNA so that we can match it."

"There's one more thing that I'd like to discuss with you two," Hawk said, addressing Perez and Nora. "In Tina's interview, a thought struck me, and I'm thinking more about it. It's probably way far out, but she mentioned a mean character by the name of

Spike, who is a newly acquired drinking buddy of Darren Hollister. She said that he was the type that would kill his mother for money. So, my thought was that we should find out who this character is."

"You think that Darren put him up to killing his brother?" Nora asked.

"Well, I don't know, just an idea. What if, while being liquored up, Darren told Spike that he would inherit a bunch of money if his brother, James, were not around? I can just picture Spike telling him that he could take care of that problem for a fee, maybe even a percentage of Darren's share. Or maybe it was Darren's idea from the beginning, and that's why he found a guy like Spike to carouse with?"

Perez and Nora exchanged glances as each thought of the possibility. Perez said, "It's definitely a long shot, but if Cynthia didn't do it, we don't have anything else to go on right now. Why not check it out? I'll ask Orlinski to search the database for anyone that used Spike as a name or nickname. The guy must have a criminal record. And I'll get Salazar and Ling to tail Darren and see if he hooks up with the guy at a bar tonight. Do you have a better description of him other than 'mean character?' Sure, would be helpful."

Hawk said, "I can call Tina and get a description of him."

"Why don't we let Nancy or Harry talk to her," Nora said. "They're the ones that have to find him." Hawk chuckled, knowing exactly what she was up to. Nora looked at him and scrunched up her nose.

As Hawk and Ricci were about to leave, Mortimer hurriedly walked into Perez's office with a slight limp. He wore exceptionally wide black pleated pants, a double-breasted dark blue blazer sporting extra wide lapels and padded shoulders. His light blue shirt was neatly pressed, and he wore his favorite red and green suspenders with a matching bow tie. Nora was glad that MacGregor was not there. She knew she would have a fit after asking him to wear clothing of this era and not of the eighties. *Where does Josephine find these for him? Must go to thrift stores to shop.*

"Oh, I wasn't told we'd be having a meeting this morning," Mortimer said, looking confused. "Did I miss something important?"

Perez gave Holliday an appraising look, and lips pressed together. He sighed, blew out his breath and turned away. Nora saw him roll his eyes and shake his head. Twisting back to Mortimer, he asked, "How are you feeling today?"

"Oh. My knees still hurt a bit, but overall, I'm all right. Thanks for asking. What's this meeting about? Does this concern the Hollister cases?"

"You didn't miss much." Perez said, "Only that Hawk and Ricci have requested an arrest warrant for the person that killed William Hollister. They're sure they found the killer."

"Oh. I'm sure it was Cynthia who did it with Sam's help. Josephine and I talked about it last night. Isn't she still locked up in Golden?"

"Yeah, they're being arraigned this morning, and once that's done, they'll be transferred to us for interrogation in relation to the Hollister murders," Perez said.

"Oh. We are sure that it was she who switched the medications and shot James and Kay. Sam admitted that Cynthia wanted him to break into the lawyer's office and steal the will. That alone shows a criminal mentality on both their parts. If they were desperate enough to do the burglary, then they were desperate enough to kill all three Hollisters."

Perez looked at Mortimer with amusement. "Boy, that Josephine of yours is quite an expert, isn't she?" He chuckled as he asked Nora to explain to Holliday what was going on with the case later. "Okay, get to work. I'll get the arrest warrant for you."

The three detectives made their way to Nora's desk while Orlinski, Salazar and Ling were summoned to Perez's office.

"The Lieutenant seems to be in a good mood today," Mortimer said. "But I don't think he appreciated my analysis of who killed the Hollisters. You think that someone else did it?"

Looking at Nora, Hawk said, "While you explain to Mortimer why we're arresting someone else, I'll give Chet Watkins a call and advise him that we'll bring him the suspect's used cup or glass and ask him to rush the DNA analysis. We'll need the match to the eyebrow hair."

While Hawk made the call, Nora told Mortimer, who Tina Dionisio saw messing around with the medication. While he looked puzzled, she also informed him of Chet's call regarding the eyebrow containing a dose of dark makeup. She told him she remembered who had heavily outlined eyebrows."

"How do we know that it was someone in the family?"

"Because, Mortimer, the hair follicle was from a female and had a familial match to William Hollister."

"Oh, so you're saying that Tina's statement was in line with the DNA and your observation of the makeup?"

"It sure looks that way," Nora said. "That's why we're waiting for the warrant so that we can pick her up."

After clicking off with Watkins, Hawk noticed a frown on the tall man's face, "What's wrong, Mortimer? Aren't you pleased that we probably found William Hollister's killer?"

"Oh, I am. I'm just thinking about Josephine. She'll be so disappointed. She was so sure it was Cynthia. Of course, I thought it was George and his wife, but she convinced me otherwise. She just doesn't like being wrong."

"If it makes you feel better," Nora said. I didn't think that Ashley would've done it, either. She fooled me, I guess."

"And you're sure now that it's Ashley Hollister?" Mortimer asked. "I didn't think she would be sharp enough to figure out how to murder a person in the manner that William was killed."

"She received plenty of information from the others that evening," Hawk said. "She admitted that she was with Darren and

Tina in the bathroom when Darren mentioned the father's allergy. Tina's conversation that the pill organizer looked just like her grandmother's focused Ashley's attention on the box. I always thought that she was smarter than she wanted us to believe. But I must admit that I didn't consider her a prime suspect in patricide."

Still looking puzzled, Mortimer asked, "Could she have shot James and Kay? Maybe she was good with a gun, just like Cynthia?"

Nora said, "It will be interesting to follow up on that. If not her, maybe one of her boyfriends who she could've connived with."

Perez walked toward them. "Okay, here it is. You can go and arrest her. I'll send a patrol unit to pick her up."

In the backseat of Hawk's Jeep, Mortimer mumbled, "I hope the uniforms come. I sure don't want to be with her back here." Louder, he said, "You don't think she'll be dangerous, do you?"

Nora said, "If we have to transport her, I'll sit with her in the back."

"Yes, please. I appreciate that." He started to sneeze, followed by three more." He searched his pockets, then said, "Nora, I don't have any tissues in this new suit Josephine bought me. May I borrow one of your tissues?"

Nora reached for her purse and gave it to him. He blew his nose, and after wiping it, he began a coughing fit. "Must be allergies." *No, it's nervous tension,* Hawk thought. *It should be an easy arrest.*

CHAPTER 53

IN THE HIGHLANDS area of Denver, they ran into extremely heavy traffic due to road repairs. With the stop-and-go, it took the detectives much longer than they had anticipated. Twenty minutes into the drive, Orlinski called Hawk.

"Okay, I have information on someone named Spike. He's in the federal database as a known nickname for Matthew Edgar Jonas from Tennessee. He was on parole for gun violations—trafficking and distributing. I called his former probation officer in Knoxville, and he told me that the case was transferred to Colorado. She gave me the name of his parole officer here and said that she is so thankful that she no longer must look at his ugly mug. Anyway, Jonas moved here about two years ago. One thing that may be of interest, the parole officer said he's really handy with guns. He bragged to the woman that he could shoot a nut out of a squirrel's mouth, ha, ha. Okay. That's all I have for now. I'll call you after I talk to the parole people here. Take care. Oh, Hawk, let's do lunch again."

"Sounds good. Name the day. And thanks for the info."

Five minutes later, Detective Harry Ling called Hawk. "Hey, Bud, this is Harry."

"I know. You're on my caller ID. What's up?"

"You on speaker? I want Nora and Mortimer to hear."

"Yup. The floor is yours."

"The ballistics report came back, and it showed that they were not shot as directly as we thought. The slug came at an angle to the left of the victims. The shot was taken from about forty feet away. That puts the shooter across the street. That's one. The second is that, as you know, Nancy and I have been going over videos from buildings and businesses around where James and Kay were shot. We think we know what vehicle the shooter was in. It's a black or very dark gray Toyota Tundra with black rims and a gray shell over the bed. We've got a BOLO on it.

"Could you see the driver?" Nora asked.

"Nope. Nor could we get a license plate number."

"Okay, copy that," Nora said. "Good work."

With the traffic easing up a bit, the detectives reached Ashley's apartment building about five minutes later. With an arrest and a search warrant in hand, Hawk knocked on the door. No one answered. He knocked again, this time louder and announced, "Police, open up." Still, no one came to the door. Nora twisted the doorknob. It was unlocked. As they proceeded to enter the semi-darkened room, Hawk's right hand fell onto his gun out of habit. He unsnapped the holster, not knowing what to expect, smelling a pungent odor of booze and seeing white powder on the coffee table. Ashley, with an unknown man, was sitting on the couch.

Upon seeing the detectives, Ashley Hollister made a run for the toilet. Nora glimpsed that she snatched a small plastic bag from the coffee table. She sprinted after her but was too late to stop Ashley from flushing the baggy with its contents down the toilet.

When Ashley turned toward Nora, Ashley's eyes were dilated, and snot from her nose formed a rivulet through the white powder underneath it, on her face an ugly, predatory look of fury. It was obvious that Ashley was in a state of cocaine intoxication—excited, agitated and perhaps violent. In a rapid nasal voice, she yelled out, "What in the hell are you doing here?! Get out of my bathroom, out of my house, and out of my life, you bitch!"

Ashley's hands trembled as rage washed color over her pale face. Her blue eyes shot fire as she slammed into Nora, pushing her into the wall. Nora shoved back, but Ashley had more strength in her seemingly frail and undernourished body than Nora imagined. She thrust Nora backward as she tried to bulldoze her way past Nora out of the small bathroom. *Where in the hell is this strength coming from? Must be the coke.*

Taking a wide stance, with all the force that she could muster, Nora thumped and pushed the furious woman hard against the wall. Once she felt that she had some control, the now-tired detective battled to secure Ashley's arms to cuff them. The woman didn't submit. She twisted and pushed back, whipping her elbows at Nora while at the same time spewing the vilest profanities. Nora held tight. Eventually, with her cheek pressed hard into the sand swirl texture of the wall, Ashley succumbed. Now that she slackened, Nora forcibly grabbed one arm at a time and twisted each behind the girl's back. "Bitch! You whore! Leave me alone! You have no right!"

Hawk and Mortimer heard the struggle in the bathroom. Hawk needed to go to Nora's aid, but the men had their own problems to contend with. A few seconds after Ashley bolted for the bathroom, a bearded, broad-shouldered, rough-looking man with long, matted hair wearing a gray sleeveless T-shirt lunged from a reclining position on the couch. He went for a Glock 9mm pistol lying at the edge of the coffee table.

Hawk zeroed in on the gun. The man was fast, but Hawk was faster and brushed the gun away, the weapon sliding across the hardwood floor. With wide, bloodshot eyes, the man's tattooed arms whipped out with the power of a mortar and struck Hawk squarely on his chest. Hawk flew backward and struck his head on the side of the kitchen counter that separated the kitchen from the living room. His weapon flew out of his hand, also sliding several feet away.

Taken by surprise, Mortimer struggled to unsnap his holster, losing precious seconds as the big man turned his attention to him. He shoved the rectangular coffee table right into Mortimer's shin, swinging at him. Mortimer avoided the punch as he backed off a step. Holding his gun, he pointed it at the man and boomed out, "Stop right there! I'll shoot. I'm warning you." The crazed man crept forward, paying no attention to the threat. Mortimer had never shot anyone in all the years that he had been a policeman, but now he had no choice. Just as he began squeezing the trigger, the man pushed the coffee table again into Mortimer's shin. The bullet went wild through the front window.

Not fazed by the loud blast and a bullet flying only inches from his skull, he plowed forward toward Mortimer, his eyes wide, bugging out of his head. Moving swiftly, he grabbed Mortimer's skinny, flabby arm, and with the strength of vice, he squeezed hard. Mortimer cried out from the pain, letting go of the weapon. With his left hand on Mortimer's arm, the gorilla of a man pulled Mortimer toward him. Then with his fisted right hand, he struck Mortimer on his left shoulder, knocking him to the floor.

Leaping to his feet, Hawk plowed into the giant—weighing at least three-hundred pounds, all muscle—with his head and right shoulder. As though he hit a brick wall, he recoiled from the failed tackle and attacked the man again. Again, to no avail. This time, the man clamped onto Hawk's throat, his large hand draped firmly around Hawk's thin neck.

Hawk repeatedly punched the man in the sides, across his kidneys, in the ribs, and even kicked him in the shins. Unable to take a breath, he visualized the end of his life. *No! There's got to be a way out.* With all the strength that he could gather, Hawk judo-chopped the man simultaneously on the ears and kicked his groin with his knee. The man finally flinched in pain and loosened his grip just enough for Hawk to free himself.

Startled by a gunshot, Nora dragged the resisting Ashley out of the bathroom. She gasped at the scene playing out before her. Mortimer was attempting to get up off the floor, and Hawk was in serious trouble, gasping for air. Nora let go of Ashley and rushed to save her partner. But Ashley, even though handcuffed, stuck her leg out and managed to trip Nora. Nora fell forward onto Mortimer, who at that moment was bracing himself on a kitchen chair for support to get up. Her collision with Mortimer caused him to cry out in pain and fall flat onto the floor.

Nora did not linger. She jumped to her feet and flew with a kick into the man's side at the moment that Hawk took a swing at him. The kick did not seem to faze him. He turned toward Nora, but Hawk grabbed his arm, swung him toward him and punched him under his chin with a right hook. A second later, Nora pounded him with kicks, spinning and twirling to give her added strength. At the same time, Hawk again socked him under the chin, followed by a left hook to his jaw. The powerful man fell back with another forceful kick from Nora.

In the meantime, as Mortimer again attempted to get up, Ashley kicked him in the side. He managed to stand and stretched his long arm and, with the palm of his hand, struck her forehead, shoving her to the floor. At that moment, the two Denver police officers had finally arrived on Perez's order to transport Ashley to jail. They immediately jumped into action and helped Nora and Hawk subdue the large man, thus allowing Hawk to handcuff him. "You guys have any leg shackles in your car?" Hawk asked one of the officers. They did, and the culprit was cuffed and shackled.

After Ashley and the man, later identified as Benjamin Waters, were taken away, the three detectives, all bruised and hurting, flopped down on the couch, all three breathing hard. After they rested and caught their breath, Nora stood and looked around at the mess in the apartment. Empty beer cans, empty wine bottles and a half-full bottle of vodka were scattered about. Nora pointed to traces of white powder on the coffee table and some on the floor. A credit card stained with powder lay on the table. With a weak voice, she said, "Just as I suspected, they were snorting when we came in, using that card for cutting cocaine. Judging by how crazy and powerful they were, I bet that the stuff isn't pure. Probably laced with amphetamines but actually more likely with a large filler of flakka to add volume."

"Whew! Whatever they took, it made them uncontrollable." Hawk said. "Mortimer, are you alright?"

Mortimer sat slumped on the couch, looking absolutely miserable. "Un, oh, ah. Well, I've been much better. Everything hurts. My left-hand feels numb, and my shoulder and arm are on fire. I'm sitting here wondering if I should say anything about this to Josephine. I don't know how she'd take it. She'll probably be very upset."

Nora chuckled. "I'm sure Josephine will survive. Well, gentlemen, let's do our search of this dump, grab what we need to convict and get the hell out of here."

Hawk bagged the 9mm pistol. Another bag was used for two beer cans that could be used for a DNA match—one had a ring of lipstick which he assumed was Ashley's. Nora bagged a black eyebrow applicator lying by the bathroom sink. She recognized the brand—PureBrow, manufactured by Jane Iredale. She was certain that it would match the makeup on the small hair follicle that Chet described. Mortimer discovered a coffee-stained copy of William Hollister's will lying underneath a stack of debt-collection notices and an eviction notice. All were bagged as well.

Massaging his hands to help the pain, Hawk asked the grimacing Mortimer, "Should we take you to the ER, and have you checked out?"

"Oh, I don't think it'll be necessary right now. Actually, the feeling is coming back to my hand, and my arm doesn't hurt as much. I don't think anything is broken in my shoulder. I just will have some big bruising. I'll wait to see what Josephine says if I need to go."

Nora said, "I didn't know Josephine was a doctor. I think you may need an x-ray."

"Oh, I don't think it's all that bad. If it gets worse, I'll go in."

Hawk said, "Okay then, let's get some lunch in a quiet restaurant with nice soft booths."

CHAPTER 54

NORA SUGGESTED a place. "Since we're in the area, I know exactly where we should go. Gaetano's is the oldest Italian restaurant in Denver. It's a really cool place, and some comfort food like spaghetti with meatballs would be just the ticket. I've got to get my energy up. Whatcha say?"

"Fine with me," Hawk answered softly, his breathing still labored from the fight.

"Oh, is it expensive?" Mortimer frowned. "Josephine told me to watch my expenses, at least until I inherit that money from my sick aunt."

Nora gave Clint a quick look, but he did not seem to be focusing on the conversation. His eyes squinted, and she knew that his head must be pounding. Poor guy. He really got clobbered by that beast and then looked at Mortimer, who stood there stooped and looking downtrodden. Nora thought of him and Josephine and didn't like what she heard. She's already counting on Mortimer's inheritance.

Addressing Mortimer, she said with an uncertain smile, "Tell Josephine not to worry. The prices are about average so that you wouldn't be spending all your money. Josephine would still have money left." After saying it, she immediately regretted the comment. It really was not her business, but she considered Mortimer, a friend and didn't want him to get hurt by that woman. "A fast-food joint would certainly be cheaper."

Mortimer did not seem to catch the drift of Nora's comment, or at least, he didn't show it. Instead, his mind was focused on the price of restaurants. "Oh, those so-called fast-food places are not so cheap anymore. Josephine doesn't like them either. She wants me to eat at home."

Annoyed at the conversation and Mortimer's stinginess, Hawk was in no mood to discuss prices and who'll pay. He needed to sit down, get a cold drink, and simply unwind. "Look, Mortimer, I'll pick up everyone's tab. So, you can enjoy the place in peace."

"Oh, that's very nice of you. But as I said before, I hate to owe anyone anything."

Hawk sighed, "Mortimer, you won't owe me. Let's go!"

Once they were seated in the car, Nora made a call to Lieutenant Perez. She explained that they had a difficult time arresting Ashley and a behemoth of a man who appeared to be her boyfriend. "Both were flying high on drugs, probably heavy on flakka, and in fighting moods. We sure had our hands full. We'll give you a full report after we have lunch."

"Oh God, there you go again. Were you hurt?"

"We'll live. See ya soon, Lieutenant."

Gaetano's was in a corner old red-brick building, probably built at the turn of the Twentieth Century, on Tejon Street and Thirty-Eighth Street. Nora pointed to the bullet-proof entry glass door that sat diagonal to the intersection as the three detectives walked in. The pleasing lighted red wall columns immediately caught their eyes. A boomerang-shaped, highly polished bar was flanked by chrome and black round stools awaiting customers. At the end of the bar, two men and a woman engaged in hearty laughter. Across the aisle from the stools were beige and black booths, while across from the bar were arched, button-tufted red vinyl booths.

With the mouth-watering aroma of Italian spices wafting in the air, Hawk hoped he would feel the pangs of hunger. He asked the waitress to seat them at the comfortable-looking red booths. Once seated, all three detectives sunk into the soft furniture, Hawk shutting his eyes for a few seconds. He felt like a whipped dog, his throat hurt, and pain hammered his head, sharp and heavy. All from the whack it received when he was pushed into the kitchen counter in Ashley's apartment. *I should be going home. I feel like shit.* " He was sure that Nora felt the same, but she did not seem to be in any distress. He was amazed at how excited she was to be in this place—like rejuvenation or something.

Out of the blue, she laughed. "Holy cow, you two look like crap. But don't worry. You'll snap out of it as soon as you get some of the delicious food down your gullets. Hey, you two, don't just sit there like bumps on a log. At least look at the menu."

Hawk opened his eyes, looked at Nora's smiling face and returned her smile. "Okay, let's go for it. I'm not very hungry, but as the French say, 'appetite comes while eating.' Or something like that."

"Oh," Nora laughed, "you want to impress us with French sayings."

Hawk cracked another smile and chuckled. "My mom says it in French. I don't know where she learned it, but she is always happy to repeat it many times."

"Your mom seems like fun. I'd love to meet her."

The heavy-set waitress with curly jet-black hair walked up carrying three glasses of water. A genuine smile graced her round, smooth face. "Welcome, folks. Have you been here before?"

Hawk and Mortimer shook heads in the negative while Nora answered, "Yes. But it was a while ago."

"Thanks for coming back. Whatcha like to drink? How about a glass of wine or beer?"

Hawk said, "Thanks, but water will be fine...actually, no. What the heck? Bring us each a glass of wine."

"Oh, no. Not for me. I don't drink alcohol. Neither does Josephine. I'll have water. And we shouldn't be drinking while we're still on duty."

Hawk looked at Nora. She shrugged her shoulders and cocked her head, raising her eyebrows. "You're right, Mortimer." Addressing the waitress, he said, "How about club soda with a twist of lime, then? And could we order now?"

Nora and Hawk both ordered the spaghetti while Mortimer asked if he could have a big hamburger. The waitress nodded and disappeared. The three detectives remained silent for several minutes as though each licked their own wounds. Finally, Nora broke the silence. "You probably don't know this, but this restaurant was kinda the headquarters of the Italian mob in Denver. It was connected to the mob in Pueblo, where it all probably began. My parents used to tell me about all this mob history at this restaurant. A while back, I googled it, and sure enough, this place was run by the Smaldone mob family. It had illicit gambling and poker games—Frank Sinatra and Sammy Davis Junior played poker here. And even the gangster Al Capone visited the place."

Hawk listened intently to Nora, then speculated, "I heard some about the place before. I'm sure there were violent incidents here in the old days. Maybe even a killing or two in the basement. There may even be ghosts down there."

He glanced at Mortimer, who suddenly appeared to fall into one of his strange trances. "What's up, Mortimer?"

Mortimer did not open his eyes or move but mumbled, "Now that you mentioned ghosts, I feel the presence of spirits. And they are not kind spirits. They're angry. Maybe we should leave."

Nora chuckled, "You're not serious, are you? Clint was just joking."

"I guess it's all right now. They told me to enjoy myself."

Hawk let out a hearty laugh. "Mortimer, are you putting us on?"

"Putting you on? What do you mean?"

"Are you joking, or can you actually communicate with a spirit?"

"I never joke. Since childhood, I seem to sense them and sometimes even hear bits and pieces of what they say."

Nora and Hawk exchanged glances, their eyes wide. Neither one believed him. Nora said, "Mortimer, you're a man of many talents."

"Oh. That's what my mother used to say."

The food arrived, and all three dug into it as though there was no tomorrow. Nora left a meatball, and Mortimer, seeing that Nora was through with her meal and assuming that she wouldn't mind, reached out with his fork and snatched the meatball. Unfortunately, he did not notice that Nora had sprinkled a few cayenne pepper flakes on her food before she began eating.

Taking a generous bite out of the meatball, his eyes popped open, as did his mouth. "Oh geez! Oh geez, oh geez," he yelped. He pointed vigorously to his open mouth! He let out a loud, bellowing sneeze followed by three quick coughs, some of the meat flying out. His eyes watered. In a panic, he grabbed his glass, spilling some water out as he drenched his mouth. Still wide-eyed, he seized Nora's remaining water and chugged that down, then he went for Hawk's water glass. With his cheeks turning red, he fanned his mouth with his hand, fighting to fill his lungs with air. Finally, over the crisis, Mortimer was able to squeeze out another "Oh geez." With his breathing choppy, he added, "I've never had anything this hot before. It was like eating a fireball. Nora, how can you possibly eat food this spicy? Wait till I tell Josephine about how hot food can be. And how awful, and it's got to be unhealthy. Must burn your insides. We don't use spices like that…no, I'll stick to hamburgers."

Both Nora and Hawk felt so badly and knew it wasn't funny, really. The man was indeed miserable, but the way Mortimer looked and the way he carried on, they couldn't help laughing. Perhaps that's what they really needed now to release the stress accumulated from the brutal arrest."

"What's so funny? Nora, you just put too much pepper on that meatball, and it just surprised me, that's all."

"I'm really, really sorry, Mortimer," Nora said. "I guess I'm just used to a little spice in my meals once in a while. I know it wasn't funny, and we shouldn't have laughed, but sometimes, you do some unexpected things. Are you okay now?"

As they walked out of the restaurant, Hawk said, "Except for Mortimer's spicy meatball, the meal was great. Good choice, Nora. I wouldn't mind coming back. Let's make a date of it."

Nora smiled. "Maybe…now let's see what MacGregor has to say about our arrest of Ashley. She'll probably tell us again to take time off. But I'm pumped up. I'm ready for another case…assuming, of course, that the DNA we have matched the DNA in the hair and the gun was the one that was used to shoot James and Kay."

CHAPTER 55

CLINT JOKES with me about a date. But he really hasn't shown me much affection. He didn't say anything when I told him that I'd like to meet his mother. As Hawk stopped at a red light on the way to the station, Nora jealously studied a young couple at the intersection pushing a baby stroller. They seemed so happy. After that, she remained deep in thought. Hawk and Mortimer conversed, but she did not hear a word. Hawk asked her a question, and she did not hear that either. Her thoughts were so concentrated. "Come back to Earth, Nora." She still did not respond.

"Nora!" Hawk shouted.

"Oh, sorry. What?"

"You were in such deep thought. What's up?"

"Oh, nothing…actually, it concerns you. But we'll talk about it later."

"Oh, oh. What did I do now?" he chuckled.

"I said we'll talk about it later," Nora said in an irritated tone. *Geez, what's that all about?* Hawk thought. *Sounds damn serious.*

As the three detectives pounded their way up the station stairs, they ran into Stanley Orlinski as he descended. Looking them over, he said with a grin on his face, "Yup. You look like horse manure. I heard that you were in a fight. Looks more like a brawl to me. Maybe now, you'll follow Captain's advice and go home." He chuckled again, "Or maybe, you'd rather join the wrestling circuit. You'd make more money." Hawk did not appreciate the comments as his body ached from head to toe. "And I want you to rest up good so that you can make it to my BBQ party this Saturday." He looked at Mortimer. "Will you and Josephine be there?"

"Oh, oh, I'll try if Josephine lets me go."

"Isn't she coming?"

"I told her about your kind invitation. She said that she's too shy around a group of people. To me, that's strange because when we met on the cruise ship, she was a ball of fire, talking to everyone and having a good time. Now that we live together, she tries to avoid people."

"That's too bad. It would be nice to meet her since you talk about her all the time. I feel like I already know her," Orlinski said. "Talk her into coming." Looking at Nora, he commented, "Maybe Nora could go to your home and convince her to come."

"Oh no! She doesn't want anyone to visit us. She simply won't open the door."

"Well, hope to see all of you. Now, I have to see about the death of a homeless man found along the Platte River. Hope it was by natural causes and not a murder. So, take care."

After Orlinski left, Nora stopped Mortimer at the landing. "You being a detective, did you ever check out Josephine?"

Mortimer squinted his eyes as he looked hard at Nora. "No, certainly not. What kind of marriage would it be if I didn't trust her?"

"In that case, I'll check her out. What's her last name anyway?"

"No. Please don't. It's about time that I got married, and I don't want to hear any bad things about her. Leave it alone. Okay, Nora?"

"All right, if that's what you want, Mortimer. But I think couples should check each other out before plunging into marriage. It's nothing personal against Josephine."

"That's my decision, Nora." The fool can't see the handwriting on the wall. I bet she'd love to sink her claws into his future inheritance, and either he doesn't care or doesn't want to admit it.

Miffed, Mortimer stomped off for the Homicide Unit while Hawk grabbed Nora's arm, "Nora, wait. What got you riled up? What were you thinking?"

"Can we talk about this later…somewhere private."

"Wow, it sounds serious."

"Clint, I'm sure they're going to send us home. When they do, let's meet over a cup of coffee. I think we need to have a serious conversation."

Hawk agreed to meet at Coffee Aroma.

Just as suspected, after listening to the messy arrest with injuries to them, MacGregor commanded the three detectives to go home. Further, she stated that she had set up appointments with the Department's medical consultants for Hawk, Ricci, and Holliday to do both physical and mental evaluations. Since all three refused to seek medical attention immediately, they were excused. As they left MacGregor's office, they overheard their captain tell Perez that she worried about Hawk and Ricci. "One of these days, their luck may just run out."

Hawk left the building with mixed emotions—angry that he had to undergo evaluations and nervous about his meeting with Nora.

Nora dreaded the get-together even more. She noticed her hands tremble as she left the parking lot and turned onto Colfax for the encounter.

They arrived at about the same time. After ordering coffee, they picked a table away from everyone else. "What is it, Nora? You look worried."

Nora tried to calm herself and took a deep breath, but her voice was a bit shaky. "Clint. I've arrived at a decision."

"Oh, what's that?"

"Did you notice the young couple pushing a baby stroller at one of the intersections on the way to the station?"

"No, not really."

"Well, I did. I want to be that woman that has the pleasure of walking with my baby on a beautiful, clear day. In other words, I want a family."

Hawk suddenly sat up straighter. His face grew grave. "What's this all about, Nora?"

"I just told you. I want a husband, and I want children while I still can. We're not getting younger, you know." Hawk stopped breathing, trying to think of what to say. He knew what this was all about, and he just wasn't sure that she was the one or that he could commit to a lasting relationship with her. Nora saw his hesitancy. "Clint, I love you and want us to be together forever…but…I'm not at all certain that will ever work out for me."

"Oh, come on, why do you even think that?"

"Because you have never told me that you loved me. I want to be loved, Clint. I can give a man all the love in the world, but I need that man to reciprocate." Clint grabbed his coffee and held it tightly with both hands, his eyes fixed on the black liquid in the cup.

"Look Nora…I…um…I'm… not sure I'm ready for a family and kids."

On the verge of tears, Nora remarked, "That's exactly what I knew you'd say. But I can't wait any longer. My clock is ticking. So, let's remain friends and partners at work and cover each other's backs, but I'm going to start seeing other men. Hopefully, I'll be lucky enough to find one that falls deeply in love with me and wants a family." She hesitated, not knowing whether to tell him about her plans. She decided that she should. "I'm going to return Seth Morgan's calls for a date and see if a spark we once had is rekindled. Just fair warning to you."

"Seth Morgan? Your former partner?"

"Yes." She saw that Hawk looked upset but wasn't sure if he was upset that she'll go out with someone else or that he would lose the convenience of having her available for an occasional get-together. "I'm sorry, Clint. Surely, you understand that I must go on with my life."

"But we've only met not that long ago. Don't you think we should try to know each other a little better before making a huge commitment like that?"

"Clint, we've seen each other day in and day out. We've spent evenings together and even stayed overnight waiting to be murdered. We've shared secrets, and we've shared our feelings. We faced danger and almost lost our lives together. I feel like I know you well. You are a good man, Clint, but as you just admitted to me, you have a problem with commitment, and I'm not sure you'll ever get over it."

"Well, let me think seriously about this before you go out with someone else."

"No, Clint. I already know your answer. If you wanted to commit, you'd tell me how much you loved me and wanted to be with me. But you didn't. And yet I know deep down inside that you do love me but are afraid to say it or show it…let's just go our separate ways, okay?"

Hawk remained silent for several minutes. He closed his eyes and rolled his head back. Finally, he opened his eyes and said, "Okay, if that's the way you want it."

"Okay, what?"

"Go ahead and see Seth Morgan if that's what you want. I need more time."

"Fine. At least we know where we stand. So, have a nice weekend. I might see you at Orlinski's."

Nora stood. A tear snaked its way down her cheek. "Goodbye, Clint."

EPILOGUE

MONICA PACHEK greeted Nora and Seth Morgan at the door. They already knew each other from work, and introductions were unnecessary. Walking through Orlinski's small house to the backyard BBQ, Monica said over her shoulder, "I'm glad you came. Everyone from the Homicide Unit is already here, and I have a few friends over as well. Stan and I have a big announcement to make later."

As Nora walked out through the sliding patio door with Seth as her escort, it appeared as though everyone suddenly stopped whatever they were doing. No one expected Nora to date anyone else other than Hawk. Nora smiled and introduced Seth to those that hadn't met him before. She noticed Mortimer standing next to the BBQ grill with Orlinski—no sign of Josephine. Standing off to the side by himself was Hawk looking upset as he stared back at Nora. Nora smiled, but Hawk did not return a smile, only nodded.

Hawk could not muster a smile. Bitter anguish crept up to Hawk's throat from his stomach. An uncanny sensation of unease, disappointment or maybe even rage came over him. *"I'm jealous…I can't believe how much Nora being with someone else bothers me. I must love her. But why can't I just tell her that?"*

Hawk could not keep his eyes off Nora as she circulated around the group of people—all smiles and laughter. Wearing a tight Robin-egg blue blouse with fitted floral pants, she looked sexy, and he wanted her. He saw Nancy come up to Nora. He knew what the conversation was about. *"What happened? They all want to know. I wonder what Nora will say."* He expected that he'd get the third degree as well, and sure enough, Orlinski and Harry strode up to him and asked what the deal was. He could only respond that they were not joined at the hip and left it at that.

Lieutenant Perez introduced his wife to Nora and Seth. Nora was surprised at how beautiful the woman looked with her long dark hair and large brown eyes, wearing leggings and a loose-fitted shirt over her trim body. As Nora approached Captain MacGregor, the captain asked how she was feeling after that brawl. Nora laughed and said, "She's fine, just a little sore." MacGregor's husband was exactly like Nora pictured him—short, chubby with a full gray mustache and uncombed gray hair that needed a trim. He wore baggy cargo shorts and a Harley-Davidson T-shirt. Rather a comical figure, Nora thought.

Orlinski and Monica were the perfect hosts, making sure that everyone was comfortable and had plenty to drink and eat. Orlinski bragged about his skills at the grill, and he wasn't wrong because the food was delicious. After everyone had a kielbasa or two, three for Mortimer, the couple announced their engagement and that everyone will be invited to the wedding at the Cathedral downtown. Orlinski uncorked several bottles of Champagne while Monica gave them each a flute for a toast.

After the toasts, Lieutenant Perez asked Hawk, Nora, and Mortimer to join him. "You can close the Hollister cases. Harry, Nancy, and I interrogated Ashley Hollister, and she confessed to switching the pills after I informed her that the DNA plus a witness statement proved that she had. She admitted that her boyfriend, Benjamin Waters, shot James and Kay Hollister after she promised him fifty percent of her inheritance. The gun that you bagged in the apartment was a match."

Nora said, "Great, so that case is done. Kinda crummy, though, that the other siblings will inherit the estate all because of Ashley's criminal behavior. None of them deserve it, especially not Cynthia." Perez said, "That's life. It is unfair, but that's the way it is." He hesitated for a minute. "But the main reason I called you over is that a few moments ago, I received a call from dispatch. Sorry to ruin your party, but this looks like a case for my best detectives. Two victims were found dead, lying on a couch in a lawyer's office in the Capital Hill area. The medical examiner is there now, waiting for you. Go!" THE LAW OFFICE MURDERS

THE LAW OFFICE MURDERS

The author invites you to take a SNEAK PEAK of part of the first chapter of the third book of the Clint Hawk and Nora Ricci murder mystery series.

CHAPTER 1

Present day: Denver, Colorado

A WOLFISH smile broke out on his clean-shaven angular face the instant Elizabeth Durand Esquire strode into his office and slammed the door shut behind her. He expected her. The rest of the attorneys and staff had left for the day, and the building was locked tight. Being Friday, the staff did not waste any time leaving for the weekend. For Elizabeth and her boss, it was now playtime—their special time to be together. The excuse for working late was that there was just too much work at the Visser, White, and Garza Law Offices, LLC.

Elizabeth returned a sultry smile, her brown eyes sparkling. She sidled over, her generous hips swaying, towards handsome Baxter Visser as he sat behind his huge cherrywood desk. He slid his high-back Corinthian leather chair from his desk just in time for Elizabeth to fall into his lap. They kissed passionately, his hands all over her curvaceous body. One kiss followed several more before Baxter motioned toward the wide tan leather sofa that stood against a walnut-paneled wall of the large office.

"Yes, yes, yes, let's go," she responded breathlessly. In a state of arousal and hard breathing, they made it to the couch. Their clothes went flying. Elizabeth barely had a chance to lay down before Baxter pounced into the waiting arms of his beautiful and highly seductive associate.

They were in the act of overwhelming lust when suddenly the door swung open. Elizabeth twisted her neck to see what was happening. Her eyes widened in terror as a black-clothed figure flew towards them. She screamed a blood-curdling shriek. Baxter crooked his head toward the assailant and strained to lift himself off the woman. It was too late. Elizabeth saw a wisp of smoke as the gun with the silencer exploded. Baxter collapsed, his weight

pinning her to the couch. A second later, still screaming, the gun
went off again.

She was dead.

***

About The Author

Victor Moss has been an attorney engaged in private practice of law since 1974 in both Pueblo and Denver, Colorado. Prior to that time, he had been an assistant attorney general for the State of New Mexico and assistant city attorney for Pueblo, Colorado. His prior books are Beware the Wolves: A Soviet WWII Love Story, No Return Home, The Soul Named Samantha, and Coffee House Murders. He lives with his wife in Highlands Ranch, Colorado.